THE HELPING RELATIONSHIP

Healing and Change
in Community Context

D1571993

THE HELPING RELATIONSHIP

Healing and Change
in Community Context

Edited by Augustine Meier and Martin Rovers

UNIVERSITY OF OTTAWA PRESS
OTTAWA

University of Ottawa Press
542 King Edward Avenue
Ottawa, ON K1N 6N5
www.press.uottawa.ca

uOttawa

The University of Ottawa Press acknowledges with gratitude the support extended
to its publishing list by Heritage Canada through its Book Publishing Industry
Development Program, by the Canada Council for the Arts, by the Canadian
Federation for the Humanities and Social Sciences through its Aid to Scholarly
Publications Program, by the Social Sciences and Humanities Research Council,
and by the University of Ottawa.

We also gratefully acknowledge St Paul's University whose financial support has
contributed to the publication of this book.

LIBRARY AND ARCHIVES CANADA CATALOGUING IN PUBLICATION

The helping relationship : healing and change in community context /
edited by Augustine Meier and Martin Rovers.

Includes bibliographical references and index.
ISBN 978-0-7766-0730-6

1. Psychotherapist and patient. 2. Psychotherapy.
3. Helping behavior. 4. Counseling.
I. Meier, Augustine, 1933- II. Rovers, Martin, 1949-

RC480.8.H44 2010   616.89'14   C2010-907224-3

Table of Contents

Introduction

Helping Others in Religious, Cultural, and Psychological Contexts

Augustine Meier and Martin Rovers

There are many stories of how people have come together to help others who have endured unexpected disasters and tragedies or suffer from some of life's pains, losses, and traumas. During the flood in Manitoba, volunteers from all across Canada came to the aid of inundated Manitobans. Hurricane Katrina (2005) marshalled help from all over the world. When a young Saskatchewan farmer died from cancer, his relatives and neighbours organized themselves to take off his harvest. Following the Columbine High School Massacre (1999), counsellors were sent to the school to help the returning students grieve the loss of their friends. The list of such stories goes on and on.

The urge to help others is ingrained in human nature and is thus as old as humanity itself. Helping others is held up as an ideal by all of the major religions and is characteristic of all societies and cultures. The scope of helping others advocated by the major religions ranges from helping the needy, the orphaned, the widowed, and the travelling to helping those who suffer from physical and psychological pain and those who strive to achieve greater self-awareness and enlightenment. The call to help others as well as the qualities of those who help others are carefully spelled out in world religions, psychotherapy books, and everyday stories to children.

The Helping Relationship and World Religions

Hinduism, also known as Sanatana Dharma ("the eternal natural law"), began in India around 1500 BC (Aiken, 1914b; *Hinduism: A Brief Overview*, 2005; *Hinduism: Origins*, 2005). It is one of the most ancient religious and spiritual systems thought to be "revealed" by God and/or realized by ancient sages. The focus of this religion is on self-perfection and on reaching salvation (moksha). Salvation is typically reached after a series of reincarnations that represents the passage from death to life, and the state in which one is reborn depends on one's actions and their results, referred to as the law of karma. There are four paths that Hindus can follow to reach moksha: the path of devotion, the path of knowledge, the path of right action, and the path of yoga. The path of right action implies acting selflessly, without any thought of oneself. Although the focus of Hinduism is on self-perfection in order to reach salvation, the Hindu is obligated to manifest the divinity within him- or herself to others. The greatest service that a Hindu can render to others is to help them manifest their own innate divinity (Sastrananda, 1997). The motto is first let us become gods, and then help others to become gods: that is, be and make. Satyanarayana (2007) states that Hindu philosophers have attached great importance to the duty of selfless and loving service to others. We should not only relieve the misery of others but also identify with them and become part of them so as to undergo their suffering and share their misery. One of the principal Hindu scriptures, Rig-Veda, states that "he alone lives for the sake of helping others" (Satyanarayana, 2007, p. 3).

Similar to the Hindu, the Buddhist strives for detachment from self and the world so as to achieve enlightenment and salvation (Aiken, 1914a; *Buddhism*, 2007; Kinnes, 2007). Buddhism was founded by Sidartha Gautama, known as Buddha, who lived in India from about 560 to 480 BC (*Buddhism*, 2007). Buddha did not leave behind anything in writing, only an oral tradition, which later was recorded in books. The chief sources of early Buddhism are the sacred books in the first two divisions of Ti-Pitaka ("triple basket"), comprised of disciplinary rules for monks, alleged discourses of Buddha, and treatises on doctrinal subjects. The essence of Buddha's teachings is contained in the four noble truths of suffering: namely, the truth of suffering, the cause of suffering, the end of suffering, and the path that leads to the end of suffering. Cravings for pleasure, material goods, and immortality lie at the root of suffering since they can never be satisfied. One can end one's suffering and the worldly cycle of birth and rebirth, and achieve nirvana, by following the steps of the noble eightfold path: right understanding, right thought, right speech, right action, right livelihood, right effort, right mindfulness, and right concentration. They can be subsumed under the themes of good moral conduct and mental development. The good and bad actions during one's lifetime determine one's karma: that is, what we experience in this life and what we can expect to experience in the next life (Schuman, 2007). A person continues to go through the life cycle of death and rebirth until he or she has achieved enlightenment or nirvana. Although Buddhists are preoccupied with their own enlightenment, they are nevertheless encouraged to be of help to others to perfect themselves, because they share humanity in common with all other people. In helping others to relieve their suffering and achieve nirvana (*Helping Others,* 2007), we must address them on their own level, using their words and gestures, and allow them, with the aid of our enlightenment, to see emerging mindfulness inside their minds. We must also have pure intentions in helping them, because if our intentions are egoistic or selfish it is not possible to help them.

The sacred book of Islam, the Quran, is replete with exhortations for proper living. They were given to the Prophet Muhammad between AD 610 and 622. The aim of the Quran is to change how an individual thinks rather than to change the social system. The book does not set out everything in detail but encourages persons to think for themselves along proper lines. One of the major exhortations of the Quran is to take care of the poor, the orphaned, the disabled, the captive, and the wayfaring. But the Quran discourages people from helping others so as to be seen by others as doing good (Quran, 2: 264, 271); charity is for those in need (2: 73). The greatest charity for a Muslim is to learn something and then teach it to others, which is best reflected in the field of education.

Judaism exhorts its followers to help the less fortunate and to accept strangers as one among themselves. It is written in the book of Deuteronomy (24:19-21; Wansbrough, 1985) that, "When you reap your harvest in your field and forget a sheaf in the field, you shall not go back to get it; it shall be left for the alien, the orphan, and the widow. ... When you gather the grapes of your vineyard, do not glean what is left; it shall be for the alien, the orphan, and the widow." The book of Leviticus (9:33-34) admonishes, "When an alien resides with you in your land, you shall not oppress the alien. The alien who resides with you shall be to you as the citizen among you; you shall love the alien as your self for you were aliens in the land of Egypt."

Christianity asks its followers to "care for orphans and widows in their distress" (James 1:27; Wansbrough, 1985), to maintain "constant love for one another ... be hospitable to one another ... serve one another with whatever gift each of you has received" (I Peter 4:8-10), and "bear one another's burdens" (Galatians 6:2). Christians are exhorted to love their neighbours as they love God, which Jesus illustrated with the parable of the Good Samaritan, who took a man beaten by robbers and left to die to an inn, where he had the man cared for (Luke 10:25-37). Christians are asked to lead a life "with all humility and gentleness, with patience, bearing with one another in love, making every effort to maintain the unity of the Spirit in the bond of peace" (Ephesians 4:1-2). Jesus himself said that it "is more blessed to give than to receive" (Acts 20:35). The theme of helping others—our neighbours—is everywhere to be heard in the sayings of Jesus.

The Helping Relationship and Society and Culture

Helping others is also characteristic of all societies and cultures since the beginning of time (Neill, McGarry, & Hohl, 1960). During the hunter/food gatherer and agriculture eras, adults passed on to their children the knowledge, life skills, and crafts to hunt and fish and to gather edible wild fruits and vegetables (Barnard, 2004; Bettinger, 1991). The elderly and the sick were taken care of by their families and communities, and the dead were given respectful burials. The elders of these communities passed on the traditional wisdom and conduct expected from all.

Major changes were brought to this society by the Industrial Revolution. There was a major shift in technological, socio-economic, and cultural conditions (Ashton, 1948; Berlanstein, 1992) that resulted in families moving to larger centres and working in factories and industries. Gradually, the training of children for jobs shifted from family to experts. Specialization became the trend. Training took place in stages, first becoming an apprentice and then becoming a journeyman, at which time the worker obtained his or her papers signalling fully fledged tradesperson. At the same time, state-funded schools emerged, and the young studied the culture and prepared for their careers (Lenzen, 1994). State-operated hospitals also began to emerge, and the sick were treated and cared for in them. So too mental hospitals, where specialists treated people with emotional problems (McGrew, 1985).

With the establishment of hospitals and patient records, and with the founding of the mental health movement, care of the emotionally disturbed shifted from family care to hospital care to community care. With this shift came a mushrooming of helping professionals to care for the institutionalized. Psychiatrists, clinical psychologists, social workers, psychiatric nurses, and clergy committed their energies to care for the emotionally troubled. Competing theories began to emerge regarding the causes and treatments of emotional disorders. The first comprehensive psychological theory was psychoanalysis, soon to be followed by other approaches, such as behavioural therapy and client-centred therapy. These varying approaches led to debates, particularly about the relative merits of the human relationship and techniques to help others. Some took the position that techniques, similar to those in medicine, were primary in treating emotional disorders. Others strongly advocated the healing role of the human relationship. Professionals still debate the relative merits of techniques and relationships in helping others to face a life crisis or emotional turmoil.

The Helping Relationship and Therapeutic Techniques

There is an emerging consensus today that both relationship and technique contribute to the healing process, but the extent to which each contributes to this process is not known (Gelso, 2005). This book, *The Helping Relationship*, takes the first stand that the relationship is an essential aspect of the healing process and that it needs to be brought back into this process. The book holds that healing takes place within the context of relationship and community. To work with someone in need primarily from a technical perspective is to dehumanize that person and disregard his or her fundamental need for relationship and community. This book presents the helping relationship from different perspectives, including the setting and context of the helping relationship, the helping relationship as learning and mentoring, and working through interpersonal issues that arise within the context of helping others. Four of the first five chapters focus on a unique aspect of the helping relationship: namely, transference and countertransference. Transference refers to the client's emotional reaction to the behaviours, actions, and/or responses of the therapist, and countertransference refers to the therapist's emotional reactions to the utterances, behaviours, and/or actions of the client.

Chapter Summaries

In the first chapter, Augustine Meier briefly summarizes the positions taken by those who advocate the therapist-client relationship, the technique, and/or the interaction of the relationship and technique to be primary in therapeutic change. Meier turns the question around and asks, what do clients take from their participation in a technique used in psychotherapy? The material used for this study consisted of the feedback of two clients following their participation in a therapeutic technique. Meier advocates more research on the psychotherapy process from this perspective.

Tricia Schöttler, in the second chapter, highlights the crucial importance of the helping relationship in and of itself and argues for its maintenance as an essential component of psychotherapy despite the trend in psychotherapy to become ever more technological. The helping relationship is described as comprising two significant components: the personal bond between therapist and client (e.g., warmth, genuineness, acceptance), and the working alliance that entails agreement between therapist and client on the goals of therapy and how they will be achieved. Schöttler cites results from empirical studies that support the impact of the therapeutic alliance on therapeutic outcome. She outlines trends in psychotherapy research such as the rigid adherence to the medical model, the development of manualized treatment protocols, and the increasing emphasis on evidence-based psychotherapies and how they impact on the significant role of the therapeutic relationship. Schöttler concludes the chapter by offering alternative paths that might serve to counteract what seems to many in the helping professions to be a growing trend toward ultimately divesting the therapeutic encounter of its inherently personal, human, and relational foundations, in effect taking the helping relationship and the therapist out of the treatment room.

In Chapter 3, Augustine Meier revisits the concepts of transference and countertransference. Both are considered to be by-products of the efforts to establish a therapeutic emotional bond.

The treatment of countertransference comprises the major part of the chapter. Currently, there is a divide over whether to consider countertransference as comprising all of the psychotherapist's emotional reactions to the client or whether to classify these responses according to a classic definition of countertransference or to a totalistic/integrative/moderate definition of countertransference. Meier offers a two-dimensional model that views countertransference on a continuum constituted by two components: the degree of awareness of one's emotional reaction, and the degree of awareness of its origin. The chapter concludes by presenting a model that explains the etiology and dynamics of both transference and countertransference.

Shelley Briscoe-Dimock, in Chapter 4, considers the therapeutic relationship to be the main vehicle to or agent for change in psychodynamic therapy. The therapeutic relationship is conceived of as comprising the therapist-client emotional bond, the goal of therapy, and an agreement on how to achieve the goals. Since the therapist and client can become emotionally engaged, transference by the client and countertransference by the therapist are distinct possibilities. Countertransference can be an interference, or it can be informative. Using her own experiences, Briscoe-Dimock addresses how one can use one's countertransference in a transformative way. Reflecting on cases in which countertransference was considered to be an interference and in which it was considered to be informative, she delineates six components or steps in positively managing one's own countertransference.

Chapter 5, by Augustine Meier, Micheline Boivin, and Molisa Meier, reports research that studied the resolution of client transference. In the study, theme analysis was applied to the transcripts of 37 counselling sessions of a young adult European Canadian female client, with a low-level borderline personality disorder, to identify the themes of separation/individuation transference, indicate how they are linked to each other, and track changes in the themes across psychotherapy sessions as reflected by a change process measure. Psychotherapeutic themes were defined in terms of polarities, with one pole representing the problem end on a continuum and the other pole representing the striving-toward end on a continuum. The Seven-Phase Model of the Change Process was used to assess change in the themes across the sessions. Low-level borderline personality disorder was defined by the DSM-IV-TR diagnostic criteria, and the degree of separation/individuation was assessed by the Process Inventory. Three classes of themes were identified: descriptive, main, and core. The research produced one core theme to which the other themes are linked. The results suggest that the themes change across therapy in a progressive manner.

In the sixth chapter, John Dimock, a psychiatrist, shares the story of his training and practice as a psychiatrist. He offers the reader a look at psychotherapy from the perspective of a psychiatrist. Dimock points out current trends, such as managed care, manualized treatments, and the need for quick and cheap treatments, that have tarnished the "mantle of the helper." He advocates for "good enough" therapy and is hopeful that the dimensional component to be added to the next edition of the DSM will help to restore psychotherapy to its rightful and honoured place.

Current research indicates similarities between the pedagogical relationship and the therapeutic relationship. Chapter 7, by Kristine Lund, focuses on how therapy is about learning: learning about self, other, and "self in relation." Drawing on recent developments in postmodern understandings of the self, complexity theory, ecology, and hermeneutics, Lund presents an "enactivist" model of cognition. She also considers the implications for therapy and supervision.

In Chapter 8, Lorraine Ste-Marie presents a model of mentoring that is applicable to journeying with students enrolled in a ministry program. The model describes the necessary qualities of a mentor, the theological, philosophical, and androgogical content of mentoring, and the focused style of interviewing with its four levels of conversation. The theological approach to mentoring is based on two foundations: on a call to fullness, and on hospitality. Philosophically, mentoring is characterized by its dialogical character, an openness to horizons of significance, originality, discovery, construction, and opposition to structures of oppression. Androgogy, in this chapter, refers to self-directed adult learning that is rooted in the fundamental human need to make meaning of one's experience. Informational learning is distinguished from transformational learning that is aimed at making changes to one's mental structures: that is, changes to how we know. The chapter illustrates the four levels of focused conversation—objective, interpretative, reflective, and decisional levels—by using a transcript from an actual meeting between a mentor and mentee. The mentoring helping relationship is educative in nature, not therapeutic.

In Chapter 9, Marsha Cutting reports on research that investigated personal and interpersonal qualities, supervisory skills, and presence of supervisors as reported by supervisees who had either a positive or a negative supervision experience. The sample was comprised of eight participants for each of the two groups. The study clearly differentiated between those who reported having positive supervision experiences and those who reported having negative supervision experiences.

Bradley Morrison, in Chapter 10, takes the concept of the helping relationship into a very different setting, that of a church or believing community. He points out that the rationale behind the movement to replace pastoral care and counselling with spiritual care and counselling, particularly in institutional settings, is misguided. He views spiritual care and counselling as having a personal focus and as being removed from the sense of community or congregation that includes its matrix of relationships, including pastor, parishioner, stranger, God, and the landscape that they inhabit. The helping relationship in a community pastorate is distinguished from other helping relationships in that the congregation is built around the claim that God is encountered, unlike clinical and institutional contexts in which any alleged encounter with God may remain private and

individually claimed. Morrison argues that the helping relationship within the pastoral paradigm allows for a more developed
understanding of community. In the last part of the chapter,
he demonstrates how the pastoral paradigm and the research of
psychotherapy might intersect. This chapter, assuredly, will generate a lot of discussion, particularly in this age when university
programs and journals are replacing "pastoral" with "spiritual."

Our hope is that the many ideas presented in the chapters will
add to the debate about the relative roles of the relationship and
technique in the transformation process and that others will pick
up the challenge and explore new vistas and thereby contribute to
a better understanding of the change process.

References

Aiken, C. F. (1914a). "Buddism." In *Catholic encyclopedia* (online). http://www.
    catholicity.com/encyclopedia/b/buddhism.html [retrieved September 2, 2007].
---. (1914b). "Hinduism." In *Catholic encyclopedia* (online). http://www.catholic-
    ity.com/encyclopedia/h/hinduism.html [retrieved September 2, 2007].
Allah All-Mighty. (Timeless). Quran. Medina Munawwarah: Hazrat Uthman Ibn
    Affan Publishers.
Ashton, T. S. (1948). *The Industrial Revolution (1760-1830)*. Oxford: Oxford
    University Press.
Barnard, A. J., ed. (2004). *Hunter-gatherers in history, archaeology, and anthropology*.
    Oxford: Berg.
Berlanstein, L. R. (1992). *The Industrial Revolution and work in nineteenth-Century
    Europe*. New York: Routledge.
Bettinger, R. L. (1991). *Hunter-gatherers: Archaeological and evolutionary theory*.
    New York: Plenum Press.
Buddhism: An introduction. (2007). http://www.pbs.org/edens/thailand/bud-
    dhism.htm [retrieved September 2, 2007].
Gelso, C. J. (2005). "Introduction to special issue." *Psychotherapy: Theory, Research,
    Practice, Training, 42*(4), 419-420.
Helping others out of suffering. (2007). http://themiddleway.net/2007/07/05/help-
    ing-others-out-of-suffering/ [retrieved September 2, 2007].
Hinduism: A brief overview. (2005). http://www.important.ca/hinduism_overview.
    html [retrieved September 2, 2007].
Hinduism: Origins, nomenclature, and society. (2005). http://www.important.ca/
    origins_of_hinduism.html [retrieved September 2, 2007].
Kinnes, T. (2007). *Tipitaka, the Pali canon of Buddhism*. http://oaks.nvg.org/tripi-
    taka.html [retrieved September 2, 2007].

Lenzen, D. (1994). "History of education." *Münster in Westphalia,* November 27.

McGrew, R. E. (1985). *Encyclopedia of medical history.* London: Macmillan.

Neill, T., McGarry, D. D., & Hohl, C. L. (1960). *A history of Western civilization.* 2 vols. Milwaukee: Bruce Publishing.

Sastrananda, S. (1997). *Perfection is in your luminous essence.* http://www.hinduismtoday.com/archives/1997/9/1997-9-24.shtml [retrieved September 2, 2007].

Satyanarayana, M. C. (2007). *Concept of sewa in Hinduism.* http://www.watermarkpages.net/ [retrieved September 2, 2007].

Schuman, H. W. (2007). *Karma in Buddhism.* http://themiddleway.net/2007/07/05/helping-others-out-of-suffering/ [retrieved September 2, 2007].

Wansbrough, H. (Ed.). (1985). *The New Jerusalem Bible.* New York: Doubleday.

I

The Therapeutic Relationship and Techniques: How Clients Bring about Desired Changes

Augustine Meier

Introduction

The twenty-first century is indeed an exciting time in which to live because of the many technological advances that pervade all segments of our society. Information technology allows us in seconds to connect to and communicate with people regardless of where they live. Technology has opened the door to outerspace exploration and has advanced medical diagnostic and surgical procedures. One stands in awe in the face of all these advances and humbly ponders whether the best is yet to come.

Fascinated by the technological advances in medicine, communication, and outerspace exploration, psychotherapists and psychotherapy researchers ponder whether there are techniques that could raise the emotionally distraught out of their pain and sorrow and into a state of inner peace and harmony with fellow man and woman. Psychotherapists have, for generations, searched for and designed techniques that would act as potent instruments in facilitating personal and interpersonal growth and change. Free association and interpretation represent the first such attempts (Freud, 1940). They were followed by empathic responding (Rogers, 1951), behaviour rehearsal, systematic desensitization (Yates, 1975), and healing images (Sheikh, 2003), to mention only a few. More current techniques include eye movement desensitization and reprocessing (Shapiro, 2001), neuro-linguistic programming (Grinder & Bandler, 1983), and emotional freedom technique (Craig, 1999).

The fascination with techniques and their potential power to render changes has sparked, over the decades, an intense and vociferous debate among psychotherapy researchers on the relative effectiveness of the therapeutic relationship and of techniques on the therapeutic change process and a successful outcome. Most therapists have found themselves on one side or the other of this ongoing debate. Today there is a growing recognition that therapeutic techniques do not have inherent capacities to bring about changes but, in tandem with the therapeutic relationship, contribute to the therapeutic change process. The unanswered question is this: how do these two factors work together to bring about the desired change? Where in the therapist-client interaction do these two factors intersect? What needs to emerge when these two factors interact so as to bring about change? It has been postulated that the interaction of these two factors contributes to positive therapeutic outcomes when they, in tandem, are able to awaken in the client that which is new and life giving and the client owns it and lives from it.

This chapter first summarizes the two positions of the debate by briefly presenting the assumptions of authors who adhere to one or the other of the two viewpoints. The chapter then addresses the theoretical and research literature concerning the interplay of the therapeutic relationship and techniques on the change process. The third part presents the thesis of this chapter, which is that the relationship and technique are said to interact when the client is able to take from them something new and life giving, owns it and lives from it, and refuses to look back. The last part presents cases that demonstrate how clients used the therapeutic relationship and the technique to promote inner healing and psychological growth and to develop more meaningful and healthier interpersonal relationships.

The Therapeutic Relationship and the Change Process

When there is a discussion about the therapeutic relationship, one typically focuses on the therapist and his or her therapeutically effective qualities and characteristics. Yet the therapeutic relationship comprises the engagement, encounter, and working together of both therapist and client. Freud was one of the first therapists to discuss the mutual commitment and collaboration of both the client and the therapist in this relationship. He stated that, when the patient and the psychoanalyst agree to engage in the psychoanalytic process, the patient promises "complete candour ... to put at our disposal all of the material which his self-perception provides ... that comes into his head, even if it is disagreeable to say it" (1940, pp. 36-38). The psychoanalyst assures the patient "the strictest discretion" (p. 36) and the application of his or her skill in interpreting material that has been influenced by the unconscious. The therapeutic relationship, in essence, comprises a real relationship (between therapist and client), a working arrangement or alliance regarding the goals of therapy and the means to achieve them, an emotional bond between therapist and client (Bordin, 1976), and client transferences and therapist countertransferences. A discussion of the therapeutic relationship, therefore, entails a discussion regarding the characteristics and quality of participation by the therapist and the client.

Therapist Qualities and Characteristics
Rogers is credited with being the first and the strongest proponent of the importance of the therapeutic relationship in the change process and outlined the necessary conditions to foster this relationship. His position is based on the assumption that the innate striving toward self-actualization leads to growth and change when this striving is supported, fostered, and stimulated by healthy human relationships (Rogers, 1966). Within this context, the person achieves a sense

of selfhood and the capacity for meaningful interpersonal relationships. Unhealthy relationships, according to Rogers, may not only interrupt or sidetrack the striving toward self-actualization but also bring about emotional problems manifested particularly by a feeling of being alienated from self and others. According to Rogers, a person can work through and rise above his or her emotional problems by being offered healthy relationships, particularly by the therapist, that reinstate the self-actualizing strivings. The process to reinstate self-actualization requires certain therapist interpersonal qualities such as respect, acceptance, and love, which generate within the person the feeling of self-worth and self-esteem. Rogers (1957) outlined what he considered to be the necessary and sufficient conditions for change: unconditional positive regard and empathic understanding genuinely experienced by the therapist. Rogers (1951) maintained that it is the therapist's affirmations that produce client changes. He stated that the "client moves from the experiencing of himself as an unworthy, unacceptable, and unlovable person to the realization that he is accepted, respected, and loved, in this limited relationship with the therapist. ... [A]s the client experiences the attitude of the acceptance which the therapist holds toward him, he is able to take and experience this same attitude towards himself" (pp. 159–160).

Rogers argued against the singular emphasis on external control and the use of techniques by therapists to bring about change (Rogers & Skinner, 1956). He maintained that every person has an innate striving toward self-actualization and an "organismic valuing process" (Raskin & Rogers, 1989, p. 170) that guides him or her in making choices on the basis of direct, organic processing situations in contrast to acting out in fear of what others might think of or expect from him or her. In brief, the therapist, through the qualities of empathic understanding, genuineness, and positive regard, supports and encourages the client to discover how to live his or her life by reinstating and responding to the self-actualizing process.

Frank (1973) also advocated the role of the human relationship in the change process. This is based on the assumption that patients suffer from demoralization and a sense of hopelessness.

Consequently, any benign human influence is likely to boost the patient's morale, which is considered to be improvement. The ingredients of the human relationship are interest, respect, understanding, encouragement, acceptance, and forgiveness.

The therapist's qualities postulated by Rogers (1957) and Frank (1973) regarding the helping relationship must be broadened to include other qualities such as the capacity for emotional bonding (Bordin, 1979, p. 254) and "empathic immersion" (Kohut, 1977, p. xxii), having a "sense of oneness" with the other, and the capacity to be "separated and individuated" (Mahler, Pine, & Bergman, 1975, p. 4). Another quality is that of "care," in the Heideggerian sense (1962), which entails a pull toward sustaining and enhancing life, be it physical or psychological. It is necessary that the therapist possess these capacities to foster the client's experience of oneness and separateness and being valued and prized within the context of therapy. Regarding the capacity for "oneness" with the other, Rogers (1986, p. 198), toward the end of his career, acknowledged that a crucial quality for the therapist is being in "touch with the unknown in oneself," which can emerge when one is close to one's inner and intuitive self. This capacity to be in touch with the unknown in oneself makes it possible to be in touch with the unknown in the client. Rogers (1986, p. 198) stated that at these moments "it seems that my inner spirit has reached out and touched the inner spirit of the other. Our relationship transcends itself and becomes a part of something larger. Profound growth and healing and energy are present." Thorne (1992, p. 22) adds that our experiences as therapists "involve the transcendent, the indescribable, the spiritual."

In brief, it is not sufficient to offer genuineness, unconditional positive regard, and empathic understanding as an outsider; rather, it is important that these qualities be offered from the position of "being able to immerse" oneself in a client's inner world (Kohut, 1977). The manner in which a therapist is present to a client will undoubtedly be determined by his or her conceptualization of the client's needs and by the client's readiness to receive the relationship.

Client Qualities and Characteristics

Clients typically begin therapy by expressing a wish or desire to deal with their personal and interpersonal problems, such as depression, anxiety, anger, or an unhappy relationship. Translating these problems into positive statements, clients wish and desire to experience the joy of life, to be calm, to be patient, to control their emotions, or to be in meaningful relationships. To be effective, the therapist must see beyond clients' problems and emotional states and recognize their underlying needs and tailor the therapeutic responses and interventions accordingly.

The thesis of this chapter is that therapeutic change is directly or indirectly related to the emergence of something new and life giving that impels the client forward. That which is life giving for the client is often explicitly or implicitly expressed in terms of realizing, accepting, and asserting one's yearnings, desires, wishes, and needs that previously were either not accessible or from which the client feared to live. Meier and Boivin (2001) argue that underlying psychological problems and emotional states are unknown, unacknowledged, and/or unmet fundamental personal and interpersonal needs. In their study on conflict resolution, for example, Meier and Boivin (2001, 2006) observed that the recognition, articulation, and assertion of human needs led to a resolution of the conflict. In a review of the literature on the influence of client variables on psychotherapy, Clarkin and Levy (2004) concluded that clients who were more needy established long-term relationships with the therapist compared with less needy clients, that clients' capacity to relate predicted outcome, and that the quality of their interpersonal relationships was directly related to favourable process and outcome. The implication is that, when clients' interpersonal needs are reasonably addressed within the context of therapy, and when clients sense that the therapist focuses on that which is meaningful and life giving to them, they tend to pursue therapy until they achieve their goals.

Personal and interpersonal needs can be organized in different ways. For example, Maslow (1970) organized human needs according to a hierarchy beginning with physiological needs, then moving to the needs for safety, belonging and love, self-esteem, and ultimately self-actualization. For the purpose of this chapter, human needs will be organized according to two interdependent sets of needs: namely, the need for "oneness" and "separateness" (Kaplan, 1978, pp. 25, 250; Mahler, Pine, & Bergman, 1975, p. 4), and the need for affirmation of self as "being competent" and affirmation of self as "being a good and lovable person" (Kohut, 1977, p. 179).

Based on their research with children, Mahler, Pine, and Bergman (1975) observed that children develop from being one with the significant other to separating from the other and becoming an individuated person: that is, becoming an individual with his or her own thoughts, goals in life, et cetera. This progression, however, is cyclical, with the child moving away to experience his or her separateness and then returning to feel connected to the significant other. Therapists such as Cashdan (1988), Kernberg (1984), and Masterson (1976) observed the same phenomenon in working with adults, particularly with borderline and narcissistic personality disorders. From this it can be safely concluded that every person has two basic needs. The first need is to be connected to a significant other, to be in a relationship, and to be loved, cherished, accepted, and valued. The second need is to be separated from the other so as to have distance and freedom to exercise one's own competency and power and thereby become one's own person: that is, to become individuated. The developmental task is to reconcile these two needs (inner forces) within the context of a relationship so that the person can be close to the other (be intimate) and at the same time remain a separate and individuated person. In brief, the inner forces for "connectedness" (oneness) and for "separateness" influence many human interactions and behaviours. Interpersonal problems among couples often hinge on a failure to arrive at a balance between the need for oneness and the need for separateness.

The second set of needs is for affirmation that one is a competent person and a worthwhile and lovable person (Kohut, 1977).

The need for affirmation of one's competency relates to being a competent worker, student, athlete, dancer, partner, father, or mother, to name a few. A sense of "omnipotence" (Kohut, 1977, p. 8) and empowerment accompanies the experience of being competent. A person also has a need to be affirmed for being a worthwhile and lovable person, one whom others like to be with and cherish. A person who has not been sufficiently affirmed when young will manifest problems of self-esteem and empowerment as a teenager and adult. Because they lack a sense of empowerment and self-worth, these persons might feel powerless and fail to develop the ability to self-comfort and self-soothe when they experience emotional hurts from what they perceive to be criticisms, put-downs, and so on.

The needs for oneness and separateness, referred to as relational needs, interact with the needs for affirmation for being a competent and lovable person, referred to as self needs. For example, it is possible for one person to feel worthless because she feels incompetent and for another person to feel worthless because he does not feel that he matters to anyone: that is, they perceive themselves to be unlovable. It is also possible that a person can feel competent as an employee but feel incompetent as a father and partner. It is essential that the therapist accurately identify the client's needs so as to foster and solidify the therapeutic relationship and to help the client move forward. For example, in working with borderline personality disorders, it is important, at the beginning of therapy, to respond to the client's need for emotional connection. To overlook this need and to ask clients to become independent and responsible for their lives would be a technical error as the clients are not ready and able to move forward until they first have a sense of connectedness with the therapist. As in normal development, the client needs to be connected before she can become separated and individuated. Therefore, it is essential that the therapist offers a personal presence and tailors his responses to the client: that is, to foster the emergence of life-giving sources.

Techniques and the Change Process

Although Watson (1913) is considered to be the father of American behaviourism (see also Bjork, 1993; Buckley, 1989), it is Skinner (1953, 1972) who articulated the principles of behaviourism and applied them to the treatment of emotional and behavioural disorders. His ambition was to develop a science of behaviour that would result in behavioural engineering. Fundamental to this engineering is the development of behavioural techniques that would bring about change. The assumption underlying the effectiveness of techniques is that all behaviours are learned and that change is brought about by learning new behaviours. This approach is based on a social learning model. It is assumed that not innate forces but external pressures, stimulants, and reinforcers determine the acquisition of new behaviours. Change is not the realization of inner potentials but the adoption of new behaviours. At the heart of learning new behaviours is the use of therapeutic techniques that are orchestrated to provide new conditions by which the client can learn new ways of functioning. It is assumed that the therapeutic relationship plays a minimal role in the change process and that the techniques are operative by themselves: that is, the technique is primary in bringing about the change.

A fundamental assumption of behaviourism is that a person is not the free agent of his or her own actions, thoughts, beliefs, and so on. Rather, a person is determined by his or her environment, which is responsible both for the "evolution of the species and for the repertoire acquired by each member" (Skinner, 1972, p. 214). Skinner contends that "environmental contingencies now take over functions once attributed to the autonomous man," and in this process the "autonomous inner man" is abolished (p. 215). This is in stark contrast to positions taken by authors such as Freud (1923), Maslow (1961, 1970), and Rogers (1951), who postulate that inner strivings and drives realized within the context of human relationships influence behaviours and actions and the development of values and attitudes. In brief, advocates of the role of techniques in the change process assume that techniques provide the conditions for learning and acquisition of both overt and covert behaviours and actions.

The Interplay of Relationship and Technique

There is both theoretical and research support for the idea that the therapeutic relationship and technique interplay to bring about therapeutic change. Behavioural and cognitive behavioural therapists, in particular, have become more articulate about the role of the therapeutic relationship in positive therapy outcome. Preliminary research, as well, supports the interactive nature of relationship and technique in successful therapy. The emerging consensus is that both the therapeutic relationship and techniques play significant roles in the change process. One factor alone is not sufficient to bring about change.

Theoretical Considerations

Although some might strongly disagree, it can be said that Freud (1940) was the first therapist to point out the interplay of therapist qualities and techniques. One of the major psycho-analytic techniques is interpretation. With regard to interpretation, Freud states that one assesses the patient's readiness to receive the interpretation before giving it and does not tell the patient everything that one knows or has discovered. As a rule, one refrains from telling the patient "a construction or explanation until he himself has so nearly arrived at it that only a single step remains to be taken" (p. 43).

According to Freud (1940), interpretation is to be supported by two counsellor qualities: respect for the patient, and empathy. Freud cautions psychoanalysts against moulding patients into images of themselves. He states that, "however much the analyst may be tempted to act as a teacher, model and ideal to other people and to make them in his own image, he should not forget that this is not his task in the analytic relationship" (p. 39). Empathy, the second psychoanalyst quality, "is a form of 'emotional knowing', the experiencing of another's inner world" (Arlow, 1989, p. 47). Freud (1913, p. 320) contends that everyone "possesses in his own unconscious an instrument with which he can interpret the utterances of the unconscious in other people." In another text, Freud (1915b, p. 194) states that "It is a very remarkable thing that the Ucs. of one human being can react upon that of the another, without passing through the Cs." In this sense, empathy is a special mode of perceiving that presupposes the ability of the analyst to identify with the patient and to be able to share the patient's experience affectively as well as cognitively. In psychoanalytic terms, empathy presupposes that the therapist's identification with the patient is transient and that the therapist maintains his or her separateness from the patient (Arlow, 1989, pp. 29–30). One might argue that the notion of empathy contradicts Freud's advocacy for neutrality: that is, for "analytic purification, surgical coolness, neutrality, absence of value judgment, mirror like reflection" (Blanck & Blanck, 1979, p. 128). Freud used these terms to convey that undisciplined involvement or too much therapeutic zeal contaminates the treatment. He did not mean by this that warmth should be absent in the analytic situation. If so, how to explain Freud's (1909) treatment of the Rat Man—"He was hungry and was fed" (p. 303)— or of the Wolf Man (1918), whom Freud supported when he lost his fortune? Blanck and Blanck (1979) say that "neutrality means simply that the analyst does not seek to impose his values upon the patient" (p. 128), and, again, "analytic neutrality refers to absence of value judgments and is not violated by caring whether the patient gets better, provided that therapeutic discipline is honored" (p. 129).

Object relations theory, an extension of classical psychoanalysis, emphasizes the importance of both the relationship and the technique in the treatment of emotional disorders (Cashdan, 1988; Mahler, Pine, & Bergman, 1975; Winnicott, 1965). The

techniques used include exploration, interpretation, and confrontation, which are delivered within the context of the traditional psychoanalyst-patient therapeutic relational characteristics of respect and empathy. Unlike the early Freudians, who
focused on transference and resistance, object relations therapists focus more on the client's relationship problems with the
therapist and with persons outside therapy. Focusing on the client's relationships is not to be confused with the therapist relational qualities offered to the client. Addressing the client's relationship problems and patterns serves as the content of therapy,
much like a person's compulsive hand washing and checking
doors are content. Muran, Safran, Samstag, and Winston (2005)
applied brief relational therapy, cognitive-behavioural therapy,
and short-term dynamic therapy for treating personality disorders. Brief relational therapy promotes cultivation of the skill of
mindfulness and tracks and treats alliance ruptures. The assumption is that brief relational therapy integrates both therapist's
relational qualities and counselling techniques and therefore
would be more effective than cognitive behavioural therapy and
short-term dynamic therapy in treating personality disorders.
The authors observed that brief relational therapy was no more
effective than the other two treatments for treating personality
disorders. Perhaps the reason is that working on relational issues
such as alliance ruptures does not engage the personal characteristics of a therapist any more than when working on other personal and interpersonal issues. Thus, other methods are required
to assess the contribution of the therapist relationship and technique to successful outcome.

One also observes recognition of the importance of the therapeutic relationship among behavioural therapists. Daldrup, Beutler, Engle, and Greenberg (1988, p. 32) accept the importance
of "therapist warmth, empathic ability, integrity, credibility, trust-
worthiness and caring" for effective therapy. They add that the
therapist has the responsibility to facilitate and create an atmo-
sphere in which these qualities become apparent. In their book on

learning foundations of behavioural therapy, Kanfer and Philips (1970, p. 465) indicate that "the therapist may enhance or detract from the effectiveness of his behavioral techniques through the impact of his own personal and interactional characteristics." In the same vein, Goldfried and Davison (1976, p. 55) state that "any behavior therapist who maintains that principles of learning and social influence are all one needs to know in order to bring about behavior change is out of contact with clinical reality."

Kohlenberg, a radical behaviourist, acknowledges the importance of the therapeutic relationship to bring about therapeutic change (Kohlenberg & Tsai, 1991). It is the authors' view that a client learns from being involved in a real relationship. They state that "a therapist who loves, struggles, and is fully involved with a client provides a therapeutic environment that evokes corresponding CRB [clinically relevant behaviours]" (p. 27). In support of their view, they cite Peck (1978, p. 173), who stated what made psychotherapy effective and successful:

> It is human involvement and struggle. It is the willingness of the therapist to extend himself or herself for the purpose of nurturing the patient's growth—willingness to go out on a limb, to truly involve oneself at an emotional level in the relationship, to actually struggle with the patient and with oneself. In short, the essential ingredient of successful deep and meaningful psychotherapy is love.

The authors also point out that therapists should adapt themselves to the needs of their clients in terms of being more active and engaged or being more passive and distant (p. 27).

Cognitive therapists such as Beck and associates emphasize the importance of the therapeutic relationship for successful outcome. Beck (1976) states that a primary component of cognitive therapy is a genuine collaboration between therapist and patient. This implies that the therapist is tuned in to the vicissitudes of the patient's problems from session to session. Beck states that the therapist characteristics of genuine warmth, acceptance, and accurate empathy (Rogers, 1951) have been found to facilitate "successful outcome" (p. 221). Beck, Rush, Shaw, and Emery (1979, p. 45), however, caution against the careless use of or overemphasis on these qualities as they might become "disruptive to the therapeutic collaboration." The authors believe that these therapeutic qualities in themselves are "necessary but not sufficient to produce optimum therapeutic effect" (45). Padesky and Greenberger (1995, p. 6) reiterate Beck and associates' comments about the interplay of therapist relationship and technique: "a positive therapist-client relationship is a critically important foundation for successful therapy." They add that "the best cognitive therapists are warm, empathic, and genuine with their clients."

Although experiential/humanist therapy adheres strongly to the effectiveness of the therapist's qualities in effecting change, some therapists have integrated formal techniques into their practice. An example is Gendlin (1981, 1996), who, based on Eastern philosophies, developed a focusing technique that helps clients to access material that is out of their awareness by paying attention to bodily felt feelings. This technique often leads to insights and new perspectives concerning a current problem and consequently to new behaviours and actions.

Research Findings

Research has demonstrated that both technique and the relationship contribute to change (Goldfried & Davila, 2005). In one study on the cognitive treatment of depression, it was observed that the use of a cognitive technique improved mood and that mood changes were associated with the quality of the therapeutic relationship (Persons & Burns, 1985). In a second study on the cognitive treatment of depression, it was observed that both the client's perception of the therapist's empathy and homework compliance were associated with positive outcome (Burns & Nolen-Hoeksema, 1992). In other studies, it was observed that exploratory strategies (Bachelor, 1991), accurate interpretation (Crits-Christoph, Barber, & Kurcias, 1993), and reflection, listening, and advising (Sexton, Hembre, & Kvarme, 1996) enhance the bond between client and therapist.

Research also demonstrated that the relationship influences the effectiveness of the technique (Goldfried & Davila, 2005). Morris and Suckerman (1974) observed that systematic desensitization carried out by warm and concerned therapists was more effective than when the same technique was carried out by cold, aloof, and impersonal therapists. In a study of cognitive therapy for depression, Castonguay, Goldfried, Wiser, Raue, and Hayes (1996) observed that the ineffective use of this treatment modality for depression occurred only in those cases where there was a strained therapeutic alliance. In two other studies, the effective use of a technique was related to a client's readiness or lack of readiness to comply with the directives of the therapist. For example, Linehan (1993) observed that, in using dialectical behaviour therapy to treat borderline personality disorders, patients were resistant to being told the things that needed to be changed or could be done better. The patients interpreted these suggestions as criticisms. Linehan recommended a balance between acceptance and change. Another study, by Beutler, Clarkin, and Bongar (2000), also observed that, for clients who have a high internal locus of control, behavioural techniques were less effective. They interpreted this to mean that persons who are told what to do feel that their freedom is being threatened and therefore do not effectively use the offered technique.

The research findings clearly demonstrate that the choice of psychotherapeutic techniques must be guided by the quality of the therapeutic relationship and by the client's readiness to change. It appears that, the stronger the therapeutic relationship, the more willing the client is to accept techniques as part of the therapeutic process. In reviewing the research on the role of therapist variables in the change process, Beutler and colleagues

(2004, p. 292) conclude that "the tendency to pit relationship factors against technical ones ... must be replaced by a more integrative and synergistic perspective."

Mechanisms and Mediating Variables in the Change Process

Thus far it has been established that the relationship and techniques interplay in the change process. What are the agents of therapeutic change? Are there mediating variables or mechanisms that power the interaction of relationship and techniques in bringing about change?

The agents, mechanisms, or mediating variables considered to be therapeutically curative are dependent to a large extent on the theory that one holds. Psychodynamic theory, for example, considers gaining insight into one's unconscious strivings, release of repressed affect (abreaction) (Freud, 1940), transference gratification (Freud, 1915a), corrective emotional experience (Alexander, 1954), holding environment and empowerment (Winnicott, 1965), activation of unconscious fantasies (Silverman, 1982), and release of bad objects (Fairbairn, 1952) to be curative and directly related to change. Behavioural and cognitive-behavioural theorists maintain that cognitive processes act as an intervening variable in the change process. However, they differ in how they see cognitive change implicated in therapeutic change. Bandura (1977, p. 79), a behavioural therapist, states that "cognitive events are induced and altered most readily by experiences of mastery arising from successful performance." However, "cognition is but one link in a behavior-cognition-environment loop that gives primacy to none of these components" (Arkowitz & Hannah, 1989, p. 152). Beck (1976), a cognitive theorist, holds that cognitions are not only mediators of subsequent emotions and behaviours but also the primary cause of them. Beck states that there is a "sequence of thoughts that intervened between the event and unpleasant emotional reactions" (p. 26).

How the Client Uses the Therapeutic Relationship to Bring about Change

How does the interaction of relationship and technique bring about the curative factors that underlie change? What does the client take from the relationship and technique interaction to achieve the curative factor and subsequent changes? It is possible to have a "good enough" therapeutic relationship and a competent delivery of a technique without their interaction translating into the emergence of a curative factor and subsequent attitudinal and behavioural changes. The two factors can exist side by side but not affect each other. What, then, makes it possible for the therapeutic relationship and technique, in tandem, to bring about therapeutic change?

The thesis of this chapter is that it is not the therapeutic relationship or the technique or the interaction of the two by itself that brings about therapeutic change. Rather, it is what the client takes from the therapeutic relationship and the technique offered that is directly linked to client transformations.

To understand how a client might take from the therapeutic relationship and technique and/or their interaction what she needs to secure the desired change, one can use the example of the digestive system and its relationship to the intake of food. A person might be given some fruit to eat, such as a pear, as part of the daily diet. The pear and how it is presented determine what can be taken but do not determine what the person actually takes from it. The pear, so to speak, offers itself to the person. It is the person's digestive system that determines what is needed and what it will take from the pear. A healthy digestive system will take nutrients, minerals, and vitamins from a pear differently than will an unhealthy system. At times, eating the pear may actually serve as an irritant, particularly when the digestive system is upset. In a similar vein, the person takes from the relationship and technique what she needs for her emotional health and/or to heal herself. It is the client who determines how the technique and relationship will impact her. The client is an active participant in the therapeutic process. Similar to food that acts as an irritant or a toxin, the interaction of technique and relationship might serve as a psychological irritant or toxin, particularly when use of the technique is ill timed and when the relationship offered is not in keeping with the client's pace and needs. For example, some clients, such as those with borderline personality disorders, require nurturing, affirmation, and bonding during the first phase of therapy. If the therapist is unaware of this need and uses a technique to challenge the client to become autonomous, the client will take very little, if anything, from the relationship and technique and will likely terminate therapy prematurely.

Illustrations of Client's Use of the Therapeutic Technique

The following examples illustrate how clients have taken from the therapeutic relationship and technique what they needed to work through their problems. All of the clients were seen by the same therapist, who uses psychodynamic theory (e.g., object relations theory and self psychology) to understand and conceptualize emotional problems and who uses experiential techniques (e.g., experiential focusing, imagery, ego state therapy) as modalities of treatment. His method of therapy is process and discovery oriented. It is process oriented in the sense that change is seen to occur in incremental steps across phases. Three of the phases are Exploration/Uncovering, Awareness, and Action/Experimentation (Meier & Boivin, 1984, 1988, 1992, 1998). The approach is discovery oriented in the sense that the therapist helps clients to uncover motives, cognitive processes, affective states, and repetitive patterns that underlie their personal and interpersonal problems and to use these insights and draw from their inner resources to bring about the desired attitudinal and behavioural changes. The emphasis on the uncovering process is for the client to access, acknowledge, and live from his or her life-giving needs, aspirations, desires, and wants, some of which were briefly described above.

The material presented in the following cases is taken from actual therapy sessions that were audiotaped for the purposes of training and research. Following the use of a technique, the therapist typically asked clients to report on their experience of the exercise: that is, report how the technique was helpful to them. From the exercise itself and from the clients' responses, one can derive what they took from the technique to help them deal with their presenting problems. Unfortunately, it was not the therapist's habit to ask clients how the therapeutic relationship was helpful to them in resolving their problems. Since the therapist used experiential techniques and proceeded in a discovery-oriented manner, one can assume that the therapist fulfilled Rogers' core conditions of empathy, genuineness, and positive regard, and Heidegger's concept of caring, and inserted the technique in the therapeutic process according to the needs of the client.

The examples presented below demonstrate how two different clients used two popular therapeutic techniques— Experiential Focusing and Gestalt Two Chair—to deal with personal and interpersonal problems.

Experiential Focusing Technique

The Experiential Focusing Technique (Gendlin, 1996) is designed to help clients pull themselves out of feeling stuck, confused, and conflicted by getting in touch with a bodily felt feeling that is assumed to embody an understanding and a direction for the resolution of the presenting concern. In this exercise, the client takes a meditative position and attitude, puts aside all daily concerns, attends to bodily felt feelings (e.g., pressure in the abdomen), allows the feeling to formulate an image, word, symbol, or picture, asks what is needed to make all of this better, and then receives and accepts that which is suggested. This technique offers clients a space where they can access the deeper layers of their concerns.

Client Background

The Experiential Focusing Technique (Gendlin, 1996) was used with Simone (pseudonym), who sought counselling because she was confused about how her childhood experience with sexual abuse—incest—affected her sexual orientation and her feelings and thoughts about lesbian sexual relationships.

Simone, in her late twenties and a helping professional, has many women friends toward whom she is supportive and with whom she is caring, loving, and intimate. In working with lesbian couples, Simone observed that they have the same degree of emotional intimacy as she has with her women friends yet, for her, emotional intimacy does not culminate in sexual engagements with her women friends. Nevertheless, something within her made her feel that, given this intimacy, such relationships would lead to lesbian relationships. Simone was confused as to why this did not occur for her and wondered whether it was related to her own sexual abuse, to enculturation, or to something else.

Summary of Session

To help Simone work through the confusion, the Experiential Focusing Technique was used. In proceeding through this exercise, Simone at first experienced tension in her stomach and abdomen, tightness in her chest, and shortness of breath. These symptoms then shifted to feeling pressure on her temples. All of the bodily sensations then left her, everything turned dark, and she became aware of her sadness. She found herself in a dark hole, like a prison, naked, sitting up with her arms wrapped around her legs, and rocking to comfort herself. She felt that she was in the hole because she was a bad person. She tried to be strong and brave.

The darkness was then broken by a small light, which allowed her to see herself. At the same time, a woman with a veiled face came up behind her, placed a blanket around her, embraced her, and took her hand, and the two then walked out of the darkness together. Simone did not know the woman, but she felt safe, secure, protected, loved, and nurtured by the woman. The woman represented that which was good and pure.

Debriefing

In the debriefing, Simone expressed how this exercise challenged and helped her to work through her confusion about her sexual orientation and her feelings and thoughts about lesbian relationships. The following is an edited transcript of the feedback part of the session. (Note that interventions/responses T33, T34, and C33 were inaudible and therefore deleted).

T29:   What was the experience like for you?

C29:   It was very powerful. There was this vivid image, and it went away, and there was the girl. I was overwhelmed with this sense of sadness and aloneness that I was not aware of (silence 25 sec). But in the beginning I couldn't get into my body. It wouldn't stay. I felt tension in my stomach, and it went to my chest, and I felt a bit nauseous, and I felt this tension in my head, nothing was static.

T30:   It kept moving.

C30:   It kept moving all over, it wouldn't stay. I couldn't make sense of it, I couldn't stay with it, it was jumping around. And then everything went black, not black, charcoal grey, except this little light at the bottom that allowed me to see me. It was like a projector, there was a ray so that I could see, and I knew that I was there. I felt that I was there, but then the light came on, and then I could see me (silence 30 sec). I am a bit amazed when I said I know that I am not bad. There was always a part of me that knew that even despite all of the actions that said that I was bad. I was always able to hang onto that feeling, that knowledge that I wasn't bad. I think that that woman that came, she looked like Mary, and she came to take me away, and she represented good, and she represented the good, and she came to rescue me.

T31: She came to nurture you, to comfort you, to take you away.

C31: And to take me to where I belonged. Take me out of the dark, to take me out of the evil, to take me out of the bad, and to take me back to where I belonged, and that is where the security and the safety [are]. I didn't know who she was, and I didn't know where I was going, but yet I knew that I was going somewhere where I belonged, I was going somewhere good.

T32: In some way she affirmed what you knew.

C32: But only I knew. You know there is a little child, and she is so tiny and so innocent and so scrawny and help-less with crossed legs as in an Indian position just rock-ing back and forth trying to soothe herself.

T35: When you look at the exercise as a whole, what do you make of it?

C35: (Silence 55 secs). I guess the exercise helps me to con-solidate that intuitive goodness. It helps to sort out my confusion and to discover myself in relation to others.

C36: Even though I was sitting there and I was in that cir-cumstance and I experienced that very dark, fearful alone place, there was that part of me, that spirit, that goodness that was affirmed and was acknowledged and was embraced by this woman.

T37: Anything else you want to say about this exercise?

C37: The woman represents the good and nurturing spirit. Even though I don't know her or where I am going, I feel I can trust where she will take me. I will be safe. She

provides what I need, my needs will be met. I liken this
to my experience with women in that with my intimate
girlfriends, who I perceive to be emotional, supportive,
caring, and affectionate, my intimacy needs are met, and
therefore the relationship is complete without sexual
engagement, whereas with men I feel incomplete without sexual intimacy which is connected to me emotionally. This would explain my confusion because, if I have
the foundation for an intimate relationship with women,
why would the natural progression not be toward sexual
intimacy? This speaks to my curiosity about the meaning
of the sexual relationship for lesbian couples.

C39:   It was a powerful experience, and it helped me to sort
out my confusion and to discover myself in relation to
others.

Comment

Using the Experiential Focusing Technique indirectly helped
Simone to clarify her confusion about her feelings and thoughts
about lesbian relationships and her sexual orientation. Through
this exercise, Simone was able to reach deep within herself, get in
touch with herself through a bodily felt feeling, reclaim her sense
of goodness, which was symbolized by the woman, and validate
her own thoughts about her relationships with women and about
lesbian relationships, although she felt pressured to feel and think
otherwise. Simone took from the exercise the experience of being
loved and being a good person and being affirmed for her intuition that her relationships with her women friends were complete
without sexual expression. These were for her the curative factors.
She also experienced that she is able to have a view on things that
differs from those of others and at the same time be loved, nurtured, and accepted by them. In other words, Simone was able to
balance the need to remain in a relationship (togetherness) and the
need to be her own person (separateness): that is, have her own
ideas and act and live according to them.

Gestalt Two Chair Technique

In the Gestalt Two Chair Technique, the client speaks to an imaginary person or to an imaginary part of self in a chair that faces the client (Perls, 1969). The task of the therapist is to keep the dialogue focused and in the here and now and to help the client listen to implicit messages. This technique is particularly useful in helping clients to express and externalize internal dialogues concerning conflicts since it offers the client an opportunity to dialogue with a significant other or part of self about a significant concern or problem. They take turns talking, and each speaks from his or her respective chair. The steps of the process leading to change usually involve confrontation, empathic understanding, collaboration, and resolution (Meier & Boivin, 2001, 2006).

Client Background

Rick, 24 years old, single, and Caucasian, requested therapy because he felt that something was preventing him from being happy, successful, and committed. There was something stopping him from being the person he wanted to be. In the pre-dialogue phase of the session, Rick pictured that which was stopping him as an invisible wall, which keeps him separated from others and tells him that he cannot have close relationships. He sensed a two-voice dialogue within himself regarding how to live his life. At this point the therapist introduced the Gestalt Two Chair Technique.

Summary of the Session

When engaged in the Gestalt Two Chair exercise, Rick began to give expression to the two voices. He called the one voice Self and the second voice Wall. He pictured Wall as keeping him from having close relationships and from being happy, successful, and committed. In speaking to Wall, Self stated that he was tired of hearing Wall tell him what to do, how to be, how to act, and to keep distant from people. In defence, Wall said that Self was just a kid and that it was Wall's job to protect him and that this was the price that Self had to pay and the pain that he had to endure. Self complained that he could no longer put up with Wall and its pressures to keep him away from people. Self expressed that he was tired of not having someone to care for and not feeling wanted, that he wanted more adventure in his life, more risk taking, and more space. Self found Wall very mistrusting of others, overprotective, stifling, and not willing to take risks and be spontaneous. Self wanted Wall to let go of control over him and to stop protecting him. Wall began to understand where Self was coming from, agreed that it was too protective, rigid, and stifling. Both agreed to work together to resolve their conflicts and differences. At the same time, Wall would learn to let go of control over Self and take more risks, and Self, for its part, would let Wall have a part in his life.

Debriefing

In the feedback following the session, Rick described his experience in using the Gestalt Two Chair Technique to work through his inner dialogue. The following is an edited transcript of that part of the session.

T59:   How do you feel about the exercise?

C59:   Pretty good right now. It is strange, you know, the Wall kept being associated with my mom, you know; I felt pretty good, felt good.

T60:   When you say good. ...

C60:   Like feel energetic or like a relief to some degree that there's that something that changed.

T61:   What is it that has changed?

C6l: I'm walking out with a ticket to risk, you know. Like what I came out with from this exchange is a ticket to risk and a ticket to learn, you know.

T63:   You have permission to risk and learn, and whatever you've learned will help you to risk.

C63:   Um-hum.

T64:   How do you see yourself? ...

C64:   Working together more than fighting each other. And it's like from both sides you get the sense of caution, but at least there's a stepping out of it. OK, we'll trust each other a bit, not totally, but we'll trust each other a bit, and we'll see how that goes, you know.

T65:   There's an opportunity to do things differently and to be different now.

C65:   Yeah. I'm really quite surprised at the emotion at the beginning and how fast it struck. It was like "Oh, what's going on here?" you know.

T66:   You experienced some unexpected deep feelings.

C66:   Yeah, yeah.

T67:   Anything else that you want to say before we terminate?

C69:   Um-hum. The image of the Wall was very appropriate. I just kind of struck out there when I started the interview, I sensed some kind of Wall there that just ah. ...

T71:   It blocked [you] from moving forward.

C71:   Well, the reason for an invisible Wall is that I could see the people playing on the other side, and I couldn't play with them, you know.

Comment

In this exercise, Rick reclaimed his "authority" over his own life: that is, he took charge of how he wanted to live his life. In his earlier years and upbringing, Rick was dominated by the wishes, desires, and demands of his mother (the Wall); she did not affirm his self-directive behaviours: that is, his desire to play and interact with his peers. In object relations terminology, Rick, in the exercise, achieved some degree of separation from his mother and exercised his sense of individuation by telling the Wall to respect his desires and wishes for adventure and risk taking. His desire to take risks is an expression of his desire to be authentic, to live his life truthfully and fully. Rick emerged from the exercise with a "ticket" to take risks, to learn, and to take charge of his life. From the Wall, Rick received affirmation for his views about the sti-fling nature of the Wall and the need to take risks if one wants to live life outside the box, beyond conventions. The curative factor for Rick was the experience of being an individuated person, for which he was affirmed.

Conclusion

From the examples presented above, one can conclude that clients were able to take from the relationship and techniques what they needed for their personal and interpersonal growth and devel-opment. The relationship and the techniques together offered something potentially helpful and challenging to the clients, who responded positively to them by taking from them what they needed. Rather than viewing the relationship and the techniques as interacting, one could speak more accurately of the relationship and techniques together interacting with the client. In this sense, the relationship and techniques become one, the techniques being extensions of the relationship.

It is useful to conceptualize, in object relations terminology, the client's underlying personal and interpersonal needs and desires in order to offer the client a challenging and growth-oriented experi-ence and to keep the exercise focused on the task at hand. Many clients' underlying problems appear to be related to relational or self issues or to a combination of them. When clients' problems are correctly conceptualized, the therapist is in a better position to offer the types of relationship and technique that challenge the client personally and interpersonally.

Since clients seemingly take from the tandem of the thera-peutic relationship and techniques what they need personally and interpersonally, it would be interesting to study these differ-ences. For example, one could design a research project in which therapists offer the same technique to multiple clients with the same diagnosis and then compare for differences within same therapist groups and between therapist groups. This research could be extended to include two or more techniques and assess for differences within same therapist groups, between therapist groups, and between techniques. For all of these studies, one could use standardized instruments to identify the nature of the gains. However, in the initial stage of this type of research, it would be important to conduct qualitative studies that analyze clients' reports on their experience of techniques and the therapeutic relationship.

References

Alexander, F. (1954). Some quantitative aspects of psychoanalytic technique. *Journal of the American Psychoanalytic Association, 2,* 685–701.

Arkowitz, H., & Hannah, M. T. (1989). Cognitive, behavioural, and psychodynamic therapies: Converging or diverging pathways to change? In A. Freeman, K. M. Simon, L. E. Beutler, & H. Arkowitz (Eds.), *Comprehensive handbook of cognitive therapy* (pp. 43–167). New York: Plenum Press.

Arlow, J. (1989). Psychoanalysis. In R. J. Corsini & D. Wedding (Eds.), *Current psychotherapies* (4th ed.) (pp. 19–62). Itasca, IL: F. E. Peacock Publishers.

Bachelor, A. (1991). Comparison and relationship to outcome of diverse dimensions of the helping alliance as seen by client and therapist. *Psychotherapy, 28,* 534–549.

Bandura, A. (1977). *Social learning theory.* Englewood Cliffs, NJ: Prentice-Hall.

Beck, A. T. (1976). *Cognitive therapy and the emotional disorders.* New York: Meridian Book.

Beck, A. T., Rush, J. A., Shaw, B.F., & Emery, G. (1979). *Cognitive therapy of depression.* New York: Guilford Press.

Beutler, L. E., Clarkin, J. F., & Bongar, B. (2000). *Guidelines for the systematic treatment of the depressed patient.* New York: Oxford University Press.

Beutler, L. E., Malik, M., Alimohamed, S., Harwood, T. M., Talebi, H., Noble, S., & Wong, E. (2004). Therapist variables. In M. J. Lambert (Ed.), *Bergin and Garfield's handbook of psychotherapy and behavior change* (pp. 227–306). New York: John Wiley & Sons.

Bjork, D. W. (1993). *B.F. Skinner: A life.* New York: Basic Books.

Blanck, G., & Blanck, R. (1979). *Ego psychology 11: Psychoanalytic developmental psychology.* New York: Columbia University Press.

Bordin, E. S. (1979). The generalizability of the psychoanalytic concept of the working alliance. *Psychotherapy: Theory, Research, and Practice, 16(3),* 252–260.

Buckley, K. W. (1989). *Mechanical man: John Broadus Watson and the beginnings of behaviorism.* New York: Guilford Press.

Burns, D. D., & Nolen-Hoeksema, S. (1992). Therapeutic empathy and recovery from depression in cognitive-behavior therapy. *Journal of Consulting and Clinical Psychology, 60,* 441–449.

Cashdan, S. (1988). *Object relations therapy: Using the relationship.* New York: W. W. Norton.

Castonguay, L. G., Goldfried, M. R., Wiser, S. L., Raue, P. J., & Hayes, A. M. (1996). Predicting the effect of cognitive therapy for depression: A study of unique and common factors. *Journal of Consulting and Clinical Psychology, 64,* 497–504.

Clarkin, J. F., & Levy, K. N. (2004). The influence of client variables on psychotherapy. In M. J. Lambert (Ed.), *Bergin and Garfield's handbook of psychotherapy and behavior change* (pp. 194–226). New York: John Wiley & Sons.

Craig, G. (1999). *Emotional freedom technique: Manual.* The Sea Ranch, CA: Author.

Crits-Christoph, P., Barber, J. P., & Kurcias, J. S. (1993). The accuracy of therapists' interpretations and the development of the therapeutic alliance. *Psychotherapy Research, 3,* 25–35.

Daldrup, R. J., Beutler, L. E., Engle, D., & Greenberg, L. S. (1988). *Focused expressive psychotherapy: Freeing the overcontrolled patient.* New York: Guilford Press.

Fairbairn, W. R. D. (1952). *Psychoanalytic studies of personality.* London: Tavistock.

Frank, J. D. (1973). *Persuasion and healing.* Baltimore: Johns Hopkins University Press.

Freud, S. (1909). Notes upon a case of obsessional neurosis. *Standard edition,* 10, pp. 153–318. London: Hogarth Press.

Freud, S. (1913). The disposition to obsessional neurosis: A contribution to the problem of choice of neurosis. *Standard edition,* 12, pp. 317–326. London: Hogarth Press.

Freud, S. (1915a). Observations on transference love. *Standard edition,* 12, pp. 157–171. London: Hogarth Press.

Freud, S. (1915b). The unconscious. *Standard edition,* 14, pp. 166–204. London: Hogarth Press.

Freud, S. (1918). From the history of an infantile neurosis. *Standard edition,* 18, pp. 7–64. London: Hogarth Press.

Freud, S. (1923). The ego and the id. *Standard edition,* 19. London: Hogarth Press.

Freud, S. (1940). An outline of psychoanalysis. *Standard edition,* 23, pp. 144–207. London: Hogarth Press.

Gendlin, E. T. (1981). *Focusing* (2nd ed.). New York: Bantam Book.

Gendlin, E. T. (1996). *Focusing-oriented psychotherapy: A manual of the experiential method.* Toronto: Guilford.

Goldfried, M. R., & Davila, J. (2005). The role of relationship and technique in therapeutic change. *Psychotherapy: Theory, Research, Practice, Training, 42*(4), 421–430.

Goldfried, M. R., & Davison, G. C. (1976). *Clinical behavior therapy.* New York: Holt, Rinehart & Winston.

Grinder, J., & Bandler, R. (1983). *Reframing: Neurolinguistic programming and the transformation of meaning.* Moab, UT: Real People Press.

Heidegger, M. (1962). *Being and time.* (J. Macquarrie & E. Robinson, Trans.). New York: Harper & Row (Original work published 1926).

Kanfer, F. H., & Philips, J. S. (1970). *Learning foundations of behavior therapy.* New York: Wiley.

Kaplan, L. (1978). *Oneness and separateness: From infant to individual.* New York: Simon & Schuster.

Kernberg, O. (1984). *Severe personality disorders: Psychotherapeutic strategies.* New Haven, CT: Yale University Press.

Kohlenberg, R. J., & Tsai, M. (1991). *Functional analytic psychotherapy: Creating intense and curative therapeutic relationships.* New York: Plenum Press.

Kohut, H. (1977). *The restoration of the self.* New York: International Universities Press.

Linehan, M. M. (1993). *Cognitive-behavioral treatment of borderline personality disorder.* New York: Guilford Press.

Mahler, M., Pine, F., & Bergman, A. (1975). *The psychological birth of the human infant.* New York: Basic Books.

Maslow, A. H. (1961). Comments on Skinner's attitude towards science. *Daedalus, XC,* 572–573.

Maslow, A. H. (1970). *Motivation and personality.* New York: Harper.

Masterson, J. F. (1976). *Psychotherapy of the borderline adult: A developmental approach.* New York: Brunner/Mazel.

Meier, A., & Boivin, M. (1984). *Manual of operational criteria for classifying counseling phases.* Unpublished manuscript, Saint Paul University, Ottawa.

Meier, A., & Boivin, M. (1988). *Counseling phases criteria: Interrater agreement and validity data.* Unpublished manuscript, Saint Paul University, Ottawa.

Meier, A., & Boivin, M. (1992*). A Seven-Phase Model of the Change Process and its research and clinical application.* Paper presented at the eighth annual conference of the Society for the Exploration of Psychotherapy Integration, San Diego, April 2-4.

Meier, A., & Boivin, M. (1998). *The Seven Phase Model of the Change Process: Theoretical foundation, definitions, coding guidelines, training procedures, and research data.* Unpublished manuscript, Saint Paul University, Ottawa.

Meier, A., & Boivin, M. (2001). Conflict resolution: The interplay of affects, cognitions, and needs in the resolution of intrapersonal conflicts. *Pastoral Sciences, 20*(1), 93–119.

Meier, A., & Boivin, M. (2006). Intrapsychic conflicts, their formation, underlying dynamics, and resolution: An object relations perspective. In A. Meier & M. Rovers (Eds.), *Through conflict to reconciliation* (pp. 295–328). Ottawa: Novalis.

Morris, R. J., & Suckerman, K. R. (1974). Therapist warmth as a factor in automated systematic desensitization. *Journal of Consulting and Clinical Psychology, 42,* 244–250.

Muran, J. C., Safran, J. D., Samstag, L. W., & Winston, A. (2005). Evaluating an alliance-focused treatment for personality disorders. *Psychotherapy: Theory, Research, Practice, Training, 42*(4), 532–545.

Padesky, C. A., & Greenberger, D. (1995). *Clinician's guide to mind over mood.* New York: Guilford Press.

Peck, M. S. (1978). *The road less traveled.* New York: Simon & Schuster.

Perls, F. S. (1969). *Gestalt therapy verbatim.* Toronto: Bantam Books.

Persons, J. P., & Burns, D. D. (1985). Mechanisms of action in cognitive therapy: The relative contributions of technique and interpersonal interventions. *Cognitive Therapy and Research, 9,* 539–551.

Raskin, N. J., & Rogers, C. R. (1989). Person-centered therapy. In R. Corsini & D. Wedding (Eds.), *Current psychotherapies* (4th ed.) (pp. 155–194). Itasca, IL: Peacock.

Rogers, C. R. (1951). *Client-centered therapy.* Boston: Houghton Mifflin.

Rogers, C. R. (1957). The necessary and sufficient conditions of therapeutic personality change. *Journal of Consulting Psychology, 21,* 95–103.

Rogers, C. R. (1966). Client-centered therapy. In C. H. Patterson (Ed.), *Theories of counseling and psychotherapy* (pp. 403–439). New York: Harper & Row.

Rogers, C. R. (1986). A client-centered/person-centered approach to therapy. In I. L. Kurtash & A. Wolf (Eds.), *Psychotherapist's casebook: Theory and technique in the practice of modern therapies* (pp. 197-208). London: Jossey-Bass.

Rogers, C. R., & Skinner, B. F. (1956). Some issues concerning the control of human behavior: A symposium. *Science, 124,* 1057–1066.

Sexton, H. C., Hembre, K., & Kvarme, G. (1996). The interaction of the alliance and therapy microprocess: A sequential analysis. *Journal of Consulting and Clinical Psychology, 64,* 471–480.

Shapiro, F. (2001). *Eye movement desensitization and reprocessing: Basic principles, protocols, and procedures.* New York: Guilford Press.

Sheikh, A. A. (Ed.). (2003). *Healing images: The role of imagination in health.* Amityville, NY: Baywood Publisher.

Silverman, L. H. (1982). The unconscious fantasy as therapeutic agent in psychoanalytic treatment. In S. Slipp (Ed.), *Curative factors in dynamic psychotherapy* (pp. 199–222). New York: McGraw-Hill.

Skinner, B. F. (1953). *Science and human behavior.* London: Collier MacMillan.

Skinner, B. F. (1972). *Beyond freedom and dignity.* New York: Alfred A. Knopf.

Thorne, B. (1992). *Carl Rogers.* London: Sage Publications.

Watson, J. B. (1913). Psychology as the behaviorist views it. *Psychological Review, 20,* 158–177.

Winnicott, D. (1965). *The maturational processes and facilitating environment.* New York: International Universities Press.

Yates, A. Y. (1975). *Theory and practice in behavior therapy.* New York: John Wiley & Sons.

II

The Fate of the Helping Relationship in the Age of Manualized Treatments: Evidence-Based Practice and Time-Limited Psychotherapies

Tricia Schöttler

I worry about psychotherapy—about how it may be deformed by economic pressures and impoverished by radically abbreviated training programmes.

(Yalom, 2003, p. xv)

Psychotherapy, as a means to give meaning to one's life, to face and conquer psychological issues, to make fundamental changes in one's life, will become remnants of memories from a dying culture.

(Wampold, 2001, p. 228)

Despite the gloomy tone of the title of this chapter, the aims of this discussion are ultimately benevolent: to highlight the crucial importance of the helping relationship, a proven medium of client change; to outline the current trends in psychotherapy research and training as they relate to the recognition, or lack thereof, of the role of this crucial factor; to speculate on the possible future of the helping relationship within this current social/political/economic climate; and to offer some alternative paths that might serve to counteract what seems to me and many others to be a growing trend toward ultimately divesting the therapeutic encounter of its inherently personal, human, and relational foundations, in effect taking the helping relationship and the therapist out of the treatment room.

What Is the Helping Relationship?

The concept of the helping relationship between therapist and client is as old as psychotherapy itself, originating in the psychoanalytic tradition and initially conceptualized as the healthy, affectionate, and trusting feelings of the client toward the therapist, as opposed to the neurotic component (i.e., the transference) of the relationship (Wampold, 2001). Many different terms have been used to describe the helping relationship, including "the alliance," "the therapeutic bond," and "therapeutic rapport." Over the years, the concept has been cross-theoretically expanded to include at least two core aspects of the helping relationship.

The first core aspect can be described as the *personal bond* between client and therapist, and it includes the qualities of any good and meaningful relationship (Martin, 2000). This aspect includes traditional Rogerian concepts such as warmth, empathy, acceptance, genuineness, respect, non-judgmentalism, patience, and sensitivity. The establishment of an effective personal bond is fundamental throughout the course of therapy but is probably most critical early in therapy, when the client is establishing a basic sense of trust and safety with the therapist. There is some evidence that the strength of this aspect of the alliance is established quickly, within the first three sessions of psychotherapy, and changes little thereafter (Eaton, Abeles, & Gutfreund, 1988). Therefore, it behooves the therapist to pay particular attention to early therapeutic experiences and the power of the first impression in establishing a solid personal bond.

The second core aspect of the helping relationship can be described as the *working alliance,* and it includes the collaborative commitment of both therapist and client to the mutual work, processes, and goals of psychotherapy (Martin, 2000). This facet of the helping relationship is more task oriented, and it involves client and therapist agreement on where they are going and how they plan to get there together. The research evidence suggests that this client-therapist epistemological agreement is a critical component in psychotherapy effectiveness, regardless of which specific epistemology the participants agree on (Wampold, 2001). As Jerome Frank noted, "therapists should seek to learn as many approaches as they find congenial and convincing to themselves—creating a good therapeutic match involves both educating the patient about the therapist's conceptual scheme, and if necessary, modifying the scheme to take into account the concepts the patient brings to therapy" (Frank & Frank, 1991, p. xv).

The helping relationship may thus be conceptualized as consisting of a variety of important components, including the client's affective relationship with the therapist, the therapist's ability to respond empathically and create basic conditions of safety and trust, and client and therapist agreement about the goals, processes, and tasks of the therapeutic process. Much research has been dedicated to exploring basic questions about the influence of these various aspects of the helping relationship on client outcome.

What Is the Role of the Helping Relationship in Client Outcome?

A large body of research evidence exists, spanning several decades, supporting the primary role of the therapeutic alliance in determining treatment outcome (Barber, Connolly, Crits-Cristoph, Gladis, & Siqueland, 2000; Horvath, 2001a, 2001b; Lambert & Barley, 2001; Martin, Garske, & Davis, 2000; Norcross, 2001; Wampold, 2001). In fact, we can say conclusively, and without any reservation, that the quality of the therapeutic relationship is far more important than whatever techniques the therapist uses (Martin, 2000). The results of two recent meta-analyses of existing research on the relationship between the alliance and outcome are illustrative of this point. In 1991, Horvath and Symonds reviewed 20 studies published between 1978 and 1990. Each study contained an average of 40 participants, involved treatments that lasted an average of 21 sessions, and used therapists with an average of 8 years of experience. The results of the aggregated statistics of correlation indicated a significant, medium-sized effect of .26, which is equivalent to saying that about 7% of client outcome was associated with the alliance. In 2000, Martin, Garske, and Davis conducted a similar meta-analysis including 79 studies published between 1977 and 1997, with similar aggregated results. They found an average effect size of .22, indicating that 5% of the outcome variance was associated with the alliance. To put these findings in context, similar meta-analyses comparing specific treatment effects and differences between treatments produce at most an effect size equivalent to saying that approximately 1% of the outcome was due to specific treatment effects. Thus, these meta-analyses suggest that the alliance accounts for at least 7 times the variance than that due to specific treatment differences.

Various theoretical explanations have been postulated as to why the therapeutic relationship is so inherently healing (see Schöttler, Oliver, & Porter, 2004, for a review). Therapist-offered conditions such as empathy, warmth, genuineness, respect, and acceptance have been conceptualized as providing clients with the freedom and safety of a warm, accepting, trusting, reliable, and honest relationship within which to openly explore and experience both positive and painful emotions and thoughts (Truax, Carkhuff, & Douds, 1964). These "personal bonding" skills and attitudes elicit authentic client exploration, reduce anxiety in clients (which in itself is reinforcing), shatter clients' experiences of isolation and hopelessness, elicit reciprocally positive affect in clients, and permit the therapist to become a personally potent reinforcer in the client's life (Carkhuff & Berenson, 1967). Furthermore, a good

therapist is able to optimally use the base of such a positive therapeutic relationship to effectively conceptualize internal client
dynamics as well as to deploy orientation-specific technical skills
(Strupp, 1986).

Other explanations of the importance of the human relationship in psychotherapy stem from the belief that the major cause of
many kinds of psychological disturbance is related to the absence
of good human relationships (Patterson, 1984). From this perspective, psychotherapy can be seen as providing a new relationship to correct the ill effects of previous negative relationships in a
client's life (Patterson, 1984; Strupp, 1986). The client undergoes
a corrective emotional experience in the context of the therapeutic
relationship, and the therapist simply becomes a better mentor
than significant figures in the patient's past (Strupp, 1986).

Henry, Schacht, and Strupp (1990) used the theory of interpersonal introjection to explain why the interpersonal and personal skills of the therapist exert such a powerful influence on
therapy outcome. The basic principle of this theory is that people
learn to treat themselves as they have been treated by others. Inter-
estingly, these authors did find evidence of a significant relationship between therapists' interpersonal behaviours and the ways in
which patients acted toward themselves. For example, there was a
high degree of correspondence between patient self-blaming and
therapist statements subtly blaming the patient.

Regardless of why it might be so, it is an undeniable fact within
the empirical research community that the therapeutic relationship heals. However, while we appear to have compelling research
support for the essential role of the relationship in client outcome,
researchers seemingly have been unwilling to go further and examine the actual components responsible for building or destroying
this essential relationship (Ackerman & Hilsenroth, 2001). We
are confident that the relationship is crucial; we are confident that
the therapist as a person must play some role in facilitating the
development of that relationship; but we are reluctant to pinpoint
what that role might be (Schöttler et al., 2004). Psychology in

particular, as a discipline, consumed with identifying, cataloguing, and measuring the personality qualities and interpersonal skills of its consumers, seems to be noticeably reluctant to turn the same level of attention toward itself. As Carkhuff and Berenson (1967) speculated, perhaps this reluctance reflects our fear of discovering that what we do is really quite magical, personal, and intangible, having much to do with who we are as human beings and less to do with who we are as psychologists.

Important Trends in Psychotherapy Research and Training

Taking a snapshot of the current state of psychotherapy research and training we can see that there appear to be at least three notable trends. These trends represent the direction in which disciplines such as psychology appear to be heading and are perhaps the biggest threats to the valuing, acknowledging, respecting, and utilizing of the therapeutic relationship. Ironically, while the empirical status of the helping relationship has never been on more sure research footing, the philosophical status of the helping relationship appears to be in serious jeopardy.

Continued Rigid Adherence to the Medical Model
The origins of psychotherapy, particularly with respect to its foundations in psychoanalysis and early behaviourism, clearly lie within the medical model (Wampold, 2001). Throughout their development, psychotherapy research and training have deviated little from the medical model and have ever more rigidly and dogmatically embraced this model in their desperate attempts to carve out a niche in an overpopulated mental health care market — a market hierarchically dominated by general practitioners and psychiatrists. There are several components of the medical model that have been directly and unquestioningly transcribed from the world of the physical body to the world of psychotherapy, with

significant implications. The most consequential component with respect to the role of the relationship in healing has to do with the notion of specificity. Specificity is a critical concept in the medical model, and it implies that it is the specific therapeutic intervention (e.g., surgery, medication) that is directly responsible for the treatment effects. Concomitantly, these specific and direct effects of the treatment are assumed to be overwhelmingly larger than any other kind of general effects in the intervention (e.g., placebo, the relationship) (Wampold, 2001). While the medical model recognizes that "non-specific" or "general" effects may be present in an intervention, they are considered incidental nuisance factors, psychological in nature, and easily distinguishable from the direct physiological and chemical effects of the intervention. Unfortunately, in the realm of psychotherapy, one cannot readily tease apart the specific effects due to the specific therapeutic ingredients (e.g., application of systematic desensitization to a phobic client) from the effects due to incidental or general factors (e.g., the helping relationship), as these effects are both psychological in nature. As Wampold (2001) concludes, what results from these differences are serious conceptual and empirical ambiguities in the realm of psychotherapy application and outcome research. Unfortunately, these ambiguities are particularly threatening to the helping relationship, which is relegated to the realm of the "nuisance," "incidental," and "non-specific" factors in this model.

The "Small Revolution" in Treatment Manuals

The use of psychotherapy treatment manuals has proliferated dramatically since the first one developed by Beck, Rush, Shaw, and Emery (1979) describing a CBT intervention for depression. This is likely because such manuals have become required components for the funding and publication of outcome research in psychotherapy (Kiesler, 1994). The notion of the treatment manual comes directly from the medical model and includes required components such as defining the targeted disorder, problem, or complaint; providing a theoretical basis for the disorder, problem, or complaint; describing the theoretical change mechanism; and specifying the therapeutic actions that are consistent with the theory, all under the rubric of specificity and the central idea that these specified treatment interventions lead to treatment efficacy. The purpose of the treatment manual is to create standardization of treatments, thereby reducing variability in the independent variable (the "operations" performed by the therapist) by eliminating the role of nuisance factors that unfortunately, once again, include components such as the interpersonal qualities and the relational and personality skills of the individual therapist and the quality of the therapeutic alliance (Wilson, 1996). Theoretically, and in accordance with the medical model, it should not matter who delivers the treatment protocol as long as the specific ingredients deemed to be directly responsible for client improvement are included.

Much research has been conducted investigating the efficacy of various manualized treatments and examining the overall impact of manualization on therapist adherence to designated protocols and therapist effectiveness. For example, Robinson, Berman, and Neimeyer (1990) conducted a meta-analysis of treatments for depression and included in their analysis approximately equal numbers of treatments conducted with manuals and without manuals. The results showed that, in directly comparing the two, the absolute magnitude of effect sizes from 11 studies that used formal manuals did not reliably differ from the absolute magnitude of effect sizes in the 14 studies in which no manuals were used.

In addition, some studies have even shown that strict adherence to the treatment manual can be detrimental to client outcome. For example, in one study, Henry, Strupp, Butler, Schacht, and Binder (1993) examined changes in therapist behaviour after a year-long manualized training program in time-limited dynamic psychotherapy. While they found that therapists' technical interventions had changed in line with the protocol, there was an unexpected decline in certain interpersonal and interactional aspects of therapy. Although the changes were not significant, the trend was toward less warmth and friendliness and greater expression of negative attitudes. After training, therapists were judged to be less optimistic, less supportive of patients' feelings, and more authoritarian. They also demonstrated less overt approval and were more defensive. Clearly, these results have disturbing implications for the therapist's ability to both value and make use of the most empirically proven "tool" in the therapy "bag of tricks," the effective establishment and maintenance of a positive helping relationship.

The Emphasis on "Empirically Supported Psychotherapies" (ESTs)

The identification and cataloguing of ESTs began in the 1990s, concomitant with an increasing emphasis on managed care in medicine and health care and the associated increasingly direct role of insurance company representatives in clinical treatment decisions (Wampold, 2001). As the use of psychopharmacological interventions in the treatment of mental disorders exploded, the medical model assured itself a particularly strong hold in the discipline of psychiatry. Psychology responded in kind, and in 1995 a task force of Division 12 in the American Psychological Association stated that, "If clinical psychology is to survive in this heyday of biological psychiatry, APA must act to emphasize the strength of what we have to offer—a variety of psychotherapies of proven efficacy" (Task Force on Promotion and Dissemination of Psychological Procedures, 1995, p. 3). Accordingly, the task force set about to identify inclusion criteria for a published list of ESTs. Although the criteria have evolved, they originated from the criteria used by the American Food and Drug Administration (FDA) to approve drugs, stipulating that a treatment would be designated empirically validated for a particular disorder provided that at least two studies showed superiority to groups that attempted to control for general effects and that the treatment was administered to a well-defined population of clients using a treatment manual (Wampold, 2001). Not surprisingly, treatments on the list include

CBT for panic disorder, exposure treatment for agoraphobia, behaviour therapy for depression, CBT for depression, interpersonal therapy for depression, and behavioural marital therapy for marital problems. Their inclusion likely reflects the fact that such treatments are inherently easier to put in a manualized form. Such manuals often do acknowledge the importance of the therapy relationship, but few go on to specify the precise therapist qualities or in-session behaviours that might facilitate the development of a curative relationship, focusing instead on the "specific" factors that are deemed to make that particular treatment better than another (Norcross, 2001).

Where Does This Leave the Helping Relationship?

The medical model continues to have a stranglehold on psychotherapy. This model, with its emphasis on specificity, manualization, and empirical support, represents a significant threat to valuing the healing nature of the therapeutic relationship. Ironically, this threat occurs despite the indisputable research evidence—it is not the specific treatments that have been shown to account for the majority of differences in client outcome, it is the alliance. Unfortunately, the helping relationship and the medical model are not good friends: the role of the alliance is relegated to "nuisance"; the factors that might help or hinder the development of a good alliance have not been well researched and hence do not readily lend themselves to manualization; and this ultimately means that the goal to "develop and maintain a good therapeutic relationship" will not likely be included in the APA's list of ESTs in the near future.

The motivation to adopt and adhere to the medical model in order to bolster the status of psychotherapy was evident right from the inception of the "talking cure," and this motivation has only become stronger in a climate of tight health care market competitiveness. Despite the clear research evidence, there continues to be resistance to fully acknowledging the crucial role of the helping relationship in client outcome. Why is this so? Some have suggested that to fully recognize this could be taken to imply that the conditions of psychological change are not the exclusive property of trained, professional practitioners (Carkhuff & Berenson, 1967). In essence, anyone with the "right" kind of personality and interpersonal skills can do this job and do it well, as long as he or she demonstrates the ability to establish a good relationship. This idea is particularly scary for a discipline that tries to hold on tightly to its rather tentative place in the mental health care system, when it is only the therapy work of psychiatrists and GPs that is covered by provincial health care plans, when the almost exclusive use of medications in treating psychological problems is increasing and only psychiatrists and GPs can prescribe them, and when private insurance health care plans are placing increasing restrictions on what mental health care providers can and cannot do and to whom they can and cannot do it. It appears that, the more distance we might put between ourselves and the "reputable" medical/scientific professions (GPs, psychiatrists), the more we may be relegating ourselves to an "alternative" status in the health care field, and the more we may ultimately be putting our own jobs in jeopardy.

Reluctance to move away from the medical model unfortunately exists among members of the various helping professions themselves. Many psychotherapy trainees prefer to learn a series of ESTs from clearly defined and structured manuals so that they can avoid the more frightening prospect of really being present with a client, of attaching to and having a meaningful encounter with another human being, and of really examining themselves and their own interpersonal/relational qualities (Wampold, 2001). One might argue that this reflects yet another disturbing societal trend toward impersonalization, detachment, and a focus on the superficial "quick fix." Similarly, within the realm of research, the unrelenting efforts of researchers to prove that their techniques are better than someone else's, while servicing the medical model, only distract the disciplines from more deeply exploring the only thing that has really been "proven" to work, the establishment of an effective therapeutic alliance. It seems that, in our efforts to carve out our niche, we may be cutting away the very thing that makes us both effective and unique. Is there an alternative?

Alternatives: Forging a Future

Wampold (2001, p. 227) notes that, "In a way, psychotherapy is a minority culture forced into co-existence with a dominant culture with different values." He goes on to describe the various alternatives for how such a minority culture might adapt to this situation, contemplating the two paths of assimilation and coexistence. He notes that, from a philosophical standpoint, assimilation into the dominant medical model culture, which appears to be the current trend, will ultimately change the fundamental nature of psychotherapy as it continues to erode the personal role of the therapist, clearly a critical factor in the establishment of the helping relationship and therefore the success of psychotherapy. Wampold optimistically postulates an alternative strategy, one of peaceful and complementary coexistence, whereby medicine and psychotherapy come to genuinely value what the other has to offer. He notes that, to accomplish this goal, it is imperative that psychotherapy adopts a new model of understanding itself, which he terms the "contextual model." He states that the contextual model understands that it is the healing context, and the meaning that the client gives to the experience, that are important. He adds that emphasis in training should be placed on the teaching of core therapeutic skills that are necessary in the establishment of a positive helping relationship—including empathic listening and responding, developing a working alliance, working through one's own issues, understanding and conceptualizing interpersonal and intrapsychic dynamics, and learning to be self-reflective about one's work. He suggests that training programs following a conceptual model would start with the teaching of these skills and then would ensure that trainees add in expertise in a variety of specific therapeutic approaches. Wampold is clear in asserting that, although the contextual model values the primacy of the alliance, it is not anathema to valuing the role of specific treatment effects. He states that the model promotes belief in treatments, but at a different level, one in which therapists realize that specific ingredients are necessary but active only in the sense that they are a component of the healing context; what is more important is that they are administered with faith and allegiance by the therapist and that they fit with the client's own rationale.

Understandably, pursuing peaceful coexistence with the world of medicine is a risky alternative for the helping professions. Nevertheless, perhaps it would be the most rewarding and meaningful path for therapists and the most beneficial for clients of these services. A contextually based psychotherapy might be seen by many clients as an alternative to the omnipresent medical model of psychological intervention and its associated "quick-fix" and impersonal context of interaction. A contextually based psychotherapy would hold on to its philosophical underpinnings as a "frontier" of meaningful human relationship and as a container for important human values of relatedness, meaning, and deep self-understanding. There is something important in this and something worth holding on to. We will all ultimately lose something in our continued unquestioning assimilation into the medical model. We will lose something empirically important, as the research evidence is conclusive that the alliance heals more than anything else, and is idealistically imperative. As Norcross (2001, p. 346) elegantly noted, impressive attempts have been made in the trend toward emphasis on technique to try to render individual practitioners as controlled variables. These efforts stand in marked contrast to "the clinician's experience of psychotherapy as an intensely interpersonal and deeply emotional experience." It is this experience that is worth valuing and preserving as the only meaningful alternative in the mental health care field.

In many Western cultures, psychotherapy is valued as a helping modality, one that can reduce symptoms, improve the quality of life, and give meaning to one's actions. Perhaps psychotherapy is indeed a myth, created by Freud and maintained by people's belief in the endeavour. In any event, it is a valuable myth and one that should be revered, cherished, and nourished, and not folded into the field of medicine, where it will be suffocated.

(Wampold, 2001, p. 231)

Although the practice of psychotherapy demands skills—both personal and technical—in the final analysis, we should be training persons, not technicians, and we should never forget—despite managed care and the technocracy of our age—that psychotherapy in the ideal sense seeks to effect healing and personality growth through an interpersonal relationship.

(Strupp, 1996, p. 138)

References

Ackerman, S. J., & Hilsenroth, M. J. (2001). A review of therapist characteristics and techniques negatively impacting the therapeutic alliance. *Psychotherapy: Theory, Research, Practice, Training, 38*(2), 171–185.

Barber, J. P., Connolly, M. B., Crits-Cristoph, P., Gladis, L., & Siqueland, L. (2000). Alliance predicts patients' outcome beyond in-treatment change in symptoms. *Journal of Consulting and Clinical Psychology, 68*(6), 1027–1032.

Beck, A. T., Rush, A. J., Shaw, B. F., & Emery, G. (1979). *Cognitive therapy of depression.* New York: Guilford.

Carkhuff, R. R., & Berenson, B. G. (1967). *Beyond counseling and therapy.* New York: Holt, Rinehart & Winston.

Eaton, T. T., Abeles, N., & Gutfreund, M. J. (1988). Therapeutic alliance and outcome: Impact of treatment length and pre-treatment symptomatology. *Psychotherapy, 25,* 536–542.

Frank, J. D., & Frank, J. B. (1991). *Persuasion and healing: A comparative study of psychotherapy* (3rd ed.). Baltimore: Johns Hopkins University Press.

Henry, W. P., Schacht, T. E., & Strupp, H. H. (1990). Patient and therapist introject, interpersonal process, and differential psychotherapy outcome. *Journal of Consulting and Clinical Psychology, 58*(6), 768–774.

Henry, W. P., Strupp, H. H., Butler, S. F., Schacht, T. E., & Binder, J. L. (1993). Effects of training in time-limited dynamic psychotherapy: Changes in therapist behavior. *Journal of Consulting and Clinical Psychology, 61*(3), 434–440.

Horvath, A. O. (2001a). The alliance. *Psychotherapy, 38*(4), 365–372.

Horvath, A. O. (2001b). The therapeutic alliance: Concepts, research, and training. *Australian Psychologist, 58*(10), 170–176.

Horvath, A. O., & Symonds, B. D. (1991). Relation between working alliance and outcome in psychotherapy: A meta-analysis. *Journal of Counseling Psychology, 38,* 139–149.

Kiesler, D. J. (1994). Standardization of intervention: The tie that binds psychotherapy research and practice. In P. F. Talley, H. H. Strupp, & S. F. Butler (Eds.), *Psychotherapy research and practice: Bridging the gap* (pp. 143–153). New York: Basic Books.

Lambert, M. J., & Barley, D. E. (2001). Research summary on the therapeutic relationship and psychotherapy outcome. *Psychotherapy, 38*(4), 357–361.

Martin, D. G. (2000). *Counseling and therapy skills* (2nd ed.). Long Grove, IL: Waveland Press.

Martin, D. J., Garske, J. P., & Davis, K. (2000). Relation of the therapeutic alliance with outcome and other variables: A meta-analytic review. *Journal of Consulting and Clinical Psychology, 68*(3), 438–450.

Norcross, J. C. (2001). Purposes, processes, and products of the task force on empirically supported therapy relationships. *Psychotherapy: Theory, Research, Practice, Training, 38*(4), 345–356.

Patterson, C. H. (1984). Empathy, warmth, and genuineness in psychotherapy: A review of reviews. *Psychotherapy, 21,* 431–438.

Robinson, L. A., Berman, J. S., & Neimeyer, R. A. (1990). Psychotherapy for the treatment of depression: A comprehensive review of controlled outcome research. *Psychological Bulletin, 108,* 30–49.

Schöttler, T., Oliver, L. E., & Porter, J. (2004). Defining and evaluating clinical competence: A review. *Guidance & Counselling, 20*(2), 46–55.

Strupp, H. H. (1986). Psychotherapy: Research, practice, and public policy (How to avoid dead ends). *American Psychologist, 41*(2), 120–130.

Strupp, H. H. (1996). Some salient lessons from research and practice. *Psychotherapy, 33,* 135–138.

Task Force on Promotion and Dissemination of Psychological Procedures. (1995). Training in and dissemination of empirically-validated psychological treatment: Report and recommendations. *The Clinical Psychologist, 48,* 2–23.

Truax, C. B., Carkhuff, R. R., & Douds, J. (1964). Toward an integration of the didactic and experiential approaches to training in counseling and psychotherapy. *Journal of Counseling Psychology, 11*(3), 240–247.

Wampold, B. E. (2001). *The great psychotherapy debate: Models, methods, and findings.* Mahwah, NJ: Lawrence Erlbaum Associates.

Wilson, G. T. (1996). Manual-based treatments: The clinical application of research findings. *Behaviour Research and Therapy, 34,* 295–314.

Yalom, I. (2003). *The gift of therapy: An open letter to a new generation of therapists and their patients.* New York: Perennial.

III

Transference and Countertransference Revisited

Augustine Meier

During the past decade, there has been increased interest in the theoretical construct of countertransference. Attempts have been made to broaden its meaning to include all of the therapist's feelings toward the client, in therapy and beyond therapy, and not to limit its meaning to the expression of the therapist's unconscious and conflicted feelings as a reaction to a client's transference. To better appreciate this trend, it is essential to revisit the concept of countertransference and to ascertain its original meaning, see how it has evolved over time, and consider the factors that have contributed to its modification.

The primary focus of this chapter is on countertransference. However, to situate countertransference within the context of the therapeutic relationship, it is important to consider the real aspects of the therapeutic relationship and transference. Therefore, the first part of the chapter presents the significant components of the therapeutic relationship. The concept of transference is presented in the second part. The third part addresses the concept of countertransference and includes classic and modified definitions, uses of countertransference, differentiating countertransference phenomena, a two-dimensional model of countertransference, and a theoretical understanding of transference and countertransference.

The Therapeutic Relationship

The therapeutic relationship comprises the real relationship, the working alliance, and the emotional bonding that occurs between a therapist and a client. In the efforts to establish a therapeutic relationship, client transference and therapist countertransference often emerge. The last two topics are treated in greater detail under separate headings.

The Real Relationship

It is imperative to differentiate between the real aspects of a relationship and the transferential and countertransferential aspects. It is safe to say that every therapeutic relationship embraces a real relationship. For example, negotiating the length and frequency of therapy sessions and determining the fee are real aspects of the relationship. The client's feeling of anger at the therapist for being late for a session and the therapist's feeling of annoyance at the client for correcting the therapist's every intervention are also aspects of the real relationship.

Within the context of psychotherapy, the real relationship is seen as having two defining features: genuineness, and realistic perceptions. Gelso and Carter (1994, p. 297) define genuineness as "the ability and willingness to be what one truly is in the relationship—to be authentic, open, and honest"—and realistic perceptions as "those perceptions that are uncontaminated by transference distortions and other defenses. In other words, therapy participants see each other in an accurate, realistic way." For Cavanagh and Levitov (2002, p. 393), the real relationship component in therapy implies that therapists are "prepared to genuinely and realistically relate to their clients" and not to hide behind their roles, duties, and responsibilities required by the therapeutic alliance.

Working Alliance

The therapeutic relationship comprises the encounter, engagement, and working together of therapist and client in the interests of the client. This engagement is also referred to as the working alliance, whereby the therapist and the client agree on the goals of therapy and the means to accomplish them (Bordin, 1976, 1983). Freud was one of the first therapists to discuss the mutual commitments of both client and therapist in this relationship. He stated that, when the patient and the psychoanalyst agree to engage in the psychoanalytic process, the patient promises "complete candour" and to put to the disposal of the analyst "all of the material which his self-perception provides ... that comes into his head, even if it is disagreeable to say it" (1940, pp. 36–38). The psychoanalyst assures the patient "the strictest discretion" (p. 36) and the application of his or her skill in interpreting material that has been influenced by the unconscious.

Kaplan and Sadock (1991, p. 573) describe therapeutic alliance as a real relationship between analyst and patient that "represents two adults entering into a joint venture. ... Both commit themselves to exploring the patient's problems, to establishing mutual trust, and to cooperating with each other to achieve a realistic goal of cure or the amelioration of symptoms."

For Greenson (1967, p. 45), the working alliance consists of the "relatively non-neurotic, rational relationship between patient and analyst which makes it possible for the patient to work purposefully in the analytic situation" (cited by Wolitzky, 1995, p. 31). The therapeutic alliance is seen as the "therapist's most important means of effective client change; it determines the success or failure of therapy" (Teyber, 1997, p. 16). A firmly established alliance encourages the client to raise difficult issues and enables the client to work through more complicated problems (Cavanagh & Levitov, 2002, p. 22).

Emotional Bonding

Within the course of psychotherapy, therapist and client form an emotional bond that fosters growth and development of the client and the resolution of his or her problems. The real relationship between the therapist and the client contains a level of intimacy that must never be confused with the intimacy associated with friendships and love relationships. The intimacy in the counselling relationship forms from the client's self-disclosures to the counsellor and from the counsellor's empathic responses to them. It is easy for clients to mistake or confuse the intimacy that this sharing with a counsellor produces with the feelings that develop for friends and lovers. Cavanagh and Levitov (2002, p. 393) add that "Counselors must therefore take special care to maintain adequate boundaries and help clients understand that the feelings of intimacy that result from counseling have little in common with intimacy produced in friendships where both partners hazard risk and disclose themselves to one another as a relationship of mutuality forms."

Transference/Countertransference
Attempts to achieve emotional bonding conjure up feelings that might be expressed in terms of client transference and therapist countertransference. In a broad sense, transference and countertransference can be considered essential aspects of every human relationship. The major difference is that the behaviours are given different names depending on whether they occur between partners, parent and child, employee and employer, or client and therapist. For example, when a child approaches her mother for a hug, we call the ensuing behaviour an act of love; however, if the client sexually embraces the therapist, we name this as an act of transference. In similar fashion, when a parent reprimands a child for unsocial behaviour such as a temper tantrum, we call this setting limits and guidance; however, if a therapist reprimands a client for not doing his homework, we call this countertransference. The difference between the scenarios is that in one situation it is expected behaviour, while in the second it is not expected or wanted behavior.

Within the context of client and therapist relationships, these emotional reactions are more complex and become more difficult to define. It is difficult to sort out an emotional response that is appropriate to the situation from an emotional response that is not appropriate to the situation. The inappropriate response of the client is called a transference, while that of the therapist is called a countertransference. In this sense, therefore, a transference and a countertransference can be considered vestiges of early childhood failures to connect with significant others in meaningful ways: that is, transference and countertransference represent early childhood relationship failures.

Transference

This section treats transference in terms of its definition, its universality, and its role in therapy. These topics are followed by a critique of this concept and cautions regarding its use in psychotherapy.

Definitions

Freud introduced the word *transference* or rather its German original (*übertragung*, which means "to carry over") in *The Studies on Hysteria* (Freud & Breuer, 1895, p. 302). The term was used to "denote a patient's inappropriate and unwarranted displacement of ideas and memories onto their analyst" (Smith, 2003, p. 109). To illustrate this notion, Freud used the example of a patient who wanted him to give her a passionate kiss to realize through analysis that earlier she had repressed her longing for a passionate kiss from her employer (Freud & Breuer, 1895, pp. 302–303).

Freud (1900, p. 562) revised this clinical definition of transference in the *Interpretation of Dreams* to form a more general psychological notion. Here transference is described as a "hypothetical and by definition an unobservable process which the charge of 'psychical energy' attached to a repressed idea becomes displaced onto an innocuous preconscious idea which is in some way associatively linked with it. The innocuous idea then becomes a proxy for the more emotionally explosive and potentially anxiety-provoking unconscious thought" (Smith, 2003,

p. 109). For example, the repressed thought of hitting a parent might be expressed in the thought of beating up a teddy bear. In this case, the energy from the parent is moved to the teddy bear and, as a result, the urge to beat up the teddy bear becomes disproportionately intense.

Freud presented the modern view of transference in *An Outline of Psychoanalysis* (1940), in which he described transference as an individual directing his or her emotional feelings toward the therapist as though the therapist was the original object that caused the feelings. Freud wrote that the patient sees in the analyst

> the return, the reincarnation, of some important figure out of his childhood or past, and consequently transfers on to him feelings and reactions which undoubtedly applied to this prototype. This fact of transference soon proves to be a factor of undreamt-of importance, on the one hand an instrument of irreplaceable value and on the other hand a source of serious dangers. This transference is ambivalent: it comprises positive (affectionate) as well as negative (hostile) attitudes towards the analyst, who as a rule is put in the place of one or other of the patient's parents, his father or mother. (pp. 174–175)

Thompson, Mazer, and Witenberg (1955, p. 619) summarize the notion of transference as "the distorted perception of the present in terms of the past, whereby the individual attributes to people in his current life the attitudes and emotions of those in his early family constellation."

Also included in the notion of transference are the client's attempts to draw the therapist into assuming different roles, such as being a rescuer, caretaker, sexual partner, and so on. This behaviour of the client has been referred to as projective identification (Cashdan, 1988). In substance, projective identification implies splitting the object and the self, projecting them onto others, and then responding to the other as if these split-off parts truly characterize the person.

Universality of Transference

Transference is a universal phenomenon and is an important factor in almost every sphere of our social, political, and religious lives (Balint, 1955). Canadians transfer feelings onto objects such as the beaver, the maple leaf, the flag, and the RCMP uniform. We see the transfer of feelings in our religious symbols and places, such as the cross (Christian), Svastika (not Swastika) (Jainist), Star of David (Jewish), and Mecca (Muslim). We project feelings onto our historical icons, such as Abraham Lincoln, John F. Kennedy, Mahatma Gandhi, Pierre Elliott Trudeau, Babe Ruth, and Rocket Richard.

Within the context of psychoanalysis and psychotherapy, transference is also a universal phenomenon. Freud (1925), the first to speak about its universality, stated that "transference is a universal phenomenon of the human mind, it decides the success of all medical influence, and in fact dominates the whole of each person's relations to his human environment" (p. 42). He added that transference is not created by analysis; rather, it is "merely uncovered and isolated by analysis" (p. 42), and earlier he noted that "psychoanalytic treatment does not create transferences, it merely brings them to light" (1905, p. 117).

The Role of Transference in Treatment

In his work with psychoanalysis, Freud (1910, p. 144) first considered that symptom removal constituted the completion of treatment. Later he entertained the thought that gaining insight into the roots of one's behaviours was the hallmark of therapeutic success. In the end, he concluded that the creation of client transference was a necessary component of the therapeutic process. Freud (1925, p. 42) stated that an "analysis without transference is an impossibility." The formation of a transference enables the client to work through the original conflict (Freud, 1940, p. 38); thus, the working through of the transference became a goal of therapy.

Transferences can be positive or negative. Positive transferences serve several purposes. First, a positive transference motivates the client to collaborate with the analyst, the person's ego becomes stronger, and the person achieves things that would ordinarily be beyond his or her power. The negative aspect is that the client gives the semblance of having recovered but in reality pushes aside his or her problems. Second, the client puts the therapist in the place of his parents and thereby gives the therapist the power that his superego exercises over his ego. Third, in the transference, the client produces with "plastic clarity an important part of his life-story, of which he would otherwise have probably given us only an insufficient account. He acts it before us, as it were, instead of reporting it to us" (Freud, 1940, pp. 174–175). Negative transferences, if not well managed, can be disruptive.

In brief, client transferences are vestiges of early childhood relationship failures whereby the client failed to establish a meaningful relationship with a significant other and continues in a repetitive manner to establish a failed relationship with a new person. Transferences represent a client's typical way of relating with others and attempts to draw the therapist into that way of relating.

Critique of the Concept of Transference
Smith (2003) provides a detailed critique of the concept of transference, asking how to differentiate it from normal responses and whether it is a protective shield for psychotherapists and an artifact of the psychoanalytic situation itself.

Differentiating Transference from Non-Transferential Phenomena
Clients undergoing psychotherapy often develop extraordinarily and inappropriately intense relationships with their therapists. Is this transference? How to distinguish a transference from a client's reaction to a therapist's behaviours or statements? To regard a feature of a client's relationship with the psychotherapist as transference, one makes the assumption that "the patient's unwholesome adult dispositions are indeed carry-overs or repetitions of childhood" (Grünebaum, 1993, p. 248). If this

behaviour is not a transference, then how does one distinguish between transference and non-transference? Greenson (1967) attempted to do this by providing criteria that identify a transference: a "transference is (a) a distinctive type of human relationship, that (b) involves the experience of wishes, feelings, drives, fantasies, defences and attitudes towards another person, that (c) 'do not befit that person and which actually apply to another' (pp. 152–153) because they belong to a past relationship rather than to a present one" (Smith, 2003, p. 113). According to Greenson, there are two qualities that characterize a transference: namely, it is "inappropriate" and "anachronistic". Attitudes that are "mature" and "realistic" and "in accord with the circumstances" are not examples of transference (Smith, 2003, p. 113). The problem with this definition is how does one define what is inappropriate? What are the criteria? Who judges what is a transference? If a therapist judges a client's behaviour to be a transference, how does one know that the therapist is not being deceived by his or her own bias? Might the therapist not be a victim of deception?

Transference as a Protective Shield for the Psychotherapist

Does the concept of transference serve as a shield to protect the therapist from "too intense affective and real-life involvement with the patient" by means of a "denial and repudiation of the patient's experience qua experience," as Szasz (1961, p. 437) contends? If this is the case, then interpretations of transference "provide a ready-made opportunity for putting the patient at arms length" (Szasz, 1961, p. 438). Shlien (1984, p. 170), a Rogerian, asserts that "transference is a fiction to protect the therapist from the consequences of his own actions." He asserts that "positive transference," in which the client falls in love with the therapist, is an entirely natural product of the three elements of the analytic relationship: "the dependency of the patient, the patient's need for sexual companionship, and the therapist's attitude of understanding" (Smith, 2003, p. 118).

Transference as an Artifact of Psychoanalytic Treatment

Might transference be an "artifact of psychoanalytic treatment" as raised by Smith (2003, p. 119)? To support his argument, Smith cites Racher (1958, p. 178), who wrote that "transference is ... an unconscious creation of the analyst. ... Just as countertransference is ... an unconscious creation of the patient." Barranger and Barranger (1996) provide theoretical support for this position by claiming that "everything that happens in the analytic situation is a product of three factors: the psychoanalytic setting, the internal world of the patient, and the internal world of the analyst, thus creating a 'bi-personal field' in which the analyst shapes the patient's experience at least as much as the patient shapes the analyst's" (cited by Smith, 2003, p. 120).

In response to the above criticisms of transference, one can say that the emotional reactions of adolescents and adults that are triggered, relived, and re-enacted because of early childhood trauma and that contaminate relationships are transferences. For example, a 35-year-old single male (Dan), the eldest of 12 children, tends to keep his distance in relationships with women. When his 12-month-younger sibling was born, Dan "unconsciously" felt that his mother pushed him aside, turned him over to his father for care, and gave to his sibling what had been his. Although loved by his mother, Dan kept a safe distance for fear of being abandoned and at the same time yearned for an intimate relationship but feared losing his sense of self. As an adult, Dan yearned for intimate relationships but maintained a distance for fear of being abandoned again and for fear of losing his sense of self. This response occurred repeatedly in his adult responses to women with whom he wanted to form intimate relationships.

Cautions in Working with Transference

The emergence of transferences within psychotherapy has not been without its difficulties and risks, and caution needs to be exercised regarding the creation of transferences within therapy and the labelling of a client response as a transference.

Creating Transferences

Although transferences are an important part of therapy, Freud cautioned against deliberately creating them. Freud (1915a), for example, is critical of doctors practising psychoanalysis who prepare their patients for the "emergence of erotic transference or even urge them to 'go ahead and fall in love with the doctor so that the treatment may make sense" (p. 161). Freud finds this procedure senseless and, in the process, the analyst "robs the phenomenon of the element of spontaneity" (p. 162). That is, Freud advocates the spontaneous emergence of client transference within the context of therapy.

Identifying Transferences

As mentioned earlier, there are no specific criteria that unambiguously differentiate a transference from an expected client emotional reaction to what transpires in therapy. Yet it is important to know whether the client's reaction is due to something that the therapist did or said or did not do or say, whether the client is sensitive to the topic and tends to misinterpret a therapist response because of past experiences, or whether it is a combination of the two. If the client's emotional response is disproportionate to what the therapist did or did not do or say in therapy, or if the client attempts to draw the therapist into an unwanted behaviour, one can assume that the client's response is a transference. This is particularly noted if the client's response is rage or feeling abandoned or if the client makes the therapist out to be more than he or she is and wishes for the therapist to protect, rescue, and take care of him or her. Having said this, I would argue that it is nevertheless important to deal with all client emotional responses and behaviours according to the clients' capacity to address them and to provide some perspective on particular issues. That is, the therapist should provide a holding environment to help the client contain his or her emotions or, in the case of idealizations or behaviours, to help the client see the therapist as a real person and to help the client become empowered.

Countertransference

The understanding of what constitutes countertransference has undergone intense examination and has been modified since it was first introduced by Freud to describe inappropriate unconscious and defensive reactions of the therapist toward the client. Two factors that lead to modification of the concept of countertransference are a consideration of the level of the client's ego organization and the client's developmental needs. Initially, the clients seen in psychoanalysis were neurotics with intact ego organizations, had the capacity for insight into the roots of their problems, and were able to use interpretations. Later the clients seen by psychoanalysts were more disturbed adults and children who had impoverished ego organizations due to traumatic pre-Oedipal experiences and required an interactive or relational therapy that provided structure, guidance, and an emotionally corrective therapeutic influence. These factors, in part, played a major role in the redefinition of the concept, countertransference, and its use in therapy.

This part of the chapter presents the origin of countertransference and its definition. That discussion is followed by topics including modification of the concept, concepts related to countertransference, differentiating countertransference phenomena, and a theoretical understanding of countertransference.

Classic Definition of Countertransference
Freud used the term "countertransference" only four times in his writings and in only two of his works (1910, 1914) (Smith, 2003, p. 120). Freud introduced the concept of countertransference in 1910 when he wrote, "We have become aware of the 'counter-transference,' which arises in ... [the physician] ... as a result of the patient's influence on his unconscious feelings, and we are almost inclined to insist that he shall recognize this countertransference in himself and overcome it ... [W]e have noticed that no psycho-analyst goes farther than his own complexes and internal resistances permit" (pp. 144–145). This has

come to be known as the classic definition of countertransference (Kernberg, 1965; Reich, 1951, 1960).

From this perspective, countertransference normally describes the unconscious, pathological, and undesirable responses of the therapist to the client's transferences that stimulate the psychoanalyst's childhood-based unresolved conflicts. The origins of the countertransference lie in the analyst's own unresolved psychosexual conflicts and tend to be Oedipal in nature. Such responses, viewed as remnants of the analyst's own unresolved Oedipal conflicts, interfere with analysis and must be resolved through training analysis and eliminated (Cashdan, 1988, pp. 27, 97; Hayes, 2004, p. 6).

Freud's definition of countertransference stemmed from his work with neurotics who were deemed to possess intact egos, capable of insight, and able to integrate the psychoanalyst's interpretation (Blanck & Blanck, 1979, p. 125). It was assumed that the patient would take responsibility for understanding, managing, and working on conflicts, anxieties, and maladaptive defences. So as not to contaminate the patient's therapeutic process, Freud cautioned the therapist against using interventions that are directive, involve advice giving, or make the therapist an equal partner in solving problems. The therapist's ability to "stay apart from actively intervening in a patient's life ... [was referred to as] ... therapeutic neutrality":

> therapeutic neutrality holds that the process of psychotherapy is the responsibility of the therapist, while the work of psychotherapy is the responsibility of the client. Therapeutic neutrality ... does not require that the therapist be a robot, a mirror, or a blank screen. The therapist is a full participant in the process through his or her interest in, curiosity about, and concern for the patient's impaired real self ... Therapeutic neutrality is not a dispassionate position. (Klein, 1995, p. 70)

"Neutrality means simply that the analyst does not seek to impose his values upon the patient" (Blanck & Blanck, 1979, p. 128).

The original definition of countertransference is still adhered to by some writers. For example, Singer (1965, p. 33) states that countertransference consists of "emotional" and "irrational" responses that interfere with therapist objectivity. Racker (1968, p. 2) considers countertransference as a "psychopathological process" in the analyst that influences his or her perception and/or interpretation of the unconscious processes of client and therapist in the therapeutic context. Hansen, Rossberg, and Cramer (1994, p. 268) state that "countertransference refers to the emotional reactions and projections of the counselor toward the client ... [and] ... may include conscious as well as unconscious attitudes of the counselor toward real or imagined client attitudes and behavior." Blanck and Blanck (1979, p. 69) view countertransference as "the unconscious feelings, both libidinal and aggressive, which are incurred by the analyst in reaction to the attitudes and productions of the analysand." Wolitzky (1995, p. 36) says that, "to the extent that the analyst's feelings or actions toward, and understanding of, the patient are influenced by the analyst's unconscious, unresolved conflicts and needs, the analyst is being biased and thereby not functioning in the best interests of the patient."

At the time of Freud, countertransference was an unacceptable psychoanalyst experience and a topic taboo to talk and write about. In a letter to Jung on New Year's Eve 1911, Freud wrote that "we must never let our poor neurotics drive us crazy. I believe an article on 'countertransference' is sorely needed; of course we could not publish it, we should have to circulate copies among ourselves" (McGuire, 1974, p. 253).

Modified Definitions of Countertransference

Beginnings of Modification
Modification of the construct countertransference has its origin in the writings of Freud (1913), Hartmann (1939), and Heimann (1950) and is a consequence of applying psychoanalysis to emotionally disturbed children and to adults suffering from emotional

problems more severe than neurosis. The notion of countertransference was extended and revised because of the pre-Oedipal emotional needs of the patient and because of the patient's impoverished ego organization.

Freud occasionally argued that all persons have an unconscious capacity to understand the unconscious concerns of the
other. He contended that everyone "possesses in his own unconscious an instrument with which he can interpret the utterances
of the unconscious in other people" (1913, p. 320). This statement implies a positive aspect of emotional knowing or, in short,
a capacity for countertransference. Thus, one can say that Freud
set the stage for an extended definition of countertransference.

A turning point in the theoretical formulation of countertransference occurred with the publication of *Ego Psychology and the
Problem of Adaptation* by Hartmann (1939). Hartmann asserted
that "the human being cannot and further must not be fully
rational. While unconscious processes with their distortions do
indeed contribute to conflict and pathology, they are also adaptive
as sources of some of our most cherished ideals–love, including
overvaluation of the object, loyalty, and the like" (cited by Blanck
& Blanck, 1979, pp. 127–128). The implication is that, despite
intense psychoanalysis, an analyst responds to a patient's material
from both a conscious and an unconscious state of mind.

Heimann (1950), in her publication *On Countertransference*, inverted the meaning of countertransference, which she
described as the psychoanalyst's unconscious sensitivity. The
psychoanalyst's "inappropriate" fantasies and emotions are said
to be evoked by a patient's unconscious conflicts and therefore
comprise an expression of the patient's psychological problems;
countertransference is the "patient's creation" (p. 77). "The analyst's emotional response to his patient within the analytic situation represents one of the most important tools for his work. The
analyst's counter-transference is an instrument of research into
the patient's unconscious" (p. 81). Heimann's approach to the
problem of countertransference became popular and is now the

dominant view in most psychoanalytic and non-psychoanalytic circles (Smith, 2003, p. 121). This view, however, is without scientific support and gives analysts "carte blanche" to "misattribute their own fantasies and conflicts to their patients' unconscious minds" (Smith, 2003, p. 121). The danger with this definition, as Klein (1946) pointed out, is that "it might facilitate the blaming of patients for the analyst's countertransference problems" (Gabbard, 2001, pp. 984–985).

Usefulness of Countertransference

Following Heimann's (1950) contention that countertransference is a creation of the client and not of the analyst, theorists and psychoanalysts began to explore how countertransference can be useful in psychoanalysis. The thought was that the analyst's emotional reactions to the patient might hold clues about important client dynamics.

Basch (1988, p. 149) thinks that the therapist's affective reaction to what a patient is saying or doing is—properly used—invaluable in coming to understand the patient. It is when the therapist is not able to decentre affective reactions to the patient's statements because of his or her unrecognized unconscious problems that these reactions interfere with treatment. Hayes et al. (1998, p. 468) believe that "the insight that may be gleaned from countertransference can deepen therapists' awareness of relationship dynamics and provide valuable information about the course of treatment." Wolitzky (1995, p. 36) states that a therapist's emotional reactions to the client's statements can be useful in pointing to "feelings that the patient might be 'pulling for' from the therapist and therefore can serve as an important guide to the interpretations offered by the therapist."

Cashdan (1988, p. 97), an object relations psychotherapist, states that countertransference "is seen as a natural response to the patient's projective identification." That is, countertransference "represents the therapist's experiential response to the patient's pathology" (p. 27). From this perspective, countertransference is a necessary and valuable part of the treatment procedure as it performs a diagnostic function and guides many of the therapist's interventions (p. 27). The therapist's emotional response, however, "is carefully monitored and used to experientially identify the precise nature of the patient's projective identification and the meta-communication that lies behind it" (p. 97).

Patterson (1966) considers countertransference to be a disturbing factor and an unavoidable impurity in psychotherapy. However, rather than dismissing it as inappropriate, Patterson "recommends that the therapist's countertransference reactions be understood and controlled" (pp. 318–319, 327).

Blanck (1976) states that countertransference can be a useful technical tool when the analyst thoroughly understands that the countertransference does not stem from his or her own infantile or neurotic responses. Blanck adds that, "when the analyst is certain that it is not he who is responding inappropriately, but that the patient is unconsciously stimulating a particular response in him, then it is technically proper to interpret what the patient is doing" (p. 70).

Abend (1989, p. 374) thinks that, rather than viewing countertransference as an "unconscious interference with an analyst's ability to understand patients," the concept needs to be broadened to include "all of the emotional reactions at work." Slakter (1987, p. 3) refers to countertransference as "all those reactions of the analyst to the patient that may help or hinder treatment." A large number of psychoanalytic writers acknowledge that countertransference is as present as transference and that it is a necessary prerequisite to successful therapy (Abend, 1989; Brenner, 1985; Greenson, 1967).

Not all psychoanalysts advocate using countertransference in direct interpersonal transactions with clients. Rather, they emphasize "understanding one's own feelings toward the patient, to engage in self-analysis in order to know why they have occurred, and, if possible, to trace them to their infantile origins and to the analyst's neurotic residue" (Blanck, 1976, p. 70).

Modified Definitions

Modifications to the definition of countertransference have in one way or another been influenced by the definition provided by Heimann (1950). Some have referred to the modified definitions as "totalistic definition," "integrative concept," and "moderate concept." All of these definitions assume that countertransference reactions arise from "the therapist's realistic, conflict-free responses to the patient's feelings and behaviors within and outside the session" (Kernberg, Selzer, Koenigsberg, Carr, & Appelbaum, 1989, pp. 21–22).

Totalistic definition: The totalistic definition of countertransference was developed substantively by Racker (1957, 1968) and elaborated by interpersonal, ego, and object relations theorists (Aron, 1996; Cashdan, 1988; Tansey, 1994). These theorists "describe the ways in which the client evokes therapist reactions, whether by 'hooking' the therapist as the client routinely does to others (Kiesler, 1996), through projective identification (Ogden, 1982, 1994) or via role responsiveness (Sandler, 1976)" (Hayes, 2004, p. 6).

Wolitzky (1995, p. 36) thinks that countertransference includes "all the analyst's emotional reactions to the patient, not just his/her transference reactions to the patient's transference." Hayes (2004, p. 6) adheres to the same view in saying that countertransference includes all "therapist reactions to a client, whether conscious or unconscious, conflict-based or reality-based, in response to transference or some other material."

These theorists share the idea that therapists must understand what clients are eliciting from them and not impulsively act on countertransference feelings. Another point of agreement is that both the therapist and the client contribute to the creation of the countertransference (Gabbard, 1995, 2001). The latter point is debatable. The client might have a role in the formation of the countertransference, but this view runs the risk of diverting attention away from the effects of the therapist's personal history in the creation of the countertransference (Hayes, 2004, p. 7).

Integrative concept: Dissatisfaction with both the classical and the totalistic views of countertransference led to a new definition known as the integrative concept of countertransference. Countertransference is defined as "therapist reactions to clients that are based on the therapist's unresolved conflicts" (Gelso & Hayes, 1998, 2001; Hayes & Gelso, 1991) and "may be conscious or unconscious and in response to transference or other phenomena" (Hayes, 2004, p. 7). This definition clearly locates the source of the therapist's reactions within the therapist, and it "encourages the therapists to take responsibility for their reactions, identify the intrapsychic origins of their reactions, and attempt to understand and manage them" (Hayes, 2004, p. 7).

Moderate concept: In accordance with Gelso and Hayes (2001), Fauth (2006) proposes the moderate definition of countertransference. He states that

> The moderate view defines CT as therapists' idiosyncratic reactions (broadly defined as sensory, affective, cognitive, and behavioral) to clients that are based primarily in therapists' own personal conflicts, biases, or difficulties (e.g., cognitive biases, personal narratives, or maladaptive interpersonal patterns ... These reactions can be conscious or unconscious and triggered by transference, client characteristics, or other aspects of the therapeutic situation (e.g., termination), but not by extratherapy factors. (p. 17)

Differentiating Countertransference

The revised definitions of countertransference do not solve the problem by using the same terms to describe all of the therapist's emotional responses, be they conscious or unconscious and be they responses from early childhood experiences or from interaction with the client. Some authors recommend a restrictive use of the term, while others propose that this phenomenon be differentiated.

Arlow (1989, p. 48) thinks that countertransference "should be reserved for those situations in which a patient and his productions evoke in the analyst conflicts relating to some unresolved childhood fantasy of his own, causing him to misperceive, misinterpret,

and misrespond to the analysand in terms of his own difficulties."
This position is in keeping with a classical definition of countertransference.

Cashdan (1988, p. 155) suggests that it might be better to
restrict use of the term to "the emotional reactions of the therapist
in response to the patient's behavior in the therapy relationship."
This definition is in keeping with that of Greenberg and Mitchell
(1983, p. 389), who define countertransference as "an inevitable
product of the interaction between the patient and the analyst
rather than a simple interference stemming from the analyst's
infantile drive-related conflicts." Defining countertransference
in this way, which is becoming more standard, makes it possible
to interpret other emotional influences in "light of the way that
they affect and possibly interfere with the countertransferential
response" (Cashdan, 1988, p. 155).

Another approach to bringing some clarity to this phenomenon is to make differentiations within it. Spotnitz (1985) distinguished between "objective countertransference" and "subjective countertransference." The former refers to what the therapist
experiences as a result of "emotional contagion" from the patient.
The latter refers to everything else and is "equivalent to Freud's
description of the countertransference" (Kirman, 1980, p. 133).
This distinction does not clarify the matter since in both forms
countertransference responses are subjectively felt. "To call one set
objective and the other subjective suggests that the therapist is able
to distinguish the quality of emotions felt at any given moment
and to identify their source. This is rarely achieved in practice"
(Cashdan, 1988, p. 154).

Klein (1995) distinguished between countertransference
acting out and countertransference in the classical sense. In
countertransference acting out, the therapist resonates with and
responds to the transference acting out of a patient. It is a reaction to what the patient is consciously or unconsciously attempting to provoke in the therapist. Transference acting out opera-
tionally means that the "patient only sees the external world as
a mirror reflection of the internal world. The intrapsychic filter

removes all that does not fit the pattern" (p. 73). The therapist's reaction is not unique to him or her but is a reaction that one might expect from almost any therapist who is unaware of the meaning of the patient's behaviour and how to manage it. Countertransference in the classic sense is a reaction that originates primarily in the therapist, not in the patient, and is a reflection of unresolved, early developmental, and interpersonal conflicts in the therapist rather than anything taking place in the therapeutic setting (pp. 84-85).

Two-Dimensional Model of Countertransference

The attempts made thus far to differentiate countertransferential phenomena have not been successful. It might be useful to view countertransference along two dimensions: the therapist's level of awareness of his or her countertransference feelings, and the therapist's degree of awareness of the origin of the countertransference. Using these two dimensions, one can think of four different combinations, or typologies (Types 1-4), the first three of which are summarized in Table 3.1. A brief description of each typology follows.

Table 3.1
Two-Dimensional Model of Countertransference:
Awareness of the Origin of the Countertransference (CT) and
Awareness of Current Experience (ER) Related to CT

Dimensions	No awareness of emotional reaction (ER): feelings, thoughts	Awareness of emotional reaction: feelings, thoughts
No awareness of origin of ER	Type 1: No awareness of countertransference or its origin	Type 2: Awareness of emotional reaction but no awareness of its origin
Awareness of origin of ER		Type 3: Aware of both the emotional reaction and its origin

Note: ER = emotional reaction.

Type 1: No awareness of countertransferential experiences: This type refers to a therapist not having any awareness of his or her emotional reactions to the client's responses. The therapist considers his response to be typical of that of any therapist in the same situation. This type overlaps with the classic definition of countertransference as the analyst's unconscious, conflict-based reactions to the patient's transference. The patient's transference triggers the analyst's childhood-based unresolved conflicts, interferes with the analyst's understanding, and provokes behaviour that meets the needs of the therapist rather than those of the client. Often Type 1 countertransference is destructive and is not an acceptable part of the therapist-client relationship. For example, a therapist might feel justified in being angry with a client, thinking that the client had it coming to him or her.

Type 2: Aware of emotional reaction but not of its origin: In this type of countertransference, the therapist is aware of her emotional reactions and realizes that something is amiss but does not have any awareness of the origins of the feelings or any control over them. For example, a therapist might feel angry at and hostile toward a client but is not aware of what is triggering this emotional reaction. The use of this type of countertransference is not appropriate for therapy. It is important for the therapist to seek help to understand its origins and to work through them.

Type 3: Aware of emotional reaction and of its origin: The therapist is aware of his or her emotional reactions and their origins and attempts to keep the countertransference in check. For example, a therapist, in listening to the story of a young mother being booted out of her home at an early age, becomes aware not only of the client's feeling of abandonment but also of his own and realizes that his feeling stems from being abandoned by his father at a young age. This type of countertransference can be of great help to the therapist in understanding the deeper issues of the client and guiding the therapy process.

Type 4: Integrated experience: The therapist is aware of the potential for a countertransferential response, but because it has been worked through earlier she is able to maintain her composure while encouraging the client to describe his or her transference and work through it. For example, a therapist who has worked through her response to loud noises and talking, which in the past meant that someone was being hurt, is able to distance herself from them and help a client work through his or her transference without being deeply affected by it.

When described according to the two dimensions and four types, countertransference is viewed as being on a continuum beginning with no awareness of the emotional reaction and its origin to full awareness of the emotional reaction and its origin. Using the 4-Type Model, one avoids trying to come up with a definition of countertransference that covers all situations. The 4-Type Model provides a good instrument for any therapist to assess the quality of his or her countertransference and to decide what action, if any, needs to take place.

Theoretical Understanding of Transference and Countertransference

The dynamics underlying the formation of transferences and countertransferences are similar in that both are triggered by an external stimulus (e.g., a statement, word, look, gesture, sound, or movement), and both are the products of unconscious or conscious internal processes: namely, introjection, interpretation, and projection. For example, if a client interprets a therapist's suggestion as an order or a demand, the client might feel pressured to act against his or her "better instincts," a childhood reminder of a domineering parent, and angrily oppose the suggestion and construe the therapist as being insensitive, unempathic, and domineering. The therapist, in turn, might not feel respected by the angry and oppositional client, become angry, feel hurt and defensive, and act out against the client. In the first part of this example, it is the client reacting against the therapist (similar to a child reacting against an insensitive and domineering parent). In the second part, it is the therapist reacting against the client (similar to a defensive and domineering parent reacting against an unsubmissive and disrespectful child). The reaction of the client is called a transference, and the response of the therapist is called a countertransference.

It is assumed that the intense interpersonal reactions between therapist and client are re-enactments of similar processes taking place within the client's and the therapist's inner worlds and that these processes become externalized when conflictual situations between client and therapist surface. That is, everyone has, to one degree or another, a "child" and a "parent" within him or her that might be in relative dialogical conflict with each other. When an external situation arises that seemingly pits the "inner child" against the "inner parent," the inner dialogical conflict can become externalized and re-enacted in client transference and therapist countertransference.

How to explain more precisely the process that leads to transference and countertransference? To explain this process, the concepts of psychic structure (or psychic organization) and dynamics (introjection, projection) are helpful. These psychic structures have received different names, such as scripts, narratives, internal working models, ego states, and cognitive structures. The dynamic structures include cognitive, affective, sensory, memory, and behavioural aspects. As well, the structures are further divided into substructures, which have been given names such as Parent, Child, Adult (Berne, 1961, 1976); Being, Self, Self-Image (Perls, 1969); and Id, Ego, Superego (Freud, 1923). The structures are perceived to be dynamic in the sense that there is a dialogical interaction among them, with each wanting to be heard, to be respected, and to have its demands honoured. When a substructure (e.g., Child or Parent) feels not heard or respected, there is the possibility for acting out behaviour (e.g., transference) or for defensive and counter action (e.g., countertransference). Thus, transferences and countertransferences emanate from the dialogical interactions of the dynamic psychic structures.

The process underlying the formation of transference and countertransference, as understood today, is best explained by psychodynamic models, particularly by object relations therapy models. Much of what has been written on countertransference originates from Freud's (1915b) early theories when the mind was construed in terms of the conscious, preconscious, and unconscious and not when Freud (1923) construed the mind in terms of three agencies: Id, Ego, and Superego. The object relations therapy models by Klein (1952/1975) and Fairbairn (1944, 1946), when combined to form one model, are particularly helpful to developmentally explain the origin of psychic structures and their dynamics, and disharmony among them can lead to countertransferential reactions.

Developmentally, the child, in the course of interactions with the significant other, has both pleasant and unpleasant experiences. Pleasant experiences originate from the child having her needs met, whereas unpleasant experiences originate from feeling frustrated over not having her needs met. Due to the infant's immature ego and perceptual processes, she experiences the parent who responds positively to her needs as being a different person from the parent who frustrates her needs. Pleasant experiences generate representations of a good parent, and unpleasant experiences generate representations of a bad parent.

Parallel to forming representations of the parents, the child also forms representations of the self. When the parent responds positively to the infant's needs, the infant experiences pleasure and feels good about the self because he feels worthy of the parent's love and care. However, when the parent fails to respond to the child's needs, the child experiences displeasure and feels bad about the self because he feels not worthy of the parent's love and care. The infant therefore forms two representations of the self, the good self and the bad self.

These representations of self and parent form the substratum of the infant's, and later the adult's, pysche and personality. Figure 3.1 depicts the psychic structures and their dynamics. Following

Figure 3.1

Endopsychic (psychological) structure according to object relations theory.

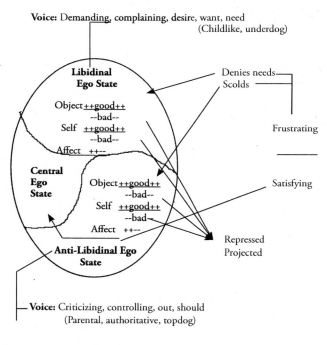

Internalizations of parent and self   **Parent**

Extrapolated from M. Klein (1959/1975), Our adult world and its roots in infancy, in *Envy and gratitude and other works, 1946–1963,* Vol. 4 (pp. 247–263) (New York: Delta); and W. R. D. Fairbairn (1944/1954), Endopsychic structure considered in terms of object relationships, in *An object-relations theory of personality* (pp. 82–136) (New York: Basic Books).

the theory of Fairbairn (1944, 1946), the psychic structure comprises three ego states: Central Ego State, Libidinal Ego State, and Antilibinal Ego State, with each having its own voice and needs or demands. The Central Ego State is present at birth and represents that which is rational, authentic, and integrative. In interacting with frustrations, part of the ego is attached to dealing with the situation and part of the ego is disconnected from the original ego state; consequently, other ego states are developed, such as the Antilibidinal and Libidinal Ego States. The Antilibidinal Ego State encompasses the internalized representations and feelings of a rejecting and critical parent, and the Libidinal Ego State comprises the internalized representations and feelings of a depriving parent. The child, however, is in a relationship with both the Antilibidinal Ego State and the Libidinal Ego State. When responding from the Antilibidinal Ego State, the child disowns his own needs and feelings and judges them to be childish and bad. The client acts like a parent toward a child. When responding from the Libidinal Ego State, the child feels helpless, powerless, inadequate, and unlovable. The client acts like a needy child in front of a domineering and rejecting parent. The child, in a sense, has internalized the real-life dialogue that took place between him and the parent and, depending on circumstances, the dialogue is skewed and dominated by the parent (Antilibidinal Ego State) or by the child (Libidinal Ego State). For example, an Antilibidinal Ego State–driven child or adult will not accept his or her libidinal needs, and a Libidinal Ego State–driven child will not accept his antilibidinal limits, restrictions, and boundaries.

When this is applied to countertransference (Types 1 and 2 as presented earlier), therapists who have not reconciled the demands of their Antilibidinal and Libidinal Ego States are not able to work with needy clients or with domineering clients. When a needy client begins therapy, therapists who are not able to accept their own neediness might want to tell the client to go and get a life, get off his or her butt, and do something useful. Therapists cannot tolerate being with a needy client because their own inner parent cannot accept the needs of their own inner child. On the other hand, when a controlling and domineering client begins therapy, therapists might equally produce a countertransference by feeling intimidated by the client and feeling inadequate and incompetent. In this case, the therapist's inner child reacts to its critical inner parent activated by the domineering client. Countertransference, therefore, can be seen as emerging from a failure to harmonize the demands and needs of the three ego states, which are in a dysfunctional dialogue with each other.

Summary

This chapter has argued that transference and countertransference, in a broad sense, are significant and normal aspects of all relationships, including therapeutic relationships. Countertransferences, when used appropriately, provide a useful understanding of the client's presenting concerns and a direction for therapeutic intervention. Much of the confusion regarding the construct countertransference stems from its roots in Freud's earlier model of the mind, which was construed in terms of the conscious, preconscious, and unconscious. The application of object relations theory (interpersonal model) to countertransference provides a better understanding of this universal phenomenon. The proposed two-dimensional model of countertransference, based on the level of awareness of the emotional response and its origin, can bring clarity into the discussion regarding the effective use of the therapist's emotional reactions in therapy and can provide a way to assess the quality or nature of a therapist's countertransference.

References

Abend, S. (1989). Countertransference and psychoanalytic technique. *The Psychoanalytic Quarterly, 58*, 374–395.

Arlow, J. A. (1989). Psychoanalysis. In R. J. Corsini & D. Wedding (Eds.), *Current psychotherapies* (4th ed.) (pp. 19–62). Itasca, IL: F. E. Peacock Publishers.

Aron, L. (1996). *A meeting of the minds: Mutuality in psychoanalysis.* Hillsdale, NJ: Analytic Press.

Balint, M. (1955). On transference of emotions. In C. Thompson, M. Mazer, & E. Witenberg (Eds.), *An outline of psychoanalysis* (pp. 471–484). New York: Modern Library.

Barranger, M., & Barranger, W. (1996). Insight in the analytic situation. In R. Litman (Ed.), *Psychoanalysis in the Americas* (pp. 56—72). New York: International Universities Press.

Basch, M. F. (1988). *Understanding psychotherapy: The science behind the art.* New York: Basic Books.

Berne, E. (1961). *Transactional analysis in psychotherapy: A systematic individual and social psychiatry.* New York: Grove Press.

Berne, E. (1976). *Beyond games and scripts: Selections from his major writings.* New York: Grove Press.

Blanck, G. (1976). Psychoanalytic technique. In B. B. Wolman (Ed.), *The therapist's handbook: Treatment methods of mental disorders* (pp. 61–86). New York: Van Nostrand Reinhold.

Blanck, G., & Blanck, R. (1979). *Ego psychology II: Psychoanalytic developmental psychology.* New York: Columbia University Press.

Bordin, E. S. (1976). The generalizability of the psychoanalytic concept of the working alliance. *Psychotherapy: Theory, Research, and Practice, 16,* 252–260.

Bordin, E. S. (1983). A working alliance based model of supervision. *The Counseling Psychologist, 11*(1), 35–41.

Brenner, C. (1985). Countertransference as compromise formation. *The Psychoanalytic Quarterly, 54,* 155–163.

Cashdan, S. (1988). *Object relations therapy: Using the relationship.* New York: W. W. Norton & Company.

Cavanagh, M. E., & Levitov, J. E. (2002). The counseling experience: A theoretical and practical approach. Prospect Heights, IL: Waveland Press.

Fairbairn, W. R. D. (1944/1954). Endopsychic structure considered in terms of object relationships. In *An object-relations theory of the personality* (pp. 82–136). New York: Basic Books.

Fairbairn, W. R. D. (1946). Object-relationships and dynamic structure. In *An object-relations theory of the personality* (pp. 137–161). New York: Basic Books.

Fauth, J. (2006). Toward more (and) better countertransference research. *Psychotherapy: Theory, Research, Practice, Training, 43*(1), 16–31.

Freud, S. (1900). The interpretation of dreams. *Standard edition,* 4 & 5. London: Hogarth Press.

Freud, S. (1905). Fragment of an analysis of a case of hysteria. *Standard edition, 7,* pp. 7–111. London: Hogarth Press.

Freud, S. (1910/1957). The future prospect of psychoanalytic therapy. *Standard edition,* 11, pp. 141–151. London: Hogarth Press.

Freud, S. (1912a). The dynamics of transference. *Standard edition,* 12, pp. 99–108. London: Hogarth Press.

Freud, S. (1912b). Recommendations to physicians practicing psychoanalysis. *Standard edition,* 12, pp. 111–120. London: Hogarth Press.

Freud, S. (1913). The disposition to obsessional neurosis: A contribution to the problem of choice of neurosis. *Standard edition,* 12, pp. 317–326. London: Hogarth Press.

Freud, S. (1914). On the history of the psychoanalytic movement. *Standard edition,* 14, pp. 7–66. London: Hogarth Press.

Freud, S. (1915a). Observation on transference-love: Further recommendations on the technique of psycho-analysis, III. *Standard edition,* 12, pp. 159–171. London: Hogarth Press.

Freud, S. (1915b). The unconscious. *Standard edition,* 14, pp. 166–215. London: Hogarth Press.

Freud, S. (1923). *The ego and the id.* New York: Norton.

Freud, S. (1925). An autobiographical study. *Standard edition,* 20, pp. 7–70. London: Hogarth Press.

Freud, S. (1940/1953). An outline of psychoanalysis. *Standard edition,* 23, pp. 144–207. London: Hogarth Press.

Freud, S., & Breuer, J. (1895). The studies on hysteria. *Standard edition,* 2, pp. 3–305. London: Hogarth Press.

Gabbard, G. O. (1995). Countertransference: The emerging common ground. *International Journal of Psychoanalysis, 76,* 475–485.

Gabbard, G. O. (2001). A contemporary psychoanalytic model of countertransference. *Psychotherapy in Practice, 57*(8), 983–991.

Gelso, C. J., & Carter, J. A. (1994). Components of the psychotherapy relationship: Their interaction and unfolding during treatment. *Journal of Counseling Psychology, 41,* 296–306.

Gelso, C. J., & Hayes, J. A. (1998). *The psychotherapy relationship: Theory research and practice.* New York: John Wiley & Sons.

Gelso, C. J., & Hayes, J. A. (2001). Countertransference management. *Psychotherapy: Theory, Research, Practice, Training, 38*(4), 418–422.

Greenberg, J. R., & Mitchell, S. A. (1983). *Object relations in psychoanalytic theory.* New York: Basic Books.

Greenson, R. R. (1967). *The technique and practice of psychoanalysis* (Vol. 1). New York: International Universities Press.

Grünebaum, A. (1993). *Validation in the clinical theory of psychoanalysis: A philosophical critique.* Berkeley: University of California Press.

Hansen, J. C., Rossberg, R. H., & Cramer, S. H. (1994). *Counseling: Theory and process.* Boston: Allyn & Bacon.

Hartmann, H. (1939). *Ego psychology and the problem of adaptation.* New York: International Universities Press.

Hayes, J. (2004). Therapist know thyself: Recent research on countertransference. *Psychotherapy Bulletin, 39*(4), 6–12.

Hayes, J., & Gelso, C. J. (1991). Effects of therapist-trainee's anxiety and empathy on countertransference behavior. *Journal of Clinical Psychology, 47,* 284–290.

Hayes, J. A., McCracken, J. E., McClanahan, M. K., Hill, C. E., Harp, J. S., & Carozzini, P. (1998). Therapists' perspectives on countertransference: Qualitative data in search of a theory. *Journal of Counseling Psychology, 45,* 468–482.

Heimann, P. (1950). Countertransference. *British Journal of Medical Psychology, 33,* 9–15.

Kaplan, H. I., & Sadock, B. J. (1991). *Synopsis of psychiatry: Behavioral sciences clinical psychiatry.* Baltimore: Williams & Wilkins.

Kernberg, O. F. (1965). Notes on countertransference. *Journal of the American Psychoanalytic Association, 13,* 38–56.

Kernberg, O. F., Selzer, M. A., Koenigsberg, H. W., Carr, A. C., & Appelbaum, A. H. (1989). *Psychodynamic psychotherapy of borderline patients.* New York: Basic Books.

Kiesler, D.J. (1996). *Contemporary interpersonal theory & research.* New York: John Wiley & Sons.

Kirman, W. J. (1980). Countertransference in facilitating intimacy and communication. *Modern Psychoanalysis, 5*(2), 131–145.

Klein, M. (1946). Notes on some schizoid mechanisms. In M. Klein, *Envy and gratitude and other works, 1946—1963,* Vol. 4 (pp. 1–24). New York: Delta.

Klein, M. (1952/1975). The mutual influences in the development of the ego and id. In *Love, guilt, and reparation and other works 1921—1945* (Vol. 3) (pp. 57–60). London: Hogarth Press.

Klein, M. (1959/1975). Our adult world and its roots in infancy. In *Envy and gratitude and other works, 1946—1963,* Vol. 4 (pp. 247–263). New York: Delta.

Klein, R. (1995). Establishing a therapeutic alliance. In J. F. Masterson & R. Klein (Eds.), *Disorders of the self: New therapeutic horizons, the Masterson approach* (pp. 69–94). New York: Brunner/Mazel.

McGuire, W. (1974). *The Freud/Jung letters* (R. Manhein and R. F. C. Hull, Trans.). London: Hogarth Press and Routledge & Kegan Paul.

Ogden, T. (1982). *Projective identification and psychotherapeutic technique.* New York: Jason Aronson.

Ogden, T. (1994). The analytic triad: Working with intersubjective clinical facts. *International Journal of Psycho-Analysis, 75,* 3–19.

Patterson, C. H. (1966). *Theories of counseling and psychotherapy.* New York: Harper & Row.

Perls, F. S. (1969). *Gestalt therapy verbatim.* Toronto: Bantam Books.

Racker, H. (1957). The meanings and uses of countertransference. *Psychoanalytic Quarterly, 26,* 303–357.

Racker, H. (1958). Countertransference and interpretation. *Journal of the American Psychoanalytic Association, 6,* 215–221.

Racker, H. (1968). *Transference and countertransference.* New York: International Universities Press.

Reich, A. (1951). On countertransference. *International Journal of Psychoanalysis, 32,* 25–31.

Reich, A. (1960). Further remarks on countertransference. *International Journal of Psychoanalysis, 41,* 389–395.

Sandler, J. (1976). Countertransference and role responsiveness. *International Review of Psychoanalysis, 3,* 43–47.

Shlien, J. M. (1984). A countertheory of countertransference. In R. H. Levant & J. M. Shlien (Eds.), *Client-centered therapy and the person-centered approach* (pp. 153—181). New York: Praeger.

Singer, E. (1965). *Key concepts in psychotherapy.* New York: Random.

Slakter, E. (1987). *Countertransference.* Northvale, NJ: Jason Aronson.

Smith, D. L. (2003). *Psychoanalysis in focus.* London: Sage Publications.

Spotnitz, H. (1985). *Modern psychoanalysis of the schizophrenic patient.* New York: Human Sciences Press.

Szasz, T. (1961). The concept of transference. *International Journal of Psychoanalysis, 44,* 432–443.

Teyber, E. (1997). *Interpersonal process in psychotherapy: A relational approach* (3rd ed.). Pacific Grove, CA: Brooks/Cole.

Tansey, T. J. (1994). Sexual attraction and phobic dread in the countertransference. *Psychoanalytic Dialogues, 4*(2), 139–152.

Thompson C., Mazer, M., & Witenberg, E. (1955). *An outline of psychoanalysis* (Rev. ed.). New York: The Modern Library.

Wolitzky, D. L. (1995). The theory and practice of traditional psychoanalytic psychotherapy. In A. S. Gurman & S. B. Messer (Eds.), *Essential psychotherapies: Theory and practice* (pp. 12–54). New York: Guilford Press.

IV

Working with Transference and Countertransference in Psychotherapy

Shelley Briscoe-Dimock

The meeting of two personalities is like the contact of two chemical substances; if there is any reaction, both are transformed.

(Jung, 1933, p. 49)

Introduction

The concept of "alliance" is rooted in psychoanalysis and Freud, who viewed the alliance as the connection between client and therapist (Horvath, 2001). Although there is no precise definition of alliance, the concept has been a topic of theoretical and empirical interest for the past quarter-century, particularly in counselling and supervision.

A review of the professional literature on the helping relationship and specifically the therapeutic alliance has consistently shown a positive relationship between client-therapist alliance and therapeutic outcome (Lambert & Barley 2001). Indeed, most therapists would agree that a positive alliance is critical to the therapeutic process. Decades of research suggest that the nature of the therapeutic relationship is the main curative component of

therapy (Lambert & Barley 2001). Current research on the therapeutic alliance suggests that the therapist's skills and personal factors most influence the alliance (Horvath, 2001).

Although there is consensus on the importance of the alliance,
currently there is no precise and/or universal definition of the
therapeutic alliance (Bordin, 1979) but an ongoing debate and
substantial disagreement among the various helping relationships
(Andrusyna, Tang, DeRubeis, & Luborsky, 2001). Despite this
lack of consensus, Bordin (1979) offers a definition of the alliance that is gaining much acceptance in the field of counselling
and psychotherapy. He defines the alliance in three related components: client-therapist agreement on the goals of therapy, client-
therapist agreement on the means to achieve the goals of treatment, and development of a personal bond in the client-therapist
relationship.

Among the various theoretical approaches that have evolved,
all with their roots in psychoanalysis and each with its own view of
the helping relationship, there is general consensus that the therapeutic relationship plays a critical role in treatment outcome and
that the ultimate goal of therapy is change. This is most apparent
in psychodynamic therapy, which views the relationship between
therapist and client, similar to Bordin's (1979) third component
of the alliance, as the main vehicle for change.

A Psychodynamic Perspective on the Helping Relationship

In psychodynamic therapy, the therapeutic relationship is the
"vehicle" for change (Leiper & Maltby, 2004, p. 70). The relationship provides a context that promotes the communication
and exploration of the relationship processes and supports
"expressive catharsis" and "insightful understanding" (p. 70).
Underlying these processes are unconscious conflicts and patterns originating from early relationships that affect the client's

current life experiences and relationships. The aim of therapy is to uncover unconscious processes and conflicts and trace them back to their roots. The therapeutic relationship creates an opportunity for clients to access and resolve their conflicts by discovering new ways of being with another person. The relationship is the agent of change, an interpersonal experience capable of producing transformation.

The psychodynamic perspective views an individual's personal relationships as consistent patterns that link similar themes to different contexts. Underlying these patterns are unconscious conflicts and their respective defence mechanisms. These conflictual patterns are rooted in the individual's developmental history and reflect formative experiences and the mechanisms developed to cope with these experiences. These patterns are re-created in subsequent relationship contexts, including current life difficulties and the relationship with the therapist. It is this last idea that forms the basis of transference, a central concept in psychodynamic theory of change. Although it is not the only medium of communication and understanding, transference is the necessary agent and the crucial link in the entire change process.

Transference and Countertransference Defined

Transference and countertransference are psychoanalytic concepts originally articulated by Freud over a century ago. In 1889, he identified the phenomenon of transference during his formation of ideas about psychotherapy and particularly in his detailed account of the infamous case study "Dora," which he published in 1905, and in his paper on countertransference published in 1910. Since that time, Freud's classical phenomena have undergone significant development and continue to generate debate in terms of both their definitions and how these concepts are used.

Throughout its development, psychodynamic theory has consistently acknowledged transference and countertransference as central concepts and paramount to the change process. The interplay between the two, in large part, constitutes therapeutic change.

Transference

In his classical definition, Freud defined transference as the client's "impulses and phantasies which are aroused and made conscious during the progress of analysis" and which "replace some earlier person by the person of the physician" (1905/1977, p. 157).

Contemporary authors define transference as the "client's reaction to the therapist based on projections deriving from past experiences with influential others" (Ladany, Friedlander, & Nelson, 2005, p. 99). Corsini and Wedding (1989, p. 600) are more specific in their definition, substituting "influential others" with "usually a parent."

Leiper and Maltby (2004) identify three features of a "transferential" relationship: when perceptions, thoughts, feelings, and actions are repeated across differing situations in ways that are not selective or discriminating; are not appropriate and may ignore or distort reality according to a fixed pattern; are not rational but idiosyncratic, oppose normal perception, and are highly emotional and "fantasy laden" (p. 71). They suggest that, when these features are present, the relationship is considered transferential.

Countertransference

Freud defined countertransference (1910/1959) as the analyst's inappropriate, unconscious, and defensive reaction to the client's transference rooted in her or his own "personal dynamics" (Ladany, Friedlander, and Nelson, 2005, p. 79).

Corsini and Wedding (1989, p. 591) define countertransference as the activation of a therapist's unconscious wishes and fantasies regarding the patient as well as the therapist's tendency to respond to clients "as though they were significant others in the life or history or fantasy of the therapist."

Ladany, Friedlander, and Nelson (2005, p. 99) view counter-transference as a naturally occurring phenomenon in all relationships. Broadly defined, it refers to "feelings a client elicits in the therapist—feelings that either reflect the therapist's own problematic transference issues or reactions to the client's attitudes, characteristics, or behaviors."

In the professional literature, two opposing definitions of countertransference currently prevail. The classical definition, with its roots in Freud and his earlier beliefs, views countertransference as counterproductive, an impediment, and an interference. The contemporary definition views countertransference as both productive and informative.

Classical View: Countertransference as Interference

In this view, countertransference is seen as an interference with the therapeutic process and a consequence of the therapist's intruding emotional difficulties. Rooted in the therapist's unconscious responses to personal dynamics, countertransference interferes with exploration of the client's inner world. The classical model views this interference as a "contaminant" of therapy whereby the therapist loses neutrality, is distracted, and is unable to identify and understand the client's issues clearly. In its worst form, and in serving the therapist's own needs and unconscious agenda, this type of countertransference can subtly or overtly exploit the client.

Contemporary View: Countertransference as Informative

On a more positive note, countertransference is seen as "informative" and "the most helpful tool in the therapist's armoury" (Leiper & Maltby, 2004, p. 78). It provides access to and awareness of what is otherwise out of consciousness; it is objective and provides a vital source of information about a client. The therapist's reaction provides a vital source of information about a client and is seen as a reality-based response to the client's presentation in the external world and in other interpersonal relationships. The therapist's reality-based response provides valuable insight into how others also respond to the client's dynamics. Thus, responses provide subtle information of which the client might otherwise not be conscious. The responses illuminate hidden features of the client's emotional world, giving the therapist access to and understanding of the client's underlying dynamics and emotional experiences (Leiper & Maltby, 2004).

Let's summarize what we know thus far. The quality of the therapeutic relationship is linked with treatment outcome. We also know that transference and countertransference are naturally occurring phenomena in therapy. Research informs us that we must be aware of transference and countertransference issues in therapy and that effective management is critical in that a lack of awareness or an inability to manage can have harmful effects on the therapeutic relationship and process.

As therapists, most of us are aware of the impact of the alliance on the change process, but few of us are taught how to effectively manage the alliance, how to work with transference or countertransference, or what to do if the alliance is ruptured. So how do we come to learn to work with transference and countertransference in order to create and maintain a positive alliance and promote change in the therapeutic relationship? How do we prevent or repair a rupture in the alliance?

Working with Transference and Countertransference

Perspectives on working with countertransference have significantly shifted since Freud's initial view of countertransference as an impediment to be avoided. In traditional classical psychoanalytic training, supervision accompanied personal analysis to help therapists maintain neutrality by coming to terms with their unconscious and "drive-based" fantasies. The overall goal of supervision was to help analysts "rid their work of intruding unconscious material" (Ladany, Friedlander, & Nelson, 2005, p. 100).

Contemporary authors recognize the necessity of identifying and working through countertransference. Arkowitz (2001) points out that, given the intimate nature of therapy, feelings of ambivalence, reactions of love and hate, and the presence of constructive and destructive forces are inevitable. Ladany, Friedlander, and Nelson (2005) point out that the vital insight into the harmful effects of countertransference on the therapeutic relationship has increased awareness of the need for effective training and supervision to deal with these concepts. Psychotherapists are being strongly encouraged to seek clinical supervision (Ladany, Friedlander, & Nelson, 2005) and preliminary personal therapy (Leiper & Maltby, 2004), features that are becoming more accepted in the field.

Theory and research recognize the importance of the therapeutic relationship and countertransference management; however, the professional literature on training therapists to work with these concepts of transference and countertransference is limited. Practice implications have been identified, and various models have been proposed as a means to work through countertransference.

Safran, Muran, Samstag, and Stevens' (2001) research addresses the repair of weak or ruptured alliances and summarizes four provisional practice implications for the therapist. First, clients may be reluctant to share negative feelings about the therapeutic relationship with the therapist for fear of a negative reaction. Hence, therapists' attunement to subtle indications of alliance rupture and exploration of the therapeutic relationship to identify what has evolved are necessary. Second, clients require an opportunity to express their negative feelings and differing perspectives regarding what has transpired in therapy. Third, therapists must be non-defensive and open to receiving the clients' expressions and must assume and identify their contributions to the rupture. Fourth, exploring clients' fears and expectations that inhibit them from discussing negative feelings may facilitate the rupture resolution process.

Gelso and Hayes (2001), in examining the literature on countertransference management and treatment outcome, point out that the existing empirical literature strongly supports the notion that acting out countertransference hinders therapy, whereas effective management aids treatment. In their research, they promote a five-factor theory originally proposed by Hayes, Gelso, Van Wagoner, and Diemer (1991) that is central to countertransference management. The first factor, self-insight, refers to the therapist's awareness of the nature of his or her countertransference feelings. The second, self-integration, refers to the therapist having an intact and healthy character structure such that identification of ego boundaries and differentiation of self from other are possible. Anxiety management, the third factor, implies that the therapist is able to manage his or her own anxiety such that it does not affect responses to the client. The fourth, empathy, refers to the therapist's ability to identify with the client and to put himself or herself in the client's shoes. And the fifth factor, conceptualizing ability, refers to the therapist's ability to theoretically grasp the client's dynamics in the context of the therapeutic relationship.

My Journey Learning to Work with Transference and Countertransference

Transference and countertransference were concepts briefly discussed in my graduate training, mostly in terms of their relevance to psychoanalytic theory. They were given little attention in my practicum or supervision. As a student trainee, I often left therapy sessions feeling overwhelmed and anxious but unable to discuss these feelings during supervision because of time constraints, a lack of openness in the supervisor to explore students' experiences, or my own underlying anxiety about discussing my feelings and my performance. Having been in personal therapy before, and feeling that I had relatively good insight into myself, I thought that supervision should have been the appropriate avenue for exploration as the supervisor had a relatively good working knowledge of my clients' dynamics and was aware of my skills and abilities as a therapist. I graduated from the program excited to venture into the world of psychotherapy, to consolidate my academic experience into practice, but I remained anxious and confused about how to work with transference and countertransference in therapy. As a result, my primary goal was to seek a clinical supervisor who would assist in my professional growth and development and specifically help me learn to work with my countertransference.

I was fortunate to find a supervisor, psychodynamically trained and orientated, who appreciated my objective to learn how to work with transference and countertransference in therapy. I soon learned that my countertransference reactions were an important part of the therapeutic and supervisory process. I came to know how countertransference can have both a positive and a negative impact on the therapeutic process as well as rupture the alliance or have harmful consequences if avoided or ignored. Through my experiences of successful resolutions, I am learning how to manage and work with my countertransference effectively.

The following case demonstrates opposing views of countertransference as both interference and informative. In the first event, countertransference was not resolved, therefore rupturing the alliance and interfering with the therapeutic process. In the second event, countertransference was informative, and successful resolution was achieved, resulting in transformation of the relationship.

Description of the Case

Juan (pseudonym) is in his mid-30s and of European descent. He was referred for therapy by his treating psychiatrist for anger, anxiety, and depression. Juan had seen two psychiatrists previously who had diagnosed him with borderline personality disorder. Predisposing events included a history of childhood trauma, including severe emotional, verbal, and physical abuse at the hands of his father. Precipitating factors included a suicide attempt, which resulted in psychiatric hospitalization, and a more recent allegation of harassment made by a female co-worker.

As an eager novice therapist, upon receiving this referral, I pulled out my DSM-IV-TR to familiarize myself with the diagnostic criteria of the disorder. I identified the following characteristics as relevant to the client's presentation: unstable interpersonal relationships and sense of self, impulsivity in self-damaging behaviour, fear of abandonment, chronic feelings of emptiness, and intense anger.

My initial reaction to the referral was feelings of anxiety and uncertainty about my clinical competence to work with a diagnosed "borderline," who, I had learned through my training, were difficult clients to treat because of their emotional intensity, and I knew that the prognosis was poor because of their lack of response to treatment. My anxiety about emotional intensity, especially anger, stems from my own experience growing up with an angry parent. However, my nature to embrace new challenges that afford opportunities for professional growth and development led me to book an initial appointment. During the assessment phase, I came to understand Juan's difficulty trusting others, his deep hurt, his intense anger primarily at his father that he directed at the external world and acted out in his interpersonal and professional relationships, his intense fear of rejection and abandonment, and his difficulty in maintaining interpersonal relationships. As a result of his recent harassment allegation, Juan fluctuated between wanting to die and wanting to harm others; he felt emotionally devastated, intensely angry, and desperate for revenge.

Example A: Countertransference as Interference
In the beginning of therapy, I used my clinical skills of empathy and compassion to strengthen the alliance with Juan, which developed surprisingly quickly. Conceptually, I recognized Juan's transference in his experience of me as an ideal mother. In an attempt to

understand his underlying dynamics, I began to explore his childhood experiences in more depth. My attempts were consistently met with much resistance and intense and escalating anger, which Juan displayed by raising his voice to the point of yelling, shaking his hands and fists in the air, and using vulgarities toward significant others. I felt myself becoming more and more uncomfortable with his escalating anger and attempted to take distance from it. However, as it intensified, I became afraid. My subconscious reaction to my fear and need to self-protect resulted in overly distancing myself from Juan, unable to relate to or understand his pain, and becoming rigid and overly direct in defining the therapeutic boundaries. Juan's transferential reaction to my countertransferential reaction was to distance and self-protect as a result of feeling misunderstood and scolded. He continued to lash out in anger at me for abandoning him emotionally. The remainder of the session resulted in a tug-of-war in which I struggled to remain in control of my fear in order to avoid further anger. Although Juan continued to attend sessions, I soon felt anxious prior to our sessions, uncertain about my ability to help him, and considered terminating therapy.

Impact on relationship and process: Juan felt that I was "pushing" him into his hurt, and he defended himself with intense anger. My fear of his anger manifested itself in my direct and hostile manner of relating. My manner led him to feel misunderstood, invalidated, and abandoned. These feelings intensified his anger and need to self-protect, which fuelled my need to self-protect, and dialogue continued. Our reactions to each other created a destructive cycle that resulted in a rupture of the alliance. Juan perceived me in a negative way, as a hostile and scolding parent. As a result, he lost trust in me and distanced himself emotionally from me.

The resolution process: As I reflected on my experience, I observed that the management of my countertransference and the successful resolution of it involved many steps. I acknowledged my countertransference and addressed my own issues with anger. I had to integrate these feelings to be able to sufficiently distance myself in sessions. By doing this, I was able to understand Juan's underlying dynamics. Namely, I was able to see his anger as a defence mechanism to ward off his underlying hurt. By addressing this with him in an empathic and validating way, I was able to help him identify this pattern in other relationships. Reassuring him that I was there for him, that I understood his anger, facilitated trust in the relationship, an openness to his inner world, and an opportunity to experience his dynamic in a healthy way. This process is summarized in Table 4.1.

Example B: Countertransference as Informative
In two future sessions, Juan openly criticized my clothing and a piece of art in my office. On the first occasion, he laughed at my attire, made a reference to the "'70s." I took his comment to mean that my clothing was out of date and that he did not like my style of dress. I did not overtly react but felt disrespected and surprised by his comment, which I thought was inappropriate and uncharacteristic of our relationship. In response to feeling disrespected, I found myself somewhat disengaged during the session in an attempt to read between the lines of his communication in search of some underlying anger or hurt that would account for what I perceived to be passive-aggressive behaviour directed toward me. After the session, I remained unaware of the nature of his comment and felt puzzled by and frustrated with my inability to understand Juan's motivation. I went over my clinical notes, recalled previous therapy sessions, but was unable to find a reason for his underlying hostility. I did not address his behaviour at the next session but found myself guarded, direct in my approach, and detached.

The second incident, two sessions following the first, Juan nonchalantly sauntered into my office and criticized a piece of art that had personal significance to me. He questioned who had given it to me and again commented that the piece was outdated. My initial reaction was feelings of disrespect and anger, which I made a clumsy effort to hide by waving off the comment. However, my

Table 4.1
Example A: Countertransference as interference

Client's transference	Therapist's counter-transference	Impacts on relationship/process	Mechanics of resolution process
— Invalidated, misunderstood, abandoned — Became resistant, angry (defence) — Experience of therapist as invalidating and scolding mother	— Fearful, disengaged, hostile (defence) — Experience of client as angry parent — Coping mechanism = suppression/avoidance	— Relational cycle; his need to self-protect triggered my need to self-protect, and reactions fed each other — Client's anger intensified the more he felt pushed and misunderstood — Therapist became direct, rigid, hostile, overly distant, contemplated termination — Alliance rupture: client lost trust, became emotionally distanced.	1. Awareness of counter-transferential reaction 2. Addressing own issues with anger 3. Taking distance from feelings in session—managing anxiety 4. Empathizing and validating client's experience 5. Understanding the client's current transference and underlying dynamics 6. Exploring client's current transference and linking this to earlier experience

countertransference manifested itself in a direct and hostile manner for the remainder of the session. I found myself overly detached and disengaged and anticipated the end of the session. After the session, I attempted to process the comment, my feelings, my reaction to it, and Juan's reaction to me. I came to realize that this was his attempt to align himself with me in the same way that Juan attempts to align himself with others in the external world. Being able to detach myself from my feelings allowed me to see that this was his style of relating and the same pattern that resulted in harassment charges being laid against him in the workplace.

After exploring my countertransference in supervision, I confronted Juan about his behaviour the following session. I pointed out this pattern of behaviour, and I let him know the impact that it had on me (e.g., "I felt uncomfortable and puzzled ... "). As we talked about the incidents, their impacts, and boundaries in relationships, he admitted that he felt "ashamed, embarrassed, and rejected." He stated that he "thought we were friends," which I normalized and pointed out the "friendly but professional nature" of our relationship. For the remainder of the session, I could sense that he was guarded; he "pulled back" and was hurt and upset with my reaction. When the session ended, I felt positive about my intervention but concerned about his reaction. Knowing that Juan felt ashamed and rejected despite my attempt to reassure him otherwise, I anticipated a difficult next session.

In the following session, Juan presented himself as guarded, defensive, hostile, and angry. He attempted to control and dominate the session and carried on superficial conversation with me. Being prepared for this reaction, I followed along for a brief period and then pointed out his tendency and need to push me away. I pointed out this "you hurt me, I'll hurt you" pattern in other relationships and anger as a defence to ward off the hurt that he initially dismissed. I again validated his feelings and reassured him that I was not rejecting him and would continue to be there for him while reinforcing the need for therapeutic boundaries. As we sat in what I perceived for him to be an awkward silence, I sensed that he was contemplating the authenticity of my response. He was considering letting me back into his "inner world" with less resistance. He let me know that this experience had affected his ability to trust me, which I validated and normalized. The session ended, and I felt positive about the experience. I felt that I had reached Juan and that he was able to receive me and experience the relationship in a new way.

In the following session, Juan presented himself as anxious, less guarded, and somewhat friendly. He opened the session with superficial conversation but within minutes began talking about his experience of the previous few sessions. Following his lead, we began to explore his experience and insights. He identified his critical pattern as an attempt to relate to others in what he perceived to be meaningful relationships. He identified the nature of the pattern as an intense need to be liked, an incessant attempt to align with people, and an intense fear of rejection. Juan developed awareness that his overcompensating behaviour was related to his intense fear of rejection. He identified an inability to relate to people in a healthy way. He concluded that, in his attempts to align with others, he ended up pushing people away with his critical and insulting behaviour. Relating this pattern to his recent allegation of harassment, he became aware that, in his attempts to be liked and to align with his female co-worker, he "crossed the line," and she took action. Juan was left feeling hurt, confused, rejected, and abandoned as a result of the allegations against him and because he was unaware of his pattern of behaviour. To ward off these feelings and to self-protect, he became hostile, angry, and vengeful.

Bringing this into our experience and the re-enactment of the pattern with me, Juan readily identified his attempt to align with me to be my friend. When I responded to his behaviour, he perceived me to be disapproving and rejecting. He was able to acknowledge and speak from his hurt, explore the negative impact on the alliance, and understand his defensive reaction in terms of his pattern of becoming angry and untrusting.

We discussed the re-experiencing of the pattern in a new way, and Juan admitted that he felt vulnerable opening up and letting me back into his psychological world but also felt positive about his increasing ability to trust, grow, and develop. He was more aware of the inappropriateness of his behaviour and respectful of the limits of the therapeutic relationship. He realized that he had learned his style of relating in his family of origin, namely from his father, who was hypercritical of and insulting toward his wife's family and others. Juan identified his difficulty with boundaries as a result of unhealthy and non-existent boundaries in his family of origin. He became aware of his consistent pattern in relationships since childhood, which he acted out in his relationship with his co-worker and subsequently in the therapeutic relationship. His ability to identify his pattern and to experience the therapeutic relationship in a new way resulted in change characterized by decreased anger, accessibility to hurt, and more compassion for self and other. This awareness enabled Juan to access his underlying hurt, accept responsibility for his behaviour, and develop compassion for himself and the woman whom he allegedly had harassed. This was for him a transformative experience.

In exploring the feelings that resulted from his new awareness, Juan felt conflicted. On the one hand, he felt positive about his ability to experience his relational pattern in a new way and positive about the insight and self-awareness that he had developed. On the other hand, he felt "ashamed and embarrassed, inadequate and socially inept," as he reflected on similar patterns in past and present relationships. I validated his feelings and suggested that we work on developing healthy boundaries and new ways of relating to others. This was the next stage of therapy. This process is summarized in Table 4.2.

Relationship to the Literature

My experience in learning to identify and work with transference and countertransference in therapy is consistent with the

Table 4.2
Example B: Countertransference as informative

Client's transference	Therapist's countertransference	Impacts on relationship/process	Mechanics of resolution
— Hurt, ashamed, embarrassed, rejected, untrusting, vengeful	— Disrespected, violated, confused, frustrated, guarded	— Client guarded, distant, hostile, angry, controlling, dominating, vengeful — Therapist guarded, direct, distant, angry, hostile, wanted session to end — Contemplated termination	1. Awareness that boundaries had been crossed and of countertransferential event 2. Assessing reaction, knowing what is mine and what is not 3. Taking distance from feelings in session 4. Empathy and validation of client's experience 5. Understanding underlying dynamics 6. Exploring and linking client's current transference to earlier experience

professional literature. The process of resolution that I identified is in keeping with Gelso and Hayes' (2001) five-factor theory of countertransference management: self-insight, self-integration, anxiety management, empathy, and conceptualization. However, I added a step.

As shown in Table 4.3, my resolution process involved developing my self-awareness; assessing my countertransferential reaction; taking sufficient distance from my feelings in order to explore my own unconscious processes and underlying dynamics, my reaction to them, and their impact on the therapeutic relationship (e.g., the client's subjective experience); empathically engaging in the client's experience; conceptualizing the client's underlying dynam-

Table 4.3
Countertransference management model

Gelso and Hayes	My process
self-insight	Awareness of countertransferential event
self-integration	Assessing my reaction/reality-based response to know what is mine
anxiety management	Ability to take distance from my feelings
empathy	Empathizing and validating client's experience
conceptualizing ability	Understanding underlying dynamics
	Exploring and linking current experience to earlier experience

ics; and exploring and linking these experiences to earlier experiences. It is this final additional step that was transformative as it facilitated the client's insight and awareness and led to a shift in the relationship patterns and the goal of change. These steps are summarized in Table 4.3.

Recommendations

I agree with Ladany, Friedlander, and Nelson (2005) in their belief that countertransference is a naturally occurring phenomenon that happens in all human relationships. I strongly support the belief that therapists who work interpersonally or relationally with clients' inner subjective experiences must also be open to their own. This openness to exploring one's countertransference can move therapy in a positive direction and deepen the therapist's self-understanding. A lack of openness or unsuccessful resolution can have serious negative consequences to the point of damaging the therapeutic relationship. Although the focus of much of the literature, including this discussion, is on the inner subjective experience of the psychodynamic therapist, I would encourage therapists of various theoretical orientations to consider countertransference as a naturally occurring phenomenon and a central feature of *any* helping relationship and to engage in subjective self-analysis and subsequent personal therapy if indicated. I believe that as helpers we have an ethical responsibility to ourselves, our clients, and our profession to ensure that we are in a healthy place to offer the help that clients seek from us.

I would also recommend that training programs put more emphasis on and resources into teaching student trainees how to work with transference and countertransference and to provide a forum where students can engage in more thorough subjective self-analysis. I strongly encourage therapists to engage in supervision with a supervisor who is clinically competent in working with transferential and countertransferential issues.

Suggestions for Future Research

Consolidating my learning into my practice as an individual therapist has been challenging but most useful. Applying my skills in my work with couples has led me to realize the benefits of using transference and countertransference in couple therapy. I often find myself relying on my countertransference to assist me in balancing the therapeutic alignment between myself and the couple and between myself and each partner. I use my countertransference to guide my intervention. For example, my countertransference provides me with insight into the individual and into the couple dynamic. It allows me to experience the impact of the partner and guides me to know when other partner involvement may be constructive or destructive.

As a couple therapist, my role is to remain neutral while consistently attempting to balance the therapeutic alignment. Given the complexity of the dynamics in couple treatment, I find myself questioning how transference and countertransference are played out in the couple context. How do they affect the alliance with each partner? Learning to work with these concepts in couple therapeutic relationships would be most beneficial. Future research might focus on the impact of the alliance on the couple-therapist relationship and on defining mechanisms for working with transference and countertransference in couple treatment.

Conclusion

In this chapter, I have attempted to define the core concepts of transference and countertransference in terms of the therapeutic process and to demonstrate how to work with them effectively. Using my own clinical experiences, I demonstrated how they can affect the therapeutic process both negatively and positively. I provided the mechanisms of resolution that facilitated my effective countertransference management. In addition to Gelso and Hayes'

(2001) process model, I proposed a final step that involves exploring and linking the client's transference to earlier experiences, a process that further promotes clients' insight, awareness, and change.

My experience in learning to work with transference and countertransference in therapy has been both enriching and transformative. My struggle to manage my countertransference has promoted my development as a therapist. My journey has transformed me and changed my view of the importance of the therapeutic relationship and the way that I work within it. It has inspired me to work effectively with transference and countertransference as a therapist. I am more aware of my reactions, more able to know what is mine and what is not, and more able to identify when my countertransferential reactions are reality based and when they are products of my own unresolved conflicts. As a result, I am more open and available to clients in their journeys toward change.

References

Andrusyna, T. P., Tang, T. Z., DeRubeis, R. J., & Luborsky, L. (2001). The factor structure of the working alliance inventory in cognitive-behavioral therapy. *Journal of Psychotherapy Practice Research, 10,* 173–178.

Arkowitz, S. W. (2001). Perfectionism in the supervisee. In S. Gill (Ed.), *The supervisory alliance: Facilitating the psychotherapist's learning experience* (pp. 35–66). Northvale, NJ: Jason Aronson.

Bordin, E. S. (1979). The generalizability of the psychoanalytic concept of the working alliance. *Psychotherapy: Theory, Research, and Practice, 16,* 252–260.

Corsini, R. J., & Wedding, D. (1989). *Current psychotherapies* (4th ed.).Itasca, IL: F. E. Peacock Publishers.

Freud, S. (1905/1977). Fragment of an analysis of a case of hysteria ("Dora"). In A. Richards (Ed. and Trans.), *Sigmund Freud: 8 case histories/"Dora" and "little Hans"* (pp. 29–164). London: Pelican Books.

Freud, S. (1910/1959). Future prospects of psychoanalytic psychotherapy. In J. Stachey (Ed. and Trans.), *The standard edition of the complete psychological works of Sigmund Freud* (Vol. 20, pp. 87–172). London: Hogarth Press.

Gelso, C. J., & Hayes, J. A. (2001). Countertransference management. *Psychotherapy: Theory, Research, Practice, Training, 38*(4), 418–422.

Hayes, J. A., Gelso C. J., Van Wagoner, S. L., & Diemer, R. A. (1991). Managing countertransference: What the experts think. *Psychological Report, 69*(1), 139–148.

Horvath, A. O. (2001). The alliance. *Psychotherapy: Theory, Research, Practice, Training, 38*(4), 365–372.

Jung, C. (1933). *Modern man in search of a soul: Problems of psychology.* Fort Washington, PA: Harvest Books.

Ladany, N., Friedlander, M. L., & Nelson, M. L. (2005). *Critical events in psychotherapy supervision: An interpersonal approach.* Washington, DC: American Psychological Association.

Lambert, M. J., & Barley, D. E. (2001). Research summary on the therapeutic relationship and psychotherapy outcome. *Psychotherapy: Theory, Research, Practice, Training, 38*(4), 357–361.

Leiper, R., & Maltby, M. (2004). *The psychodynamic approach to therapeutic change.* London: Sage Publications.

Safran, J. D., Muran, J. C., Samstag, L. W., & Stevens, C. (2001). Repairing alliance ruptures. *Psychotherapy: Theory, Research, Practice, Training, 38*(4), 406–412.

V

Working through the Transference of an Unresolved Separation/ Individuation Pattern: A Case Study Using Theme-Analysis

Augustine Meier, Micheline Boivin, and Molisa Meier

A primary developmental task for a child is to become emotionally bonded with a significant caregiver (e.g., mother) and then, in due course, to separate from her and to individuate and become his or her own person (Mahler, Pine, & Bergman, 1975). A failure to achieve this developmental task may mark the person's relational pattern in that he or she may develop a fear of getting close to people or of feeling abandoned when pushed to pursue independence. A person with this pattern can also alternate between getting close to and taking distance from a significant person. This relational pattern—referred to as an unresolved separation/individuation pattern—is often repeated with and/or transferred to significant others, including the psychotherapist.

This study investigated the working through, within the course of psychotherapy, of the transference of an unresolved separation/individuation pattern of a client with a low-level borderline personality disorder. The first part of this chapter presents the definitions of key words, and the second part presents the research study.

Definitions

Transference

A transference refers to a client directing his or her emotional feelings toward the therapist as though the therapist were the original object that caused the feelings (Freud, 1940/1949, p. 38). When transferential feelings are associated with memory, motives (e.g., wishes, yearnings), expectations, and attempts by the client to draw the therapist into a pattern of relating associated with the original target of the client's feelings, the pattern is referred to as "Transference Relationship" (Lorand, 1944, p. 298), "Projective Identification" (Cashdan, 1988, p. 52), or "Cyclical Maladaptive Pattern" (Butler & Strupp, 1991, p. 87). The transference of an unresolved separation/individuation onto another qualifies as a Transference Relationship, Projective Identification, or Cyclical Maladaptive Pattern since it is repeated and distorts and undermines a client's current and future relationships.

Borderline Personality Disorder

A borderline personality disorder is described by the *Diagnostic and Statistical Manual of Mental Disorders* (DSM-IV-TR, Code 301.83) as "a pervasive pattern of instability of interpersonal relationships, self-image, and affects, and marked impulsivity beginning by early adulthood and present in a variety of contexts" (American Psychiatric Association, 1994). Associated with this disorder are acting-out behaviours, which can include frantic efforts to avoid real or imagined abandonment, unstable self-image or sense of self, impulsivity (e.g., substance abuse), suicidal threats or self-mutilating behaviour, inability to regulate affect, chronic feelings of emptiness, and paranoid ideations. The underlying dynamic in borderline personality disorder consists of a primitive defence against achieving self-activation or the emergence of the real self for fear of abandonment. The low-level borderline personality client has the same underlying dynamic as the DSM-IV-defined borderline personality disorder but differs from the latter in that it does not manifest acting-out behaviour (Masterson, 1991). Sperry (1995) differentiates between a borderline personality disorder and a borderline personality style, which is considered to be a maladaptive interpersonal pattern. Using this as a reference point, the low-level borderline personality client can be perceived to lie somewhere between a borderline personality disorder and a borderline personality style.

Separation/Individuation

Separation/individuation refers to the developmental process through which an infant/child moves from a bonded (symbiotic) relationship with a significant caregiver to separating from the caregiver and developing his or her own individuality (Mahler, Pine, & Bergman, 1975). A significant point in this process is the rapprochement phase, during which, if it is successful, the child acquires the skills to regulate emotions and impulses, to self-comfort and self-soothe, to see self and others as whole persons rather than in terms of good and bad, to integrate impulses and yearnings with a positive sense of self, and to replace the defence of splitting with the defence of repression (Masterson, 1976, 1991).

A failure to adequately negotiate the separation/individuation process, particularly the rapprochement phase, might lead to deep-seated emotional disturbances, ego and self impairments, and relational problems. These disturbances, impairments, and relational problems can include a difficulty to comfort and soothe oneself when emotionally injured, a difficulty to regulate affect and personal and interpersonal needs and wishes, a tendency to idealize or depreciate self and others, and an inclination to relate to others as they are needed rather than as persons in their own right. These experiences are often accompanied by feelings of anger, worthlessness, and guilt when they assert their autonomy and by feelings of being intruded upon and violated when they comply (Masterson, 1976, 1991). Such patterns are often seen in borderline personality disorders, including low-level borderline personality disorder. These unresolved patterns may be projected onto a significant other, including the therapist.

An unresolved separation/individuation pattern (Mahler, Pine, & Bergman, 1975) stems from the failure to achieve self-activation and the emergence of the real self (Masterson, 1993). This failure, which is construed as a developmental impairment of the self, can result from several different factors, including genetic defects, separation stress, and parents' difficulty in supporting the child's individuative and emerging aspects of self (Masterson, 1991, p. 288). From a developmental perspective, such children are usually brought up by a parent or parents who reward their children for compliance with their wishes and punish them with withdrawal of their affection when the children assert their autonomy (Masterson 1976, 1991).

This study investigated how a client projected onto the therapist an unresolved separation/individuation pattern and then through the process of therapy resolved this pattern.

Selection of Theme-Analysis as Research Method

Theme-analysis was chosen as a research method to investigate the resolution of a client's projected separation/individuation pattern onto the therapist. Theme-analysis is a qualitative research method that analyzes transcripts of therapy sessions according to themes and then tracks the evolution of the themes across the sessions in terms of phases (Meier & Boivin, 2008). This research method was selected because the goal of the research was to identify the themes (constituents) of a projected unresolved separation/individuation pattern and to trace the working through of these themes across the course of therapy. This research method was used effectively to study the achievement of greater selfhood (Meier & Boivin, 2000) and to investigate the working through of depression (Meier, Boivin, & Meier, 2006). The research question was: does the evolution of themes follow a progressive course in a successful psychodynamic/ humanistic-oriented psychotherapy when applied to the working through of a separation/individuation transference of a low-level borderline personality client?

Method

The research method used by Meier and Boivin (2000) and Meier, Boivin, and Meier (2006) in their studies was applied to this study.

Participants

Client

The clinical material comprised the transcripts from 37 consecutive 1-hour audiotaped psychotherapy sessions of a female European Canadian young adult client, Gloria (pseudonym), who had a graduate degree in the helping profession. She sought psychotherapy to help her separate from a primary caregiver, to become a person in her own right, and to work through her feelings of loss and grief in being transferred by her previous therapist. The 37 sessions represent the last of the therapy sessions. It was during these sessions that the client explicitly transferred onto the therapist the unresolved separation/individuation pattern and worked to resolve it.

Gloria was brought up in an upper-middle-class home characterized by emotional deprivation. Her parents, both high-placed professionals, were emotionally distant from her and her siblings, and they did not acknowledge their accomplishments and affirm them as persons. Her father expected certain behaviours from her, and if she opposed him he put her down and/or retreated. Although she was angry at her father, her feelings of guilt would not allow her to let go of him, hurt him, and "take advantage of a young child." As for her mother, Gloria perceived her to be domineering and laying guilt trips on her, which left Gloria feeling trapped, helpless, and resentful. Within the family, there was little affirmation for self-directed behaviour and autonomy. Gloria, however, felt affirmed as a person and for her accomplishments by her maternal grandparents, whom she visited annually and who loved her without conditions.

Therapist and Therapy

The therapist (senior author), male, Canadian, was an experienced and doctoral-level psychodynamic/humanistic-oriented clinical psychologist who had a part-time private practice and worked full time in a university graduate counselling program. The therapist paid attention to the client's subjective experiences and to the client's current reality and used attending and focusing skills, advanced empathic responses (Ivey, 1983), and linking statements (Meier & Boivin, 2000) to address the client's explicit and implicit messages. Task-direct imagery (Meier & Boivin, 1994) was used to help the client better understand her inner experiences and the nature of her relationships, to express her thoughts, feelings, and yearnings, and to individuate and become empowered, competent, and assertive.

The client and the therapist were actively engaged in the therapeutic process and worked in the here-and-now. The client set the agenda for each session. The therapist explored and challenged the client's transferences and resistances to move forward. The therapist constantly checked back with the client to ascertain what she was experiencing and processing, particularly when she demonstrated changes in tone of voice, mood, behaviour, and so on (Meier & Boivin, 2000).

Research Measures

DSM-IV-TR

To assess for the presence of borderline personality disorder, the DSM-IV-TR was administered at the beginning of therapy and again at the termination of therapy. Prior to therapy, Gloria met the criteria for borderline personality disorder on the DSM-IV-TR, but she did not meet the criteria following therapy. As well, the client met the criteria for borderline personality style (Sperry, 1995) at the termination of therapy.

Separation/Individuation Process Inventory

The Separation/Individuation Process Inventory (S-IPI) (Christenson & Wilson, 1994) was used to assess for disturbances in the separation/individuation process. The S-IPI is a 39-item instrument that produces a single score. The items are responded to on a 10-point Likert scale. The mean score for a sample of patients diagnosed with borderline personality disorder was 201, with a standard deviation of 65.6. A sample of "normal" university employees produced a mean score of 120.6 and a standard deviation of 40. The authors suggest a cutting score of 190 to distinguish persons with separation/individuation problems from those without such problems. Scores higher than 190 on the S-IPI indicate separation/individuation problems. The S-IPI has excellent internal consistency and has demonstrated known-groups validity.

Theme-Analysis (TA)

Theme-analysis (TA), an innovative research method, combines both a qualitative component and a quantitative component. As a qualitative method, theme-analysis develops themes from transcripts of psychotherapy sessions and tracks changes in these themes across the sessions. To accomplish this task, TA engages in four interrelated operations: (a) segmenting transcripts into meaning units, (b) developing themes, (c) identifying the object (target) of a theme, and (d) describing change in a theme (Meier & Boivin, 2008). These four operations are summarized in Table 5.1 and are described in detail in *The Manual for Theme-Analysis* (Meier and Boivin, 1998a). As a quantitative method, theme-analysis correlates the two variables, phase and session, for a selected number of themes. The resulting correlation indicates the degree to which the themes are worked through in a progressive movement.

The Seven-Phase Model of the Change Process

The Seven-Phase Model of the Change Process (SPMCP) (Meier & Boivin, 1998b) was used to track changes in the psychotherapeutic

Table 5.1
Summary of the four operations of theme-analysis

Operation 1: Segmenting transcripts of psychotherapy sessions into meaning units

1. Segment the transcripts into meaning units (composed of one or more sentences) that comprise three components: a theme, an object of the theme, and a change (referred to as a phase) on a theme.
2. Assign a new meaning unit when there is a shift from one theme, object, or phase to another theme, object, or phase.
3. A meaning unit may be coded for one or more themes, objects, and/or phases.
4. A meaning unit may be explicitly or implicitly embedded within the segment.
5. A meaning unit must provide sufficient information so that the client's experience of the theme (e.g., a problem, insight, action) can be assessed.

Operation 2: Developing themes

1. Derive themes from the summarized meaning unit (client statement).
2. Express themes in terms of bi-polarities, with the problem representing one end of the continuum and the striving-toward representing the other pole.
3. Define themes using psychology and English-language dictionaries.
4. Develop four levels of themes: descriptive, first-order, second-order, and core.

Operation 3: Identifying the objects of the themes

1. Assign an object to each theme.
2. An object may be animate (e.g., person, group) or inanimate (e.g., earthquake).

Operation 4: Determining change on themes

1. Assign a phase, using the SPM, to each theme-by-object meaning unit.

Source: Meier, A., and Boivin, M. (2000). The achievement of greater selfhood: The application of theme-analysis to a case study. Psychotherapy Research, 10(1), 62. (http://tandf.co.uk). Copyright 2000 by the Society for Psychotherapy Research. Reprinted with permission.

themes as they evolved across the sessions. The SPMCP comprises seven phases: problem definition, exploration, awareness/insight, commitment/decision, experimentation/action, integration/consolidation, and termination. The conceptual definitions for these phases are presented in Table 5.2. The combined seven phases represent a progressive movement in working through psychotherapeutic themes. The SPMCP has very good inter-rater reliability and capacity to detect psychotherapeutic change (Meier & Boivin, 1998b).

Procedures

Selecting Research Subject and Transcribing Interviews

The research subject was selected, from a pool of clients, on the criteria that he or she was seen in long-term therapy (35 sessions or more), manifested separation/individuation problems, was diagnosed with low-level personality disorder using the DSM-IV-TR, the interviews were audiotaped, and the psychotherapy had a successful outcome. Gloria was the first client selected from the pool to meet the stated criteria. She was administered the DSM-IV-TR and S-IPI before and after treatment. Successful therapy outcome was determined by comparing pre-treatment to post-treatment results on the S-IPI and on the DSM-IV-TR diagnostic criteria (APA, 1994) for low-level borderline personality disorder. Gloria's score on the S-IPI prior to treatment was 205, and following treatment it was 130. The difference between the two scores is considered to be significant. Gloria met the criteria for low-level borderline personality disorder on the DSM-IV-TR (Code 301.83) prior to treatment but not following treatment. The findings on the two measures indicate that she had a successful therapeutic outcome.

The transcripts from the audiotapes were prepared in accordance with the defined standards by Mergenthaler and Stinson (1992). The transcripts were read and corrected by verifiers while listening to the audiotaped sessions. The corrected transcripts were then printed for segmentation and coding (Meier & Boivin, 2000).

Table 5.2
The Seven-Phase Model of the Change Process

Phase 1: Problem Definition: The client presents and discloses personal
and/or interpersonal difficulties, concerns, feelings, et cetera. The
therapist helps the client to identify and articulate the parameters
of the problem in terms of its nature, intensity, duration, and
extent. Psychotherapy goals are established.

Phase 2: Exploration: The client, with the help of the therapist,
uncovers the dynamics of the problem in terms of its etiology and
maintenance with reference to affective, cognitive, motivational,
and behavioural constituents. The style of relating to others is
examined. This phase represents a shift from complaining and
emoting to that of wanting to understand better the presenting
problems and concerns and to bring about change.

Phase 3: Awareness/Insight: The client has a better understanding of
how unexpressed feelings, inappropriate cognitions, unfulfilled
needs and wants, and lost meanings are related to the present
problem. This new perspective (e.g., insight, awareness) provides a
handle for taking responsibility for self and a direction for change.
The uncovering process leads to a new perspective on the etiology,
maintenance, meaning, and significance of the problem.

Phase 4: Commitment/Decision: The client implicitly or explicitly
expresses a determination to change behaviours, manner of
relating, and perspectives and assumes responsibility for the
direction of his or her life.

Phase 5: Experimentation/Action: The client responds, relates, feels,
behaves, and thinks in new and different ways and in accordance
with the new perspective. He or she tries out (experiments with)
the new awareness in everyday life situations. The experimentation
takes place between therapy sessions and/or is rehearsed within
therapy sessions.

Phase 6: Integration/Consolidation: The client undertakes his or her
own and solidifies those new actions, feelings, perceptions, and so
on that are consistent with her or his sense of self.

Table 5.2 (continued)
The Seven-Phase Model of the Change Process

Phase 7: Termination: The client, having achieved the counselling
   goals, prepares to live without the support of the therapy sessions.
   The client's feelings regarding termination are addressed and
   worked through.

Source: Meier, A., and Boivin, M. (2000). The achievement of greater selfhood:
The application of theme-analysis to a case study. *Psychotherapy Research, 10*(1), 60.
(http://tandf.co.uk). Copyright 2000 by the Society for Psychotherapy Research.
Reprinted with permission.

Research Assistants

The three authors and seven research assistants, who were mature
graduate students in counselling, comprised the research team.
The research assistants were trained to use theme-analysis (Meier
& Boivin, 1998a) to segment transcripts into meaning units,
develop and label themes, and determine the themes' objects and
the SPMCP (Meier & Boivin, 1998b) to code themes for phase
of change. Training continued until the research assistants reached
a high level of consensus, which was defined as agreement by at
least four of the seven on segmenting transcripts into meaning
units, developing and labelling themes, determining objects, and
providing a phase for each theme. The training to use the SPMCP
and TA took about 25 hours for each instrument.

Segmenting Transcripts, Developing Themes, and Identifying
Objects

The transcripts of the therapy sessions were segmented into meaning units, and themes and objects were developed and coded
according to the four operations summarized in Table 5.1. Prior to
commencement of the research proper, the research team prepared
a catalogue of themes and objects by coding the transcripts taken
from the 3rd, 12th, 23rd, and 31st sessions. It was assumed that
these sessions would generate a representative sample of themes

and objects for the client being studied. The themes were defined for their bipolar quality using psychological and English dictionaries (Chaplin, 1973; Reber, 1985; *Webster's*, 1989). These preliminary catalogues of themes and objects were available to code the 37 transcripts. As new themes and objects emerged during the analysis, they were added to the original sets of themes and objects and appropriately defined. The transcripts were presented to the research team in a scrambled fashion, and all of the client's identifying information was removed from the transcripts, including the date of the session.

The following is an example of a bipolar second-order theme and its definition: *enmeshed versus separated:* feeling entangled, embroiled, ensnared, and overinvolved versus feeling at liberty, free to go, without obligation, without constraint, independent, healthily detached.

Determining Change

Change was defined as "a progressive forward movement through the seven phases of the SPMCP for a given theme" (Meier & Boivin, 2000, p. 65). At the same time that themes were extracted from the transcript, they were coded for phase using the SPMCP. Each member of the team independently segmented the transcripts for meaning units, identified the (descriptive) themes and their respective objects, and coded the themes for phase. When they completed their codings for each of the transcripts, the research team met to determine one theme, object, and phase for each of the meaning units (segments). In such meetings, the research assistants presented their codings first to avoid any undue influence by the authors on the research assistants. Interjudge discrepancies were discussed until a consensus was reached (Meier & Boivin, 2000).

Ethics

The Saint Paul University Research Committee and the Saint Paul University Ethics Committee approved the research project.

The client provided a written consent to participate in the study. To safeguard the privacy of the client, personal information was either removed or altered, and confidentiality of the client was protected by coding the audiotaped and written material.

Results

The purpose of this study was to answer the following question: does the evolution of themes follow a progressive course in a successful psychodynamic/humanistic-oriented psychotherapy when applied to the working through of a separation/individuation transference of a low-level borderline personality client? The first task in answering this question was to form a hierarchy of themes, and the second task was to select themes from this hierarchy for study.

Formation of a Theme Hierarchy

A theme hierarchy was formed using the procedures described by Meier and Boivin (2000). The analysis produced 137 descriptive themes and identified 31 objects. To determine which descriptive themes and objects to include in the study, theme x object frequency distributions were computed and summarized in the form of tables and graphs. Themes and objects that appeared fewer than seven times across the combined sessions were excluded. The reason for this criterion was to make it possible for each theme to be coded once for each of the seven phases, to include objects that were an important target in working through themes, to include the more meaningful themes in the analysis, and to establish a meaningful pattern as to how themes are worked through. This process produced 87 descriptive themes and 18 objects.

The two dominant targets for the combined themes were the mother (26.3%) and the therapist (27.7%). Accordingly, the descriptive themes pertinent to the two objects were reduced to higher-level themes using conceptual similarities as a basis (Giorgi, 1985). In the first step, the members of the team independently developed second-order themes for the two objects. The members then discussed their differences and prepared one set of second-order themes. These procedures were repeated to form third-order and core themes. The results were 24 second-order themes, 9 third-order themes, and 1 core theme for the object mother, and 25 second-order, 11 third-order, and 1 core theme for the object therapist. These data are presented for the objects mother and therapist, respectively, in Figures 5.1 and 5.2.

Several comments are in order regarding these figures. First, the descriptive themes are represented by the oval shapes on the left-hand side of the table. Second, themes are given a one-, two-, or three-word name that represents the problem pole of the theme. Third, the lines with arrows indicate the direction of reduction. Fourth, the successive reduction of themes produced a core theme, fear of being abandoned. The striving toward pole of the core theme was the desire to be embraced, befriended, and cherished.

Regarding the core theme, Gloria became aware of her fear of being abandoned in the third session, in which she spoke about the "little part" of herself (line 28) from which she is struggling to live (phase 2). To live from this part implies giving up the security of the past (line 284); changing relationships (line 322); not letting what others have to say matter (line 349), including the therapist (line 325); and becoming the "primary in her own life" (line 354). In the seventh session, an imagery exercise was designed to help Gloria address her "enmeshment" with the therapist and her fear that what is going well in her life will be taken from her. In her imagery, she visualized herself and the therapist in a meadow, and she gave a bouquet of flowers to the therapist, yet at the same time she feared that he would return the flowers—which to her represented the relationship—thereby abandoning her (lines 165–305). Later Gloria sensed a tug of war between herself and the therapist, with the therapist "holding her back" and at the same time "pushing her out" (session 22, lines 245–275). By the end of therapy, her fear of being abandoned was greatly diminished. Gloria became aware that the therapist "would be here; that I didn't

Figure 5.1
Descriptive, second-order, third-order, and core themes and their
relationships for the object mother

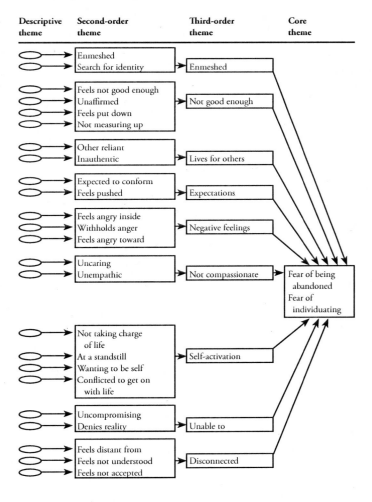

Figure 5.2
Descriptive, second-order, third-order, and core themes and their
relationships for the object therapist

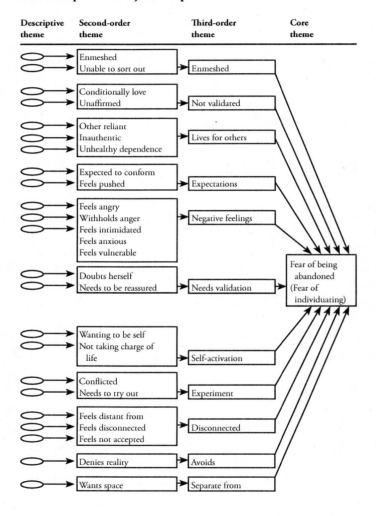

have to worry about that. You weren't going to disappear into the woodwork. I could come and talk here, it wouldn't upset you, you wouldn't be angry" (session 36, lines 191–193). The imagery exercise with Gloria holding the flowers generated the beginning of many experiences (themes) worked on in therapy described below. It launched her pursuit of autonomy.

The hierarchy of themes extracted from the clinical data represents Gloria's attempt to ward off the feeling of abandonment and reflects her efforts toward separation and individuation.

The Evolution of Themes across Sessions for Objects Mother and Therapist

Eight themes associated with separation/individuation were studied for the objects mother and therapist for their evolution across the sessions. The themes included enmeshment, expected to conform, not measuring up, not good enough, feeling pushed, other reliant, need for reassurance, and wanting to be self. Tables and figures were constructed using the SPSS scatter plot program (Norusis, 1993) to indicate where, in the sessions, each theme x object combination was located. Mother refers to "self in relation to mother," and therapist refers to "self in relation to therapist." The themes studied are organized according to the two objects.

Object Mother

Six of the eight themes studied for the object mother include enmeshed with, other reliant, not good enough, not measuring up, expected to conform, and wanting to be self. The working through of these themes is presented in Figures 5.3 and 5.4. Because of limited space, the descriptive data for two of the themes are presented here.

Enmeshed with versus separated from. This theme was addressed 22 times in 10 different sessions with all but two being in the last 10 sessions. The theme evolved across the six phases. Gloria introduced this theme as a problem in session 6 (line 345, phase 1), stating that, "for the first time, that was not okay" for her mother

Figure 5.3
Change on ??? Themes by Object Mother

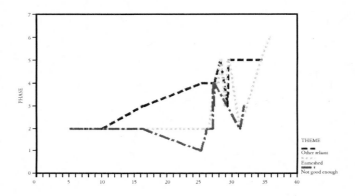

Figure 5.4
Change on ??? Themes by Object Mother

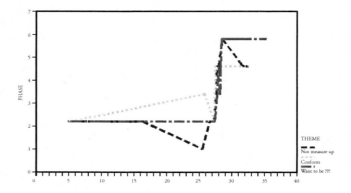

to expect her to feel, think, and behave like her mother wanted
her to: that is, to be enmeshed with her mother. In session 9,
she explored her intense anger toward her mother (phase 2). She
said, "I have really been angry ... like I've never been angry in
my life before. ... I was afraid that I would never get rid of my

anger" (lines 369–371). In session 26, she stated that "I will not put myself through that one more time. ... I find that I'm moving further and further out of this sphere" (lines 373–374). Again in session 27 (line 278), Gloria stated that to relate to her mother was to risk "being wiped out again." In sessions 28 and 29, Gloria made the commitment to separate from her mother and to be her own person (phase 4). Gloria stated, "I've got to separate the messages that I am getting from her" (session 28, line 250), and "I have to take a stand for myself in my own personhood, this is who I'm going to be, and this is how I'm going to relate" (session 29, line 43). In session 30 (line 42), she acknowledged being "very aware of myself as a separate adult person" (phase 3). In sessions 30, 32, and 35, Gloria reported how she had experimented with being "separate from" her mother (phase 5). She added that, "by individuating, I think I have narrowed our relationship. It's gone on to a new level with the realization on my part that we're not going to have intimacy" (session 30, lines 299–300, phase 5). Toward the end of therapy, Gloria became aware of how she had solidified her individuality (session 30). She stated that "I knew I was a separate person, and once I knew I was a separate person I could start running all sorts of things through me. ... So a lot of things happened that gave me the opportunity to try out by myself" (session 36, lines 505–506, 515, phase 6).

Not measuring up versus being good enough. Although this theme was addressed in sessions 6 and 17, it was worked through mostly in 6 of the last 10 sessions. This theme was first addressed in session 6, where it was explored for its meaning (phase 2). For all of her life, Gloria had felt that she was not good enough and never measured up to her mother's expectations to feel, think, and behave like her mother. Gloria stated, "I mean, even now the things she likes, the things that are okay, that she'll claim, anything that's good comes from her. Anything that is not good comes from my father or is mine intrinsically" (session 6, lines 271–273, phase 2). In session 17, Gloria became aware that she does not have to do things her mother's way. She said, "I mean that's what she did. ... It was over, and I'm starting a new life. ... I just knew that would kill me, and it was the first time I really knew, that for me [to maintain mental] health was going through it slowly and having to grieve it" (lines 148–153, phase 3). She returned to this theme 10 sessions later, stating it to be a problem (session 26, phase 1). Gloria reported that "I always had a feeling and from listening to my mother talk when we were small, it was as if there was this war, and there was her way of doing things and thinking, and there was the other way, it was this constant who is going to win the war. I mean, my mother still thinks like that" (lines 146–151, phase 1). In sessions 27 and 28, she continued to explore this theme (phase 2). She stated, "it's only in relation to her that I have this overwhelming feeling that nothing is worthwhile. What I want, what I need, what I'm doing, who I am" (session 28, lines 51–53, phase 2). Gloria became aware that she was not the only one responsible for maintaining the relationship. She said, "Why do I have to do all the reaching out? She also knows where I am. If she wants me, why can't she call me?" (session 28, lines 215–217, phase 3). In the same session, Gloria took the stand that she will not tolerate her mother describing her as "being second best" (line 260, phase 4). As for being second best, Gloria stated that "my way of being is very different, but I'm very well hooked into a value system that's exactly the kind of value system that I choose to have" (session 29, lines 150–152, phase 5). In sessions 32 and 33, Gloria saw herself as measuring up to her mother and expressing her commitment to continue to seek this from her mother. She said, "I mean, I just know I don't need this anymore, this is not particularly good for me. I don't need not to be respected" (session 32, lines 210–211, phase 4).

Object Therapist

Six of the eight themes studied for the object therapist include: enmeshed with, feels pushed, other reliant, expected to conform, needs reassurance, and wants to be self. The working through of these themes is presented in Figures 5.5 and 5.6. Because of limited space, only two of the themes are presented here.

Figure 5.5
Change on ??? Themes by Object Therapist

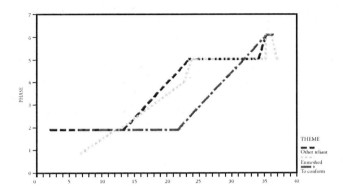

Figure 5.6
Change on ??? Themes by Object Therapist

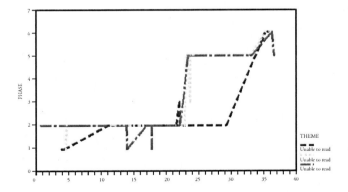

Enmeshed with versus separated from. This theme was worked on 28 times in 10 different sessions with 8 of the sessions comprising the last third of the sessions. The theme was introduced as a problem in session 7. Gloria commented on a long period of silence in therapy wherein she felt isolated, experienced a huge

chasm between herself and the therapist, did not know how to
deal with it, and felt intruded upon. She said, "What happened
was not that there was a great distance but that there wasn't any
distance. You had crossed into my world. I don't think that happens very often, and that was okay, but it ... didn't help" (session
7, lines 20–23, phase 1). This theme came up again in session
13, where Gloria explored her relationship with the therapist.
She wanted to know how to separate herself from the therapist
and to have her own world. She reported, "You can help me
move into it, and that it's different from your world, but it's
mine, and it's good just because it is mine. I don't know what
to do" (lines 72–73, phase 2). In the same session, she added, "I
can be my own person and live my own life, [and] you couldn't
stop me" (lines 234–235, phase 2). In session 23, Gloria made
a decision to separate herself from the therapist, saying, "I can't
be smothered anymore" (line 224, phase 4) and "I just know
that my distancing myself is absolutely essential for being my
own person" (line 234, phase 4). In the following session, she
went a step further and acted out her commitment by saying
to the therapist, "I can't back off on this one and that if you
can't come along with this or don't want to come along with
this then we're off" (session 24, lines 324–325, phase 5). Gloria
continued her efforts (phase 5) to separate from the therapist
in sessions 25–27, 30, 34, and 36. In session 25, she stated
that "this is the place [therapy] where I've grown up" (line 40),
"I'm being an active party in getting out of the nest" (line 56),
and "I want you to like the fact that I'm disengaging ... the life
that I'm building" (line 144). In session 26, Gloria stated that
"with you [therapist] I can come apart. ... I can individuate with
you ... because you can individuate with me" (line 52, phase
5). In session 27, she added that "our relationship has changed
... radically. I have a lot of space to move around in" (line 38,
phase 5). Gloria stated that when she individuated she needed
the therapist to "be actively present rather than passively sitting there" and that "I didn't need you anymore, and you didn't

need me anymore" (session 30, lines 306–311, phase 5). The achievement of separation and individuation brought about mixed feelings. In achieving separation, Gloria felt "very sad and very happy and excited about being a separate person," but at the same time she felt sad that she had left behind "the only shelter I've ever known" (session 34, lines 210 & 220, phase 5). In session 36, she expressed how she integrated her new actions and feelings into being a separate person. She stated, "I knew, I mean it was almost an intuitive knowing, that in order to do all those things we had to become untangled" (line 75, phase 6). In session 37, Gloria again expressed her sadness over knowing (phase 5) that it was her time to separate from the therapist in order to be her own person. She reported, "I have been experiencing this in an ongoing basis. It's kind of this idea in terms of goodbyes but in order to move into my world and in my person" (lines 334–336, phase 5).

Feeling pushed versus feeling free to be. Gloria reported two contradictory experiences regarding her relationship with the therapist: namely, she felt that he wanted her to remain enmeshed, and at the same time she felt pushed (challenged) to be her own person. The theme of feeling pushed was worked on 17 times in six different sessions, with most of the work taking place in session 22. This theme was introduced as a problem in session 5. Gloria expressed her anger toward the therapist, saying, "I think you pushed me. I didn't want to talk about that ever ... I feel violated ... I'm not talking about something that I can fix" (lines 11, 29—35, phase 1). She explored this theme in session 12, saying, "I had this picture ... of two things being polarized ... You not picking up how tired I am. I can't go around. I can't" (lines 59, 97–101, phase 2). This theme was explored again in session 22. In session 23, Gloria struggled to resolve inner conflicts and polarities, indicated that she was making little progress, felt pushed, and was unwilling to fight with the therapist. She stated, "I see that I need much more of a say in what's going on" (line 35, phase 3). Gloria felt upset when her need for space was counterbalanced by her feeling of being pushed by the thera-pist. She stated, "I find it very upsetting that I have to deal with the devastation of what happens here on the way home. We're going to have times where we can't uncover or talk about themes because all there is is fear. And that is just really new" (session 23, lines 50–51, 56–58, phase 2). This theme was explored fur-ther in session 30. In session 36, Gloria reported a very different experience regarding being pushed by the therapist. She stated, "The caring scared me. If you had pushed that too hard, you would have spooked me. I probably would have left. It wasn't that you had no expectations of me, but I always had the feel-ing that I never disappointed you. You didn't push. But I was never disappointed in you" (lines 215–217, 223–224, phase 6). Her experience of caring and nudging in a context of nurturing helped her to resolve this issue. Gloria reported, "who I was was good enough, that I'm a 7 and you're [37], therefore you should be [30] years better than I am, which is what my experience before was" (session 36, lines 393–395, phase 6).

To further assess the progressive movement in working through the themes, the authors performed a (paired) correla-tion between phase and session for combined themes across all of the sessions, the 12 themes for the two objects taken together and the 6 themes for the two objects taken separately. A Pearson r of .66 (rsq = .44) was obtained for the combined themes across all of the sessions. A Pearson r of .75 (rsq = .56) was obtained for the combined 12 themes for the two objects. When taken separately, a Pearson r of .57 (rsq = .33) was obtained for the six themes for the object mother, and a Pearson r of .86 (rsq = .73) was obtained for the six themes for the object therapist. These findings are consistent with the Pearson r correlations obtained by Meier and Boivin (2000) and Meier, Boivin, and Meier (2006) in two previous studies. The strong positive correlations together with the qualitative data support the notion that themes are worked through in a progressive course.

Discussion and Conclusion

This study provides rich descriptive and qualitative data regarding the working through of a separation/individuation transference in a therapeutic setting. The working through was studied in terms of psychotherapy *themes* and their *objects* and *phases*. In this limited space, it is possible only to provide a few comments regarding the resolution of the separation/individuation issue.

First, in the 37 sessions, 18 objects were the target of Gloria's efforts to work through the separation/individuation issue. Yet two of the objects, mother and therapist, accounted for almost 50% of the frequency with which the various objects were addressed, with mother and therapist being equally the targets of the client's therapeutic work. With regard to the separation/individuation problem, Gloria perceived the therapist in the same way as she perceived her mother. She worked through the separation/individuation issue simultaneously with both the therapist and the mother (Figures 5.3 to 5.6). The themes worked on for the two objects were the same, with the exception that for the mother alone Gloria addressed the themes of not measuring up and not being good enough, and for the therapist alone she addressed the themes of feeling pushed and needing reassurance. With the therapist, Gloria worked directly and in the here-and-now on the separation/individuation issue. She needed reassurance from the therapist, but she also needed him to challenge her to become her own person. According to psychodynamic theory (Masterson 1976, 1991), a failure to work through a developmental task often marks subsequent significant relationships and is often projected onto significant others, including the therapist. Gloria projected her difficulty in separating from her mother, rather than from her father, onto the therapist. For Gloria, the issues of separating from the mother and from the therapist were similar. The relationship with the therapist was the trigger for the emergence of the unresolved separation/individuation problem that was developed, at least in part, in her relationship with her mother.

Second, the resolution process entailed two conflicting forces: yearning for connection and intimacy, and yearning to be independent and autonomous. Gloria's perception was that, for her to measure up and be good enough, she had to conform and be reliant on significant others, including her mother and the therapist. Yet she was impelled from within to move in the direction of becoming herself. She also feared that, if she pursued separation/individuation, she would be abandoned (the core theme). She needed reassurance from the therapist that he would be there with her as she pursued separation/individuation. The data demonstrate that, as Gloria worked through the themes of enmeshment, not measuring up, being pushed, other reliant, et cetera, she also moved progressively toward separating and individuating and tempering the feeling of abandonment. Both the descriptive and the statistical data indicate that Gloria progressively worked through the themes associated with the separation/individuation issue.

Third, this study produced descriptive, second-order, and third-order themes that appear to be at the service of the core theme. In its bipolar definition, the core theme is a fear of being abandoned when asserting one's self needs, yet desiring to be embraced and cherished when pursuing these needs. The result is that the person remains enmeshed, lives for others and their expectations, and is disconnected from others and self. Fear of abandonment is a defence against pursing self-directed behaviour. This fear was not worked on directly but indirectly by addressing the themes of enmeshment, other reliant, and so on and by helping Gloria to become empowered to deal with these issues. By working through these themes, which warded off the fear of abandonment, Gloria was able to achieve a sense of independence: that is, she was able to achieve separation and individuation.

Fourth, much of the therapist-client activity for the first 20 sessions entailed exploration of the client's presenting themes. Things began to change in a dramatic way after session 20. During sessions 22–23, the client began to address her problematic relational pattern. She experienced the therapist as "holding her back" and at the same time "pushing her forward." In resolving this pattern and the underlying fear of abandonment, the client became aware of her self needs and developed the courage and the skills to pursue these needs, which led her to become more autonomous.

Fifth, the working through of the themes shows a general pattern of progressive movement. The working through of a theme began with phases 1 and 2, then progressed to phases 3 and/or 4, and terminated with phases 5 and/or 6. This general forward movement through the phases is consistent with Meier and Boivin's (2000) and Meier, Boivin, and Meier's (2006) findings that, in the achievement of greater selfhood and in the resolution of depression, clients progressed through the seven phases. These studies link successful therapy to the forward movement through the phases. Similar to the previous studies, the current study observed a link between the phases and successful therapy.

Sixth, the core theme, fear of being abandoned versus the desire to be embraced, befriended, and cherished, emerged full force in sessions 22–23. This is consistent with psychodynamic theory, which interprets themes such as enmeshment, other reliant, conforming, and so on as coping strategies to avoid being abandoned (Masterson, 1976, 1991). These compliant behaviours, according to Winnicott (1962/1965), lead to the development of a "false self." As the layers of the coping strategies are identified, addressed, and worked through, the underlying feelings and yearnings emerge, which for Gloria were the fear of abandonment and the desire to be embraced, befriended, and cherished. Working through the fear of abandonment leads to autonomy (Mahler, Pine, & Bergman, 1975) and, according to Winnicott, the development of a "true self."

This chapter has presented the research findings from a study that applied theme-analysis to the transcripts of one client working through her transference of an unresolved separation/individuation pattern. Theme-analysis can uncover themes that constitute a phenomenon and track the course taken to work through the themes across objects and sessions. As well, a significant attribute of theme-analysis is its ability to uncover the core theme to which the other themes are related. Despite its limitations, which have been summarized by Meier and Boivin (2000), theme-analysis is a promising innovative research method to study the psychotherapeutic change process.

References

American Psychiatric Association. (1994). *Diagnostic and statistical manual of mental disorders (DSM-IV)*. Washington, DC: Author.

Butler, S. F., & Strupp, H. H. (1991). The role of affect in time-limited dynamic psychotherapy. In J. Safran & L. Greenberg (Eds.), *Emotion, psychotherapy, and change* (pp. 83–112). New York: Guilford.

Cashdan, S. (1988). *Object relations therapy: Using the relationship*. New York: Norton & Company.

Chaplin, J. P. (1973). *Dictionary of psychology*. New York: Dell.

Christenson, R. M., & Wilson, W. P. (1994). Separation-individuation process inventory. In J. Fischer & K. Corcoran (Eds.), *Measures for clinical practice: A source book* (2nd ed.) (pp. 550–552). Toronto: Free Press.

Freud, S. (1940/1949). *An outline of psychoanalysis*. London: Hogarth Press.

Giorgi, A. (1985). Sketch of a psychological phenomenological method. In A. Giorgi (Ed.), *Phenomenology and psychological research* (pp. 8–22). Pittsburgh: Duquesne University Press.

Ivey, A. E. (1983). *Intentional interviewing and counseling*. Monterey, CA: Brooks/Cole.

Lorand, S. (1944). The technique of psychoanalytic therapy. In S. Lorand (Ed.), *Psychoanalysis today* (pp. 295–303). New York: International Universities Press.

Mahler, M. S., Pine, F., & Bergman, A. (1975). *Psychological birth of the human infant*. New York: Basic Books.

Masterson, J. F. (1976). *Psychotherapy of the borderline adult: A developmental approach*. New York: Brunner/Mazel.

Masterson, J. F. (1991). Comparing psychoanalytic psychotherapies. In J. F. Masterson, M. Tolpin, and P. E. Sifneos (Eds.), *Comparing psychoanalytic psychotherapies* (pp. 285–294). New York: Brunner/Mazel.

Masterson, J. F. (1993). *The emerging self: A developmental, self, and object relations approach to the treatment of the closet narcissistic disorder of the self*. New York: Brunner/Mazel.

Meier, A., & Boivin, M. (1994). *Description and application of task-directed imagery*. Paper presented at the Annual Conference of the American Association for the Study of Mental Imagery, Newport Beach, CA, June 16–20.

Meier, A., & Boivin, M. (1998a). *Theme-analysis: Theoretical foundation and procedures for labeling psychotherapeutic themes and determining their objects and phases*. Unpublished manuscript, St. Paul University, Ottawa.

Meier, A., & Boivin, M. (1998b). *The Seven Phase Model of the Change Process: Theoretical foundation, definitions, coding guidelines, training procedures, and research data* (5th ed.). Unpublished manuscript, St. Paul University, Ottawa.

Meier, A., & Boivin, M. (2000). The achievement of greater selfhood: The application of theme-analysis to a case study. *Psychotherapy Research, 10*(1), 57–77.

Meier, A., & Boivin, M. (2008). Theme-analysis: Procedures and application for psychotherapy research. *Qualitative Research in Psychology, 5*(4), 289–310.

Meier, A., Boivin, M., & Meier, M. (2006). The treatment of depression: A case study using theme-analysis. *Counselling and Psychotherapy Research 6*(2), 115–125.

Mergenthaler, E., & Stinson, C. (1992). Psychotherapy transcription standards. *Psychotherapy Research, 2,* 125–142.

Norusis, M. (1993). *SPSS: SPSS for Windows base system user's guide.* Chicago: SPSS.

Reber, A. S. (1985). *The Penguin dictionary of psychology.* New York: Penguin Books.

Sperry, L. (1995). *Handbook of diagnosis and treatment of the DSM-IV personality disorders.* New York: Brunner/Mazel.

Webster's third unabridged encyclopedic dictionary of the English language. (1989). Toronto: Random House.

Winnicott, D. W. (1962/1965). Ego integration in child development. In D. Winnicott, *The maturational processes and the facilitating environment* (pp. 56–63). New York: International Universities Press.

VI

The Medical Model of Psychotherapy: In Historical Perspective

John Dimock, MD

One usually goes to a doctor when one is sick. That has been true for time immemorial. Hua T'o was, according to the annals of the later Han Dynasty, an excellent Chinese surgeon who practised around 220 AD. He possibly used opium dissolved in wine as his anaesthetic. Western medicine was introduced to China in the early 17th century, while Emperors Fu Hsi, Shen Nung, and Huang Ti were said to have founded the art of healing long before. Tao—the method of maintaining harmony between this world and the beyond—was subdivided into heaven, earth, and man. The psyche or maintenance of one's ability to see this harmonization was probably the closest the Chinese came to the modern concept of psychotherapy.

When one, as a doctor, orchestrated this harmonization process, one assumed the "Mantle of the Healer," according to my old teacher, Dr. Sarwer-Foner. As a young resident, this was the mantle that I proudly bore. I was the provider of care, the modern medical therapist. I wasn't aware that this could simply be seen from the point of view that this mantle was a herb with a wide range of uses, from bleeding to dysentery, due to tannins contained in the plant. Or, more esoterically, the reference was to the doctor, assuming upon graduation some power or other that influenced the healing relationship.

With the modern preference for health care to be a teamwork concept, the Mantle of the Healer would simply place the physician as leader of the team. The mantle begins to tarnish when considering the economic constraints on medicine today, which, certainly in the United States and increasingly here in Canada, would place leadership in the hands of the economic provider (government or insurance company usually). Another blow is firmly laid by development of the Internet, which gives patients the knowledge to increasingly challenge the health care provider, which, in my opinion, is a healthy development. Yet another salvo of blows comes from the increasing diversity of opinions about the healing process, with the insistence that healing be a quick and cheap process.

Internet sites packed full of information, particularly in specialty areas such as psychiatry, create great pressure. Much of psychiatry is very subjective and based upon years of experience. In a culture dominated by the impulsive, quick fix mentality, experience tends more and more to count for little. The old "father image" is under attack, particularly when traditional marriages break up in 50% of cases and relationships are based on shorter periods of time. Hence, the experienced father is passé, and the impulsive, toothy-grinning bearer of instant relief is "in." This, in my opinion, is related to a more paranoid element of society— after all, the guy next to you on the subway may suddenly explode! Hence, the best solutions to one's problems come from oneself, and the toothy-grinned is second best if you can't seem to find that nirvana on the net.

The traditional psychotherapist is under attack. Yet there are many who still seek out therapy. Waiting lists only get longer. There is an explosion, probably also related to the information highway, of knowledge of that which affects the "Tao." The physician has the edge in this scramble for help, not necessarily because of traditional turning to the healer processes, although tradition plays a large role. In Canada, the support of government in terms of universal health schemes has, at least so far, meant that the availability, albeit after a long wait, of free therapy from a psychiatrist has placed the physician in many people's eyes as the person to seek for therapy. However, that cannot last forever, as more clamour for therapy and fewer psychiatrists are trained since the training is so expensive. Rumours abound about the imminent limitation on the number of therapy sessions, as is already done by managed care in the United States.

Indeed, the psychiatrist has largely become either a consultant or a "med checker"—15 minutes are billed as the psychiatrist assesses the effectiveness of medication and side effects thereof and makes adjustments based on these rushed observations. Repeated four times an hour for 8 hours a day, this is far removed from the hour-a-day therapy sessions of traditional psychoanalysis—from 8 to 32 patients a day sounds like a dream for administrators burdened by huge waiting lists, but what is the evidence that this system is any more helpful to the patient?

Before we can answer that question, we need to know if we can even quantify "help." Many patients simply benefit from having someone listen to them—often for the first time in their lives. Therapy is a narcissistic process, and what better way to improve your narcissism than have a good listener as a therapist? A good intervention, made at the right time (usually when affect is heightened in the therapy session), can be invaluable, but just listening can be just as effective. Unfortunately, when, how, or even if one makes an intervention is very difficult to study. The type of intervention remains a problem. Short-term dynamic therapy would require dynamic interpretations based on Oedipal material, according to Sifneos (1979). Malan (1963) would argue for the importance of transference interpretations linked to parents.

Freud (1963) himself said that statistics were of little use in psychoanalysis because the patients were too complex and their number too small. Here he delineated factors relevant to the outcome of psychoanalysis, factors that essentially involve the patient, treatment (interventions), personality of the therapist, and circumstances of treatment (cost, transport, etc). The criteria of outcome and the measurement of change remain the biggest problems in "measuring" the psychotherapy process.

Success, as Freud would say, means that the neurosis would disappear, but others would say that the symptoms or behaviours would change. Problems are associated with patients being unable to deal with the characteristics of the therapist, good therapists being said to be committed to their patients with a lot of empathy. Patients, particularly those with parental deprivation, may be unfamiliar with these concepts and reject them, leading to patient-therapist transference issues that confound analysis of outcome.

Hence, therapy can never be a process of the application of a set of preconceived techniques, and neither is it a process depending solely upon the charisma of the therapist. How, then, can it be used to achieve things such as "the capacity to be alone" (Khan, 1965).

Terr et al. (2006), in a majestic paper about child psychotherapy, discuss a vital concept involved in this process of "good-enough" therapy. They discuss the "formulation" as the working psychological explanation for a patient's feelings, mentation, and behaviours as opposed to the "diagnosis"—the synthesis of history, observation, and tests such that there is an indication of a certain medical condition treated in a certain prescribed fashion. If you like, these are the "art" and the "science" of psychotherapy. Their examples of "turning points" in psychotherapy should put a smile on any psychotherapist's face, as we all remember our own periods of breakthrough—perhaps because such insights are indeed artistic pearls that happen all too infrequently in therapy. They are discussing child therapy, but their insights are just as relevant to adults in my opinion.

Unfortunately, we are faced with a dilemma in this discussion. As eloquently discussed by Joyce, Piper, Ogrodniczuk, and Lamarche (2006), medical psychotherapy can, these days, be cognitive behaviour therapy, short-term dynamically orientated, behavioural therapy, or a whole host of other types of therapy. These authors review hundreds of randomized clinical trials to identify empirically supported treatments but point out that, although these studies refute Eysenck's (1952) original comments that psychotherapy was no more effective than doing nothing for patients, most are based on the medical model. As we have seen in this model, a specific disease entity, disorder, or problem can be identified and is classified using the *Diagnostic Statistical Manual of Disease* (DSM).

This nosology, some say, is more useful to lawyers than to doctors and is dehumanizing, and many say that the specific patient's vulnerabilities and quality of life are more important than specific pure diseases. The medical model requires that the etiology of the disorder be identified and that a formulation likely to produce change be identified. The therapeutic actions required for the mechanisms of change are then written in stone in the DSM. But the design is therefore symptom specific and not therapy specific. Single pathways are usually identified, yet psychiatric symptoms are of complex origin, usually with different interventions often over years being required—studies are usually brief, and these time parameters are therefore not considered.

The National Institute of Mental Health (NIMH) has tried to carry out controlled clinical trials of psychotherapy in an effort to answer the dilemma outlined above. It developed manualized programs of therapy in an effort to control variables and pointed out programs that focus on effectiveness of treatment (those of Jacobson & Christensen, 1996; Seligman, 1996) and the efficacy of psychotherapy relative, for instance, to medication (Hollon, 1996).

Efficacy assumes a causal connection between outcome and treatment as treatment methods are tightly controlled. Effectiveness is more clinically real, stressing external validity. It is also less clinical trial like and is therefore open to more criticism. Again we are back at the fundamental issue of psychotherapy as art or science or both. Many say that a DSM-type approach to the medical model forming the basis of psychotherapy means that the DSM should be altered to stress the interactive aspects of psychiatric conditions. The NIMH studies, using statistically derived "perfect" psychoanalytically orientated psychodynamic and cognitive therapies, showed that elements of both were used by both. Albert Ellis, who died as this chapter was reaching conclusion, would not be pleased. Yet a recent paper in the *American Journal of Psychiatry* indicates that psychodynamically orientated psychotherapy is more effective than cognitive therapy in panic disorders.

Effective therapy is probably therefore an art, and so-called master therapists (after the NIMH studies) are those who are experienced in the arts and, probably most importantly, are good listeners. A patient will not make the connections alone — a good therapist must point them out, and an excellent history-taking technique, malleable enough to obtain the necessary information from even the most difficult patient, is vital. That makes "perfect" therapies so laughable, as no two humans are alike, and hence the vitally exciting component of therapy, the fact that no two therapies are the same, is lost—as Professor Myre Sim (1981), my first psychiatry teacher, said, "all truth is dissolved in the average." History taking is the art of psychiatry—best taught by Dr. Hyman Caplan, child analyst, who wrote seminal papers in the 1970s on diverse subjects such as the reasons children spit.

According to the medical model, therefore, how does psychotherapy work? Nowadays it would be hard to find a modern therapist who doesn't use a combination of psychotherapy—of whatever kind—and psychopharmacology. The capacity to form so-called procedural memories seems to begin at birth, whereas verbal or declarative memory begins much later. Procedural memory seems to control our moral judgment, indeed much of our personality formation. One may have no declarative memory of the hundreds of times one's parents responded to concerns expressed as a child, yet such concern or "bonding" helps one to form open, trusting relationships. The absence of such concern may preclude one from accepting help as an adult. Procedural memory may be altered by psychotherapy through the process of "transference" and the relationship to the therapist. How psychotherapy affects memory may be central to how psychotherapy works.

This chapter would not be complete without a discussion on the dimensional aspects of diagnosis to be included in the fifth edition of the *Diagnostic and Statistical Manual of Mental Disorders,* due to be published in 2011. At a conference in Maryland last summer, it was proposed that a dimensional aspect to a diagnosis of a disorder be introduced—everything to do with the quality of that diagnosis rather than the nature of the disorder itself. A categorical diagnosis only says if the disorder is present or not. A dimensional diagnosis might include different parameters, such as symptom count, duration, severity, and certainty of diagnosis, among other things. There are many advantages to the dimensional approach from the research perspective, with greater ability to see, for instance, "effects of treatment."

A categorical approach to eating disorders may not differentiate between a cognitive behavioural approach and a self-help approach to treatment, but a dimensional one considering, for instance, occurrence rates of binging and purging might do so. These approaches clearly show the complexity of human functioning and, it is to be hoped, will be transparent and easily used by clinicians. This should go a long way toward ensuring the future of the medical model of psychotherapy.

References

Eysenck, H. (1952). The effect of psychotherapy: An evaluation. *Journal of Consulting Psychology, 16,* 319–324.

Freud, S. (1963). *Three essays on the theory of sexuality.* New York: Basic Books.

Hollon, S. D. (1996). The efficacy and effectiveness of psychotherapy relative to medications. *American Psychologist, 51,* 1025–1030.

Jacobson, N. S., & Christensen, A. (1996). Studying the effectiveness of psychotherapy: How well can clinical trials do the job? *American Psychologist, 51*(10), 1031–1039.

Joyce, A., Piper, W. E., Ogrodniczuk, J. S., & Lamarche, C. (2006). Psychotherapy research at the start of the 21st century: The persistence of the art versus science controversy. *Canadian Journal of Psychiatry, 51,* 797–809.

Khan, M. (1965). The capacity to be alone. In D. Winnicott (Ed.), *The maturational process and the facilitating environment: Studies in the theory of emotional development* (pp. 29–36). London: Hogarth Press.

Malan, D. (1963). *A study in brief psychotherapy.* London: Tavistock.

Seligman, M. E. P. (1996). The effectiveness of psychotherapy: The consumer reports study. *American Psychologist, 51*(10), 965–974.

Sifneos, P. (1979). *Short-term psychotherapy and emotional crisis.* Cambridge, MA: Harvard University Press.

Sim, M. (1981). *Guide to psychiatry* (4th ed.). New York: Longmans Press.

Terr, L., Fornari, V., Jetmalani, A., Livingston, R., Powers, J. H., Robson, K., & Jellinek, M. S. (2006). When formulation outweighs diagnosis. *Journal of the American Academy of Child and Adolescent Psychiatry, 45*(10), 1252–1263.

VII

The Helping Relationship:
A Context for Learning

Kristine Lund

David is a 29-year-old man who has come in for counselling because he is having difficulties maintaining a long-term relationship. He has had numerous relationships. He reports that he is receiving a consistent message that he is distant in the relationship, and his partners find it difficult to feel close to him.

Susan and James have been married for 7 years. They have one daughter, Hanna, 18 months old. They have come in for counselling because they "seem to argue about everything these days."

These common presenting issues elicit a variety of therapeutic responses, such as solution focused, cognitive behavioural, or psychoanalytic theory, to address unresolved issues from childhood or family of origin patterns that are influencing the client's current relationships. More recently, therapists have looked at client issues from a systemic perspective, especially narrative and constructionist, and in particular have worked to build on client strengths to address current concerns.

What if counselling is simply about learning? What if the presenting concerns that clients bring to counselling are more about opportunities for learning than about indications of dysfunction, pathology, or problems to be solved? How would that change our approach to counselling? Would our perceptions of the counselling process be different? Would we change the way in which we engage clients?

As a result of my experience as both a pastoral counsellor and a pastoral counselling teaching supervisor, I believe that the therapeutic relationship is central for client healing and change. I also assume that those who come for counselling have been unsuccessful in their attempts to effect change and healing for themselves. Clients have been unable to integrate environmental or developmental challenges that they encountered in their lives. So they come to counselling hoping that the counsellor will be able to help them.

Counselling as Hermeneutics

To understand counselling as learning, it is important first to understand that counselling is essentially hermeneutical. In short, hermeneutics is the art of interpretation. Smith (1991) observes that hermeneutics has a long history. We know that there was a school of interpretation in ancient Alexandria and that Aristotle used the term in one of his writings. Etymologically, the word *hermeneutics* is derived from the name and character of the Greek god Hermes, the messenger of the gods. His character was also one of a trickster. Therefore, hermeneutics carries within it a sense of wonder or revelation, of recognizing new understandings of the previously perplexing and paradoxical. Hence, hermeneutics is cautious of becoming overly certain.

Hermeneutics recognizes the importance of understanding what it means to be human as we share it relationally with not only other humans but also all of creation. It recognizes that truth is not fixed once and for all and that no one method can predetermine the location of truth or one authority say the way things "really are." As Weinsheimer (1985, p. 9) suggests, a motto for hermeneutics might be that "truth keeps happening."

Davis (1996) observes that hermeneutics has historically been concerned with the "text." Initially, the text was a sacred writing. Later the notion of text was expanded to include literary and legal documents. More recently, the concept of text has come to mean life itself. This reveals a shift from biblical and literary hermeneutics being concerned with uncovering the truth in a written text to more recent branches of hermeneutic thought. Included in this shift of the meaning of text is noted philosopher Martin Heidegger's (1975) conviction that being and interpretation are inseparable. As rhetoric specialist Timothy Crusius (1991, p. 5) states, "Interpretation ... is human being, our mode of existence in the world."

An etymological understanding of the term "text" expands our wisdom beyond the contention of text as simply referring to written works. Davis (1996) notes that

> originally, however, "text," like "web," was used to describe things woven, and so the metaphor of "life as text" does have a particular richness. Considered alongside the more popular "literature as text" metaphor for example, the image of intertwined linguistic threads forming a tightly woven narrative fabric foregrounds the roles of language, of storytelling, and of rereading in the construction of our respective understandings and identities. The textual metaphor also offers an image of the interweaving of our selves in the fabric of our culture. To engage in hermeneutics—to interpret—then, is to tug at the threads of this existential text, realizing that, in tugging the texture of the entire fabric is altered. Put differently, hermeneutics does not reduce us to powerless victims of historical forces. Rather, it offers hope for the future in the recognition that our lives are shaped not just by the events of the past, but also by our projects and our projections. (pp. 19–20)

This phenomenon is an element of what Varela, Thompson, and Rosch (1991) call the "fundamental circularity" of existence. We did not create our world, yet we find ourselves in it. We come to know our world as we live in it, interact with it, and reflect on both the world we live in and our experiences.

As a result of this "situated existence," we work out the possibilities that exist for us by virtue of being "thrown" (to borrow Heidegger's term) into a particular cultural, historical, and familial world. Consequently, hermeneutic inquirers do not seek to maintain the stance of a detached observer providing an objective account because they recognize that their involvement simultaneously is affecting and being affected by the situation. As a therapist, I know that my understanding of counselling, and specifically my clients' understanding of counselling, changes in part because of our (therapist's and clients') efforts to understand it. Hermeneutical inquiry cannot be understood as a linear process. Rather, the mode of inquiry is more circular, recursive, and reflective. The unifying theme in hermeneutics is a persistent questioning of our taken-for-granted modes of speaking and acting.

Heidegger's (1975) view of the human person is helpful here. His concept of person includes a view of "being in time" that is radically different from more traditional Western notions of time. Heidegger sees that human experiences of the world take place within a structure of past, present, and future. He notes that the only way we can understand the "now" that is new is through the "forestructure of understanding," which has been created by past experience. Heidegger's student, Hans-Georg Gadamer (1979), expanded on this idea by arguing that we need a framework from which our thoughts and actions can begin. He notes that "the first was to reinstate in a positive way the manner in which prejudgement is a necessary requirement for all understanding" (p. 193). When two individuals engage in a conversation, they need to bring about a "fusion" of their different perspectives into a new understanding that is then held in common. If this does not occur, then the two individuals will be unable to successfully communicate with each other. Counselling can provide opportunities for clients to recognize the "forestructure of understanding," which might be facilitating or hindering their ability to make meaning of their current experience.

Attentiveness to language then becomes a central part of developing a hermeneutical attitude. How does the client use language? What language does the therapist use in response to the client? If hermeneutics is about the basic interpretability of life, then both client and therapist are intimately involved in the interpretive task. The therapeutic relationship becomes the context in which meaning is created and not simply reported.

Selfhood

From a modernist perspective, the self is believed to exist within clear boundaries. Hard work and discipline in following the practices of self-disclosure and self-representation offer a way to fully know ourselves. Many current educational and counselling practices continue to be influenced by this modernist understanding of the self and consequently are oriented toward the goal of providing individuals with the knowledge deemed necessary for reaching their potential. In my undergraduate degree in psychology, I spent a lot of time in the lab "running rats," measuring their responses, predicting outcomes, and consequently "proving" theories of learning. Having been a child of immigrant parents and living in the time of the feminist movement, I also experienced familial and cultural pressures to reach my potential. That potential was to be found in education and career aspirations that were to be achieved on one's own.

While modernist conceptions of identity do not assert that the self is static, there tends to be an assumption of some "essential" self, one that is unique to the individual and remains static across situations. Davis, Sumara, and Luce-Kapler (2000, p. 167) observe that, "although one's relationships, behaviours, and thoughts may vary dramatically across such roles, one's identity is not seen to vary or be context-sensitive. Rather such roles are seen as aspects of a multifaceted, but unified person." Therefore, from a modernist perspective, the highest achievement is to be a self-made person: independent and in touch with who you are.

From a postmodern perspective, Usher and Edwards (1994) note that writers in the field of adult education state that

> There is an increasing recognition that all knowledge-claims are partial, local, and specific rather than universal and historical, and that they are always imbued with power and normative interests—indeed that what characterises modernity is precisely the concealing of the partiality and rootedness of knowledge-claims in the cloak of universality and value-neutrality. Thus in post-modernity there is a rejection of universal and transcendent foundations of knowledge and thought, and a heightened awareness of the significance of language, discourse and socio-cultural locatedness in the making of any knowledge claim. (p. 10)

Davis, Sumara, and Luce-Kapler (2000) observe that in postmodern discourse it is important to recognize that one's knowledge of things and one's knowledge of self do not pre-exist one another. Rather, they are "continually co-emergent phenomena" (p. 169). They argue that how we understand the self is developed around a belief that personal identity emerges from a variety of "signifying systems that include oral and written language paintings, television, the Internet, all forms of media advertising, songs, dances, gestures, and so on" (p. 169).

> The suggestion that identities are in flux does not mean that they are fragmented and incoherent. What is rejected in postmodern conceptions of the self is not the ideal of a stable identity, but of a fixed identity. Post-modern discourses do not accept the modernist assumption that the self exists in some essential form that remains unchanged as it passes through experience. Instead, one's sense of personal identity is understood to emerge from one's involvements in signifying systems

and practices—and in some ways to be contained in these systems and practices. (p. 170)

Self-understanding and self-identity then depend on one's personal narrative remaining coherent and continuous. Crisis situations and other turning points in life often challenge our current
self-understanding and raise questions of identity. At these times,
individuals are often required to reassess their understandings of
self. They may discover that their previously held belief in their
identity as continuous and unchanging was nothing more than
an old story. An old story that until this point in their lives had
worked well enough is now found to be lacking. These ideas regarding self-understanding and self-identity remind me of when I was
22 years old and my father suddenly died of a heart attack. Until
his death, I had understood myself to be a strong and independent
individual. The feelings of grief and loss were unlike any other feelings I had ever experienced. They shook the very foundation of my
self-understanding and self-identity. My old self-understanding was
challenged. In time and in the context of supportive relationships
that created space for conversations about the old self-understanding and my current experience, a new self-understanding emerged.
    Kerby (1991) adds to the discussion when he suggests that
human existence both individually and collectively is embedded
in an ongoing history. In the telling of that history from an autobiographical perspective, individuals recognize themselves as "the
implied subject generated by the narrative" (p. 7). Self-narration is
not simply a mirroring of the past but also an interpretive activity.
Kerby writes, "The meaning of the past is not something that is
fixed and final but something that is being continually prefigured
and updated in the present" (p. 7). However, this interpretation of
the past is always selective and retells the past from the perspective
of the present.
    A narrated past generates a greater sense of personal identity
because it is directed by the individual's interest in the current
experience. Kearney (2002) notes that

> when someone asks you who you are you tell a story. That is, you recount your present condition in the light of past memories and future anticipations. You interpret where you are now in terms of where you have come from and where you are going to. And so doing you give a sense of yourself as a *narrative* identity that perdures and coheres over a lifetime. (p. 4)

Kerby (1991, p. 28) observes that "what we regularly remember from the distant past is often just a repeatable token or icon taken for the real thing." What then becomes important is the meaning of the past for the individual now. Therefore, the past only has meaning in the present narrative. Kerby contends that what makes personal identity personal is that it identifies life with all its particularities. He notes Gadamer's hermeneutic principle of "effective history" and writes that

> We are finite historical beings whose understanding is mediated by and made possible through our history. We have no transcendental standpoint from which the past may be seen without interference of "subjectivity" (the present). This means that there never was such a pristine or finished meaning to the past; a supposedly "true" meaning that we ought now to recapture or coincide with, that we might once and for all pin down. In matters of the past we cannot escape the historicity of our gaze and our interests. However, this position need not lead to total relativism where anything goes, where any interpretation will do, for the past we would recapture is woven into the same fabric that guides our understanding. ... The past, ... if our analyses are correct, should be viewed as part of our lives, and because life is unfinished so is the meaning of the past. (p. 131)

Therefore, the past is seen to be constructed through language and social contact, as being a coming together of meaning rather than an unchanging reality. Throughout history, human experience has been interpreted through the most recent discoveries, whether understanding the human body as a well-made clock or most recently understanding the human mind as a computer or learning as "inputting information." Underlying all these associations is an assumption that humans are like machines and that our world can be understood from a mechanical perspective. While great intellectual discoveries have been gained from this perspective, it has created fragmentation and reduction, a tendency that has failed to recognize the differences between complicated and complex systems.

Davis, Sumara, and Luce-Kapler (2000) contend that it is possible to understand all complicated systems such as clocks, engines, or computers through knowledge of their parts. However, some complex systems cannot be fully understood by examining their particular elements because these elements are alive and dynamic. The boundaries of complex systems are much less clear than those of complicated systems. It is much easier to know where a machine, such as a car, stops than where an economic system, or a relationship between two individuals, begins and ends. Davis and colleagues argue that, in order to "understand the identity of a complex system, one must look at its embeddedness and its intertwining, not at its boundaries" (p. 174).

Knowing how complicated and complex forms are so significantly different creates an important new way of understanding human identity. Davis, Sumara, and Luce-Kapler (2000, p. 174) observe that "events of self-identification are not always about distinguishing an 'I' from a 'not-I.' In fact, it may be that most events of self-identification are about becoming part of a 'we.'"

Learning

Mezirow (1994), a researcher in adult education, developed his transformative learning theory as a result of his study of women returning to school in the late 1970s. His research has stimulated significant discussion in the field of adult education. He defines transformative learning as "the social process of construing and appropriating a new or revised interpretation of the meaning of one's experience as a guide to action" (pp. 222–223). The process of making meaning is shaped and circumscribed by meaning structures. The theory of perspective transformation looks at the revision of these meaning structures that results from further experiences. Mezirow (2000) sees critical reflection as essential to transformative learning. Mezirow has recently adopted the phrase "habits of mind" to refer to what in an earlier work he named "meaning perspective" (Mezirow, 2000). This phrase can serve as a metaphor for the conceptual and rational approach that privileges the cognitive. Yorks and Kasl (2002, p. 185) further suggest that "a theoretical framework that emphasizes a balance among multiple ways of knowing is captured more appropriately with an alternative phrase, *habits of being.*"

Yorks and Kasl (2002) describe a process in which persons strive to become engaged with both their whole person knowing and the whole person knowing of their fellow learners. They call this "learning-within-relationship" (p. 185). They observe that

> Engagement with one's whole person knowing requires critical subjectivity while developing capacity for the skilful practice of multiple ways of knowing. Engagement with the whole person of fellow learners requires interacting with others through the same balanced mix in ways of knowing—through affective and imaginal modes of psyche, as well as conceptual and practical. To share with one another one's own experiential knowing ... requires striving to nurture a field of empathic connection. Such a field of empathic connection establishes a group habit of being. (p. 185)

Yorks and Kasl (2002) note that the preconditions of trust, solidarity, security, and empathy are required for any facilitation of reflection. They believe that empathy is the precondition for trust, solidarity, and security, so they concentrate their attention on empathy.

Recent neurobiological findings support earlier studies on transformative learning theory. These studies recognize feelings to be an integral part of the process of perspective transformation. Researchers therefore recommend that feelings be given equal weight alongside critical reflection and rational discourse.

In addition to the understandings of transformational learning, Davis and Sumara (1997) draw on recent developments in complexity theory, ecology, and hermeneutics to present an "enactivist" model of cognition. While they direct their attention to the public school context, their understandings are well suited to adult learning and counselling. They observe that knowledge has tended to be seen as if it were an object, a "third thing" (p. 3). As an object, then, knowledge can be manipulated, stored, and grasped. They suggest that, instead of viewing knowledge as an object, it should be understood as action or "better yet knowledge-as (inter)action" (p. 4). Following Gadamer's (1990) understanding that a conversation cannot be predetermined but emerges in the process of the conversation, Davis and Sumara (1997) argue that understanding emerges in a similar fashion. In the unpredictable process of a conversation, each participant is affected in ways that were not foreseen at the beginning. Consequently, our understandings of the world and self-identity are recast. This has significant implications for the therapeutic relationship and the counselling process.

Davis and Sumara (1997) note that Merleau-Ponty, a French phenomenologist (1962), studied patterns of interacting and described the relationships among individuals involved in conversations as "coupling." Maturana and Varela (1991) have named this concept "structural coupling." Davis and Sumara (1997) note that, while these phrases suggest a "commingling of consciousness, of cognitive abilities, and of lived actions, none suggests that personal integrities or subjectivities are abandoned. ... [I]t is in the 'coupling' of identities ... that there arises a possibility for actions/ understandings to emerge that likely could not have been achieved by either participant independently" (p. 4).

Davis and Sumara (1997) argue that these ideas are not new and have been influenced by ecological theorists who have studied the relationships of organisms to one another. The important implication for counselling is the recognition that seeing the client "as situated *within* a particular context is limiting. Rather the cognizing agent is recast as *part of* the context" (p. 4). Therefore, as the client learns, the context changes, and the reverse is true: as the context changes, so does the context of the client. The factors that contribute to the therapist-client relationship are intimately, ecologically, and complexly related.

Following Varela, Thompson, and Rosch (1991), Davis and Sumara (1997, p. 5) have named this understanding an "enactivist theory of cognition." Echoing the words of Merleau-Ponty (1978), they assert that "the starting point for such a theory is a 'complex fabric of relations,' fundamentally and inextricably intertwined with all else—both physically/biologically and experientially/phenomenologically" (p. 5).

Davis and Sumara (1997, p. 6) therefore consider that "learning is 'occasioned' rather than 'caused' that is, we regard [client] learning as dependent on, but not determined by the [therapist] teacher." Since understandings are "situated in" and "co-emerge" in complex webs of experience, it is not possible to identify the causes of any particular action. This does not mean that deliberate efforts are not of use; rather, the therapist's activity matters to the extent that it occasions action. The therapist participates in but does not determine the client's learning.

Implications for Therapy

To return to the scenarios at the beginning of the chapter: how do hermeneutics, selfhood, and learning inform therapy with these clients? When clients live their lives in relationship, they experience their limitations. This is what customarily brings clients in for therapy. These experiences are often painful or frustrating and may be either acute or chronic in nature. These limitations create occasions for learning. At the beginning of the therapy process, clients often view these occasions as something to get rid of or avoid at all cost. At this point, it is particularly important for the therapist to be able to recognize the occasion for learning that is being presented by the current life situation. Hopefully, in time, the client will also be able to recognize and engage these limitations as opportunities for learning as well.

When David and Susan and James come in for counselling, they will want to tell the counsellor stories of their experiences. Kearney (2002, p. 133) reminds us that "Life is pregnant with stories." This is particularly true when there are challenges in our lives. In listening to a client's recounting of his or her experiences, it is important for the therapist to recognize that, in the current telling of the story, life is being lived. It is not simply a recounting of historical facts. So a stance of curiosity is important for both counsellor and client. What happens in the retelling of the experience? How is the current experience challenging the old self-understanding? What new understandings begin to emerge in the midst of the conversation? While the client may come with particular expectations regarding the outcome of therapy, often unexpected and surprising changes occur. How is the conversation changing both the client and the therapist?

Through listening, the counsellor recognizes that learning is more than simply modifying behaviour through experience. If modifying behaviour is the goal of therapy, then the role of the therapist is simply to provide appropriate experiences that induce the desired modifications in behaviour. Certainly, this has been an approach taken in the field of psychology and counselling. If we assert that learning is "due to experience," then the responsibility for things learned is placed outside the client. However, if one recognizes the therapeutic relationship as the context for learning, then it follows that we cannot simply frame learning in terms of modification of behaviour. Learning, while conditioned by particular circumstances, is a result of the client's own complex structure. Change occurs in the being of the client, with events or experiences acting as triggers rather than causes. What has the client already learned about himself and his context from the challenging experience? How is it informing his current situation? What is the therapist learning about herself in this session?

From this discussion, what is the impact on the therapy session? Does the therapist simply sit back and let the client discover what it is he needs to discover? No, I believe that, if we take hermeneutics and the enactivist approach to learning seriously, a different engagement is required of the therapist. Therapy becomes more about expanding the space of the possible and creating the conditions for the emergence of the as yet unimagined than about perpetuating entrenched habits of interpretation. Therapy is not about convergence onto a pre-existent truth but about divergence—about broadening what is knowable, doable, and beable. The emphasis is not on what is but on what might be brought forth. Therefore, therapy is a recursively elaborative process of opening up new spaces of possibility by exploring current spaces. This requires openness to what emerges and recognition that in the midst of the conversation new meanings are made.

Therapy is dynamic and impacts all levels of human existence. Never a personal or even an interpersonal activity, therapy touches on all of what is.

References

Crusius, T. (1991). *A teacher's introduction to philosophical hermeneutics.* Urbana, IL: National Council of Teachers of English.

Davis, B. (1996). *Teaching mathematics: Toward a sound alternative.* New York: Garland Publishing.

Davis, B., & Sumara, D. (1997). Cognition, complexity, and teacher education. *Harvard Educational Review, 67*(1), 105–125.

Davis, B., Sumara, D., & Luce-Kapler, R. (2000). *Engaging minds: Learning and teaching in a complex world.* Mahwah, NJ: Lawrence Erlbaum Associates.

Gadamer, H-G. (1979). *Truth and method* (W. G. Doepel, Trans.). London: Sheed and Ward.

Gadamer, H-G. (1990). *Truth and method.* New York: Continuum.

Heidegger, M. (1975). *The basic problems of phenomenology* (A. Hofstadter, Trans.). Bloomington: Indiana University Press.

Kearney, R. (2002). *On stories.* New York: Routledge.

Kerby, A. P. (1991). *Narrative and the self.* Bloomington: Indiana University Press.

Maturana, H., and Varela, F. (1987). *The tree of knowledge: The biological roots of human understanding.* Boston: Shambala.

Maturana, H., & Varela, F. (1991). *Autopoiesis and Cognition.* Boston: Shambala.

Merleau-Ponty, M. (1962). *Phenomenolgy of perception.* New York: Routledge.

Merleau-Ponty, M. (1978). *Phenomenology of perception* (C. Smith, Trans.). London: Humanities Press.

Mezirow, J. (1994). Understanding transformation theory. *Adult Education Quarterly, 44,* 222–232.

Mezirow, J. (2000). *Learning as transformation: Critical perspectives on a theory in progress.* San Francisco: Jossey-Bass.

Smith, D. (1991). Hermeneutical inquiry: The hermeneutic imagination and the pedagogic text. In E. C. Short (Ed.), *Forms of curriculum inquiry* (pp. 187–209). New York: State University of New York Press.

Usher, R., & Edwards, R. (1994). *Postmodernism and education.* London: Routledge.

Varela, F., Thompson, E., & Rosch, E. (1991). *The embodied mind.* Cambridge, MA: MIT Press.

Weinsheimer, J. (1985). *Gadamer's hermeneutics: A reading of truth and method.* New Haven: Yale University Press.

Yorks, L., and Kasl, E. (2002). Toward a theory and practice for whole-person learning: Reconceptualizing experience and the role of affect. *Adult Education Quarterly, 52,* 519–535.

VIII

Mentoring:
Educating for Mental Growth

Lorraine Ste-Marie

Mentoring is generally understood as a relationship between two people aimed at enabling a wide range of learning, experimentation, and development. Although mentoring is becoming increasingly recognized as a significant aspect of both personal and professional development today, the mentoring-type relationship has existed in all of human history. This is well exemplified in the characters of Mentor and his mentee, Telemachus, in the ancient Greek story of *The Odyssey* (Daloz, 1999, p. 17). In the past 25 years, there has been an increase in the use of formal mentoring programs in the workplace as well as in academic and professional programs of study.

In the workplace, mentoring usually involves partnering experienced individuals who have an understanding of the organization and its culture with persons who are new to the organization and in some cases new to a particular profession. In some businesses, mentors may hold a managerial focus to enable mentees to understand and meet the organization's expectations; others may serve to help a younger and less experienced employee move up the corporate ladder. In some institutions, such as hospitals and schools, mentors often have a supportive focus, acting as role models, coaches, and advisors to new professionals. In these cases, the aim of the mentoring relationship is to enhance both the mentees' competencies and the environment in which the professionals work. In academic and professional programs of study, the mentor usually holds a developmental focus, offering mentees support in integrating new learnings and gaining new awarenesses. This type of mentoring serves both personal and professional development of the person as well as ongoing development of the person's context. While the particular goals of various mentoring programs may be different, the key element for all is that mentoring is a helping relationship that is educative, not therapeutic, in nature. A helping relationship that is therapeutic serves mainly to alleviate one's psychological suffering (Kegan, 1994, p. 258). An educative helping relationship mainly serves one's mental growth (Laske, 2006). Mentoring for mental growth aims at expanding the mentee's current ways of making meaning by providing opportunities to become more aware of himself, his context, and the network of relationships that have contributed to the construction and maintenance of his particular ways of knowing. Mentoring for mental growth aims at development of the whole person.

My own understanding of and focus for mentoring have been shaped by my experience of mentoring in a professional program of study in the Centre for Ministry Formation at Saint Paul University in Ottawa, Ontario. The centre offers vocational discernment and an integral ministry formation process for persons preparing for professional ministry as lay or ordained ministers. Integral ministry formation includes spiritual, human, intellectual, and pastoral formation. The centre's vocational discernment and formation process aims at the growth of the whole person— body, heart, mind, and spirit (Saint Paul University, 2006, Section 5). Ministry formation is both personal and ecclesial: personal in the sense that it honours each individual's call as unique; ecclesial in the sense that the exercise of ministry is deeply interconnected with the life of the Christian community from which the candidate for ministry comes for formation and to which he returns to serve as a professional minister.

In an integral formation process, there are different forms of one-on-one accompaniment such as pastoral supervision, psychological counselling, spiritual direction, and mentorship. While each form of accompaniment has some overlap with the others, each has a specific focus. Pastoral supervision is centred on building skills and competencies and deepening the candidate's ministerial identity within her place of ministry. Psychological counselling focuses mainly on the candidate's mental health as it impacts on relations with self and others. Spiritual direction—also referred to as spiritual mentorship—is one of the means of integration in a formation process that involves the whole person. However, its main focus is on the candidate's relationship with God in the context of her life, ministry, and everyday relationships.

The mentor sits at the juncture of the candidate's personal and ecclesial realities, accompanying him in his personal journey and intentionally representing the wider ecclesial community according to his vision and experience of ministry. Assuming the role of companion or guide, the mentor accompanies the mentee in the "development and integration of various professional, social, personal, sexual and ideological elements" of his personal and ministerial identity (Eurich-Rascoe, 2000, p. 348). This type of mentorship recognizes that all learnings—cognitive, affective, pastoral, or spiritual—affect the whole person.

In this chapter, I present three approaches to mentoring—theological, philosophical, and androgogical—each of which gives us a lens for understanding development of the whole person. The theological approach that I have chosen affirms the fundamental call to all of humanity to reach our fullest potential and presents hospitality as a space for accompanying others in their quest for fulfillment and truth. The philosophical approach to mentoring is based on Charles Taylor's ideal of authenticity, from which Taylor draws out six characteristics of authentic human life that must all be potentially operative in our movement toward fullness of life. The androgogical approach to mentoring situates this helping relationship in the context of adult education, in which transformative learning aims at mental growth and greater capacity for reflective judgment. Finally, I propose the focused conversation method as a structure for the mentoring conversation. Rooted in an understanding of human processes as complex and holistic, the focused conversation method is an intentionally structured discussion that "flows from a natural internal process of perception, response, judgment and decision" (Stanfield, 2000, p. 22). At the end of the chapter, I provide a sample mentoring conversation based on this method that demonstrates the role of the mentor in offering a space for encountering truth and its ensuing demands for fullness of life. To ensure gender inclusivity, I use masculine and feminine pronouns interchangeably for both mentor and mentee.

Theological Approach to Mentoring

I propose two theological approaches to mentoring, both of which are interconnected and each of which is important in its own right. The first is the call to the fullness of life, to reach our fullest potential, to be fully human. This fundamental truth is captured in the well-known phrase "The glory of God is the human person fully alive!" which dates back to the second century AD. Each person is called to develop her own potential to the fullest extent possible in moving toward a fuller realization of her mission or purpose. This call sits on the backdrop of the call to become fully human, a call that is made to all of humanity. This is the horizon out of which the Christian is called to choose and act. As Jean Vanier points out, human life is a journey of growth toward wholeness, a growth in which both individual and world are affected. "To grow is to emerge gradually from a land where our vision is limited, where we are seeking and governed by egotistical pleasure, by our sympathies and antipathies, to a land of unlimited horizons and universal love, where we will be open to every person and desire their happiness" (1979, p. 105). While it is true that even the best mentoring relationships do not guarantee that the mentee will reach her potential, effective mentoring allows for the "development of [our] personal consciousness and inner freedom. In this way, we become more fully human, more fully alive" (Vanier, 1998, p. 53).

The second theological foundation of mentoring is hospitality. The term "hospitality" conjures up a number of images—stranger, host/ess, guest—all of which point to hospitality as a foundational human practice of welcoming family, friends, and influential contacts. From a theological perspective, the purpose of hospitality is to create a space, a welcome environment for encounters with God. This attitude presupposes a belief that God is alive and present, even in places or circumstances that are experienced as strange, barren, and inhospitable. In our biblical texts, God uses "the stranger to introduce us to the strangeness of truth" (Palmer, 1993, p. 74). To be inhospitable to strangers or strange ideas, however unsettling they may be, is to be hostile to the possibility of encountering truth. To be hospitable is to create a space for deep listening to the truth as it is being articulated and becoming potentially transformative. Parker Palmer, writer and proponent of holistic higher education, equates the term "space" with the "emptiness of desert" (1993, p. 70). It is in the space of the desert that the mental constructs of our reality are encountered, deconstructed, and transformed. It is in the space of the desert that we receive each other, our struggles, our newborn ideas with openness and care. Hospitality gives us the "space both to be and to become" fully human agents (p. 70). As artisans of hospitality, mentors enjoy and appreciate mentees, each with her unique gifts of grace. This is a space in which the mentee's talents are named and honoured so that they can flourish.

In modern English, the word *hospitality* implies only one end of an exchange between guest and host—two words we consider as antonyms. The Latin word *hospes,* which means both "guest" and "host," reveals the two-way nature of the relationship. When fearful strangers become guests, "guest and host can reveal their most precious gifts and bring new life to each other" (Nouwen, 1996, p. 218). The two-way nature of the mentoring relationship is evident in the way that it is often experienced as a mutual learning experience (Daloz, 1999, p. 245; Eurich-Rascoe, 2000, p. 345). While the mentee typically expects that the mentor will be the teacher or the guide, the mentor also learns from the mentoring partnership. However, just as true welcoming is more interested in the needs of the guest than the preferences of the host, effective mentoring attends to meeting the needs of the mentee, not those of the mentor (Englander, 2005, p. 15).

Philosophical Approach to Mentoring

Taylor's ideal of authenticity offers us a philosophical approach to mentoring in which mental growth is a journey toward self-fulfillment. For Taylor, self-fulfillment is an authentic moral ideal of "being true to oneself" (1991, p. 15). To be true to ourselves, we must have the capacity to "draw up [our] own life-plans" (Taylor, 1989, p. 25). However, we cannot do so unless we develop our potential to articulate and reflect on the moral ideals out of which we choose to live. When we articulate our ideals, we open the way for claiming them, for correcting them, and for deepening their meaning in our lives. For Taylor, articulacy has a moral point in that it empowers us to live up to our ideals in fuller and more integral ways (1991, p. 22). Despite the negative effects of our Western culture, which Taylor describes as being "simultaneously narcissistic and authentic," he names "authenticity" as the contemporary ideal in our quest for self-fulfillment (1991, p. 16). Taylor offers a framework for this ideal based on six characteristics for full human agency. This framework is helpful for situating the purpose and practice of mentoring.

The first characteristic upholds the dialogical character of human life. Holding together both autonomy and inclusion as intrinsic to human nature, Taylor affirms that it is through language that we become fully human agents, capable of defining ourselves. Using the term "language" to encompass not only the spoken word but also art, gesture, and love, Taylor (1991, p. 33) draws out three important functions of language that highlight the importance of the mentoring conversation for mental growth. In the first function, language serves both to bring out explicit awareness and to realize a new kind of awareness (Taylor, 1985, p. 263). When we express an idea or a feeling, not only do we become more explicitly aware of having it, but we also open ourselves to the potential of transforming what we have expressed (Taylor, 1985, p. 233). The effective mentor knows that, when we articulate our reality in a new way, often the meaning we give to it also changes.

Language's second function is to constitute and shape the public space—the *entrenous*—between people. In the very act of putting something between us, it becomes visible—a visible object for both persons to reflect on together (Taylor, 1989, p. 35). It is in the *entrenous* that mentor and mentee reflect together on "what" the mentee voices. The third function of language is to create and open us up to issues that remain hidden until they are articulated (Taylor, 1985, p. 263). Language is a consciousness-raising activity. It is in giving voice to our concerns and ideals that they exist and are a concern for us. Furthermore, the language we use to express our concerns shapes the meaning we give to our reality and constitutes what is real and true for us (Taylor, 1985, p. 270). Taylor's concern for reflexivity and articulacy is a concern for mentoring in which we presuppose that all humans are partly formed by both our self-interpretations and our conversations with others. Effective mentorship provides the space for articulating, reflecting upon, and critiquing the ideals, concerns, and assumptions that undergird her behaviours and choices.

The second characteristic of the authentic self is openness to horizons of significance. Horizons of significance are the "background of intelligibility" for that which matters in our lives (Taylor, 1991, p. 37). All of us live out of our own particular horizons of significance that give meaning and orientation to our choices and actions. All persons who try to define themselves meaningfully have to exist in a horizon of important questions that originate from beyond the self (Taylor, 1991, p. 40). These horizons can be but are not necessarily based on a particular religious vision. While the structures of our horizons are shaped and reshaped by our social, historical, and cultural conditions, they offer us significance for our very existence. In its authentic form, the stance of openness to horizons of significance is lived in dialogue with others and calls us to responsible human living. Effective mentoring enables the mentee to become clearer about "the significance things have for [her] in virtue of [her] goals, aspirations, purposes" (Taylor, 1985, p. 218). These ideals form the meaning structures through which she interprets her experience as she strives toward self-fulfillment.

These first two characteristics of the authentic self provide the basis for the four other elements—originality, discovery, construction, and opposition to structures of oppression—all of which must be potentially operative in our movement toward fullness of life (Taylor, 1991, p. 66). Originality upholds the uniqueness and creativity of each human person as she attempts to define herself meaningfully in a horizon of important questions. We cannot be true to ourselves unless we are true to our originality. Attentive to the danger of ego-centrism and social atomism, Taylor stresses our need to pay attention and clarify the demands emanating from beyond the immediacy and narrowness of our selves. Self-discovery is intrinsic to the process of becoming more fully the person that each has the potential to be. This denotes a movement from homogeneity toward fulfilling our purpose. While construction may at times include deconstruction and reconstruction of our identities and practices, the dialogical nature of the process against the background of our structures of meaning guides our quest for authenticity and truth. In our struggle for authenticity, we may find ourselves at odds with rules that until now have defined our existence. Our attempts to oppose and free ourselves from both internal and external structures of oppression are necessary steps for mental growth. The mentoring relationship is a public space for noticing and reflecting on the structures that either enable or disable the mentee's development.

Authenticity, as expressed in the deeply interconnected six characteristics of the full human agent (dialogical self, horizons of significance, originality, construction, self-discovery, and opposition to structures of oppression), allows us to live (potentially) "a fuller and more differentiated life, [which is] more fully appropriated as our own" (Taylor, 1991, p. 74). However, we cannot move toward the ideal of authenticity on our own. For Taylor, an intimate space in which "intense relations of self-exploration are going to be identity-forming" cannot be considered dispensable (1991, p. 52). Mentors have a privileged space for becoming engaged in the concrete lives of mentees as they express their pain, hopes, and dreams for authentic ways of living.

Androgogical Approach to Mentoring

Androgogy is adult learning in which adult educators guide learners in connecting with and expanding what they already have as a knowledge base. It presupposes that learners are autonomous, self-directed, and have a tremendous amount of life experiences (Kegan, 1994, p. 274). The mentoring experience out of which I speak in professional and academic programs presupposes that the mentee is capable of self-directed learning; however, we cannot assume that all adults are ready for engaging in such a learning process. Some adults prefer a pedagogical approach to education in which learners rely on the educator to direct the learning through the mode of knowledge transmission. Adults who engage in androgogical learning often seek out learning opportunities in order to cope with life changes. Their learning objectives may be personal and professional, such as wanting to get a better job, or they may focus on social or organizational change.

As adult education, the broader purpose of androgogy is to help adults "make more informed choices by becoming more critically reflective as 'dialogic thinkers' (Basseches, 1984) in their engagement in a given social context" (Mezirow, 2000, p. 30). While this broader purpose can support and expand the learner's particular objectives, adult educators must recognize the difference between the two. Even though adult educators are never neutral with respect to their own goals and agendas for change, it is not their place to indoctrinate. As adult educators, effective mentors ultimately aim to create learning opportunities for mentees so that they may become freer and more participative in discourse in their respective social or organizational contexts.

Adult education is rooted in the fundamental human need for making meaning of experience. The process of meaning making is situated in a constructivist approach to human development in which an individual's very construction of reality is determined by her mental structures. Mental structures are our meaning systems and frames of reference through which we interpret reality and make our truth claims. All humans, both individually and collectively, make meaning of our outer and inner experiences through mental structures. Mental structures are the *form* or the lens through which we make sense of the world and take action. They work as systems, each with its own inner logic, which regulates our thinking (cognitive), feeling (affective), and ways of relating in both the interpersonal and the intrapersonal dimensions of our lives (Kegan, 1994, p. 29).

We generally make meaning by integrating new experiences into what we already know. Whether or not we are even conscious of our own meaning systems, the process of meaning making in itself is value laden. Those values are influenced by a number of factors in our own history, including the events and relationships in our families and communities of origin, culture, and our unique personalities. In the process of meaning making, we continuously move through the motion of dis-embedding and re-embedding ourselves in more complex and inclusive structures of meaning. The conditions that make meaning making a learning process are both external and internal to the learner.

Androgogy and Forms of Knowing

As androgogy, mentoring makes the distinction between *inform*a-tional and trans*form*ational learning. Informational learning is aimed at changing *what* we know by bringing new content into the form of our existing ways of knowing. It fits into the *form* of the learner's existing frames of reference. Transformational learn-ing is aimed at changes in our mental structures, which are changes in *how* we know. Compared to informational learning, transfor-mational learning is always, to some extent, an epistemological change in that the form or existing mental structure is at risk of change. One of the primary goals of transformative learning is to enable learners to engage in challenging experiences that call for the changing of old habits. Both forms of learning are "expansive and valuable, one within a pre-existing frame of mind and the other reconstructing the frame itself" (Kegan, 2000, p. 49).

Transformational learning has both individual and social dimensions. It demands that we be aware of how we have come to knowledge and values that lead us to our perspectives. In trans-formational learning, learners have the opportunity to become critically aware of their own tacit assumptions and expectations as well as those of others. They also have the opportunity to assess the relevance of those expectations and assumptions to interpret or to give meaning to their experiences. Because transformational learning can be an intensely threatening emotional experience, the mentor must be attentive to the mentee's current capacities and needs for support in order to safely risk change in a manner that undergirds her convictions, values, and familiar ways of making meaning (Mezirow, 2000, p. 7).

When a mentor provides opportunities for transformational learning, she can enhance the mentee's capacity for mental growth as he develops greater capacity for critical reflection on the per-spectives and biases of the facts as they are presented. Transforma-tional learning is a necessarily collaborative endeavour in that both mentor and mentee are invested and intentional in the process.

Taking the lead, the mentor seeks to collaboratively build what Kegan calls a "consciousness bridge" toward another mental structure, a higher order of consciousness (1994, p. 278). In doing so, she firmly anchors both ends of the bridge and creates a safe space for openly welcoming what Palmer has called the "strangeness of truth" (1993, p. 74).

Androgogy recognizes the "crucial role of supportive relationships and a supportive environment" for developing our potential as fully human agents (Mezirow, 2000, p. 25). Effective mentorship can provide that form of crucial support—a space that is trustworthy for the mentee to critically reflect on her perspectives and emotions as well as to experiment with new meanings as they emerge in reflection and discourse. I now turn to the focused conversation as a means for providing such learning opportunities.

Mentoring as Focused Conversations

In my own work as a mentor and in the training that I offer mentors, I have found the focused conversation method derived from the Canadian Institute of Cultural Affairs (CICA) an effective structure for the mentoring conversation. Like Taylor, CICA is concerned about our contemporary problem of inarticulacy, the loss of our capacity to talk with one another, find deeper meaning, and "think together as part of a larger community" (Stanfield, 2000, p. 1). CICA offers the focused conversation method as a response to this problem.

Conversation can be experienced in a number of ways, ranging from idle chit-chat to a serious conversation. Idle chit-chat is conversation without a focus. While this broad range of conversations has its place in different aspects of our lives, the mentoring conversation is meant to be focused. There are fundamental differences between focused and unfocused conversations. The latter type inhibits the quality of mentoring as it can keep circulating the same information or uncritiqued truths and habits, thus perpetuating ineffective or unproductive behaviour. Unfocused conversations keep us from getting the deep information needed in order to gain a better understanding of each other and the issues being discussed, thereby maintaining distinct positions on issues (Stanfield, 2000, p. 8).

In contrast, focused conversations generate commitment and build relationship, drawing out the participants' energy and desire for learning. Focused conversations can help participants to notice patterns and make connections with other events and issues. They help to generate creativity and build a vision, thereby deepening our identities as life-long learners (Stanfield, 2000, p. 6). As Stanfield notes, "asking questions is a powerful tool in many professions" (2000, p. 18). Mentoring is one such profession. Mentoring for mental growth aims at fostering a climate of genuine inquiry, a collaborative climate in which it is safe to say "I don't know" or "Let's take a deeper look at this together." As persons who accompany others in their ongoing development, mentors need good questions that go to the heart of our concerns rather than the right answers.

A focused conversation has no specific content to teach. It is a "conversation" that is a shared search for truth; there are actually no right or wrong answers. The questions are open and contentless, often beginning with words such as *how, what, which,* or *why* (Stanfield, 2000, p. 21). This does not negate questions that can be asked with a simple yes or no or a single right answer. These questions can be helpful and are needed in situations that address "technical," simple, and easily fixable problems. However, mentoring conversations, which are both supportive and educative, serve to increase the mentee's capacity for living in complex and often not easily fixable situations.

A focused conversation consists of four levels of conversation designed to reach the depths of the topic being addressed. Each level has different questions and a different focus. The objective questions come first; they are basically meant to determine the data. The next level, the reflective questions, calls forth personal reactions, internal responses, feelings, and associations. The third

level, the interpretative questions, leads the person into an external response, to go a little deeper and broader than his internal
response. Reflective questions focus the conversation in search
of insights, learnings, and patterns of meaning (Stanfield, 2000,
p. 18). The following excerpts of a mentoring conversation give
an example of using this method of focused conversations. While
names and events are fictitious, the concerns raised in this type of
conversation for professional ministry formation are real.

A Focused Conversation

Deborah is 52 years old. She retired from a managerial role in the
public service, in which she was well recognized for her competencies in human resources and collaborative leadership. Prior to her
retirement, she became more involved in a variety of ministries
in her parish, one of which is adult faith development. She has
been studying theology for two years, first casually out of personal interest. In the past year, she has become more systematic
in her theological studies and has entered the Centre for Ministry
Formation to develop skills and competencies for pastoral ministry. One of her main learning goals was to find and use her own
voice as a woman engaged in ministry in her church. Her mentor
is a Roman Catholic lay woman who, prior to becoming a member of the centre staff, had acquired several years of experience in a
variety of lay pastoral leadership roles in the local diocese.

Following are excerpts of a focused conversation between Deborah and her mentor.

Opening
How we begin a mentoring conversation usually sets the tone for
the entire discussion. Generally beginning by situating the conversation in a particular context or by drawing on previous experiences and conversations, the mentor opens the space for the mentee to talk about a particular issue or concern.

Mentor:	Welcome, Deborah. The last time we met you were preparing for leading a meeting in your parish. How was that experience for you?
Deborah:	I was afraid you were going to ask. Part of me does not want to talk about it, and another part of me wants to.
Mentor:	You seem a little upset.
Deborah:	A little? I am more than a little upset.
Mentor:	Shall we spend our time today looking at what happened? We might both have something to learn from what you lived.
Deborah:	OK. But just thinking about it makes me feel so angry and frustrated. I don't even know where to begin.

Deborah has given the mentor a cue to move into a more focused conversation.

Objective Level
The focus of the objective level questions is to put the mentee's concerns into the public space between mentor and mentee. Here the focus is on the facts, the observable data, the external reality.

| Mentor: | Why don't we begin with what happened. Tell me about the event itself. Let's look at what has led to your feeling this frustrated. |
| Deborah: | I formally welcomed them and asked one of our weekly participants to read the gospel. We took a few moments of silence, and before I could open the conversation Guy jumped right in with his own version of how that passage is "officially" interpreted by the church. I should not have been as surprised as I was. Whenever Guy is there, he acts like he has a need to take the floor. He has a habit of jumping in with his own version |

of dogma. Usually, he does not do it right at the
beginning. This week he did, so I was really taken
aback.

Mentor: What happened then?

Deborah described the situation in which Guy preached his
own interpretation of the reading as the official truth. In response
to the mentor's questions, she talked about other team members'
attempts to enrich the conversation while she remained silent. She
named her experience as being frozen in place. Prompted by the
mentor's questions that focused on the facts, the external data,
Deborah named several concerns: her leadership and the way in
which the team exercises its leadership, her experience of being
judged because of her divorce, as well as her care for one of the
participants, whom she saw as experiencing Guy's lecture as a
judgment. If there is no shared understanding of what is being
discussed, then the various comments will seem disconnected, and
both parties will need to guess at what the other knows (Stanfield,
2000, p. 26).

The mentor finished with the following question to ensure that
they were focusing on the same issue.

Mentor: Is there a specific word or phrase that stands out
            for you as you recall that experience?

Deborah: Oh, yes! When Guy said "This passage is the truth
            on which the church does not recognize divorce,"
            I was absolutely flabbergasted. I had thought we
            would have an opportunity to talk about the pas-
            sage in a way that people could share their own
            experiences and understandings, not just sit and
            receive the "truth" from an authority figure. Guy
            seemed to be towering over all of us, standing in
            judgment of her, of me, and all who have had
            marriages that failed. I am livid that he had the
            gall to do such a thing.

After being reasonably satisfied that all the relevant facts have been named, the mentor used Deborah's last line to move into the next level of conversation.

Reflective Level

In this level, the focus is on the internal relationship between Deborah and what she has shared as data or facts. The goal of these questions is to reveal the initial responses through questions that relate to feelings, moods, emotional tones, memories, or associations. This level of questions opens the mentoring conversation to the world of intuition, memory, emotion, and imagination (Stanfield, 2000, p. 27).

Mentor: Deborah, you say that you are livid that he had the gall to do such a thing. Did you feel livid right there, when you heard him speak and the others question him?

Deborah: Oh, no. Not at the time. In fact, I felt like I had been squashed, pushed into a corner, chastised, and silenced. The meeting got off track right from the beginning, and I felt powerless to take the reins.

Mentor: When did you start to feel livid?

Deborah: When I realized where he was going with the church's stance on divorce. I felt my blood pressure rising.

Mentor: What came to mind for you as you felt your blood pressure rising?

Deborah: (taking a deep breath) I could hear the words of my own mother, who refused to understand why I had to leave my first husband. I know what it is like to be shamed into not having a perfect marriage. I've been through that, and I thought I had finished dealing with this issue in therapy. Yet his words seared me. I looked at Emily, and that is

> when I became livid. I could not help but think of
> what his words were doing to her.

Mentor: Sounds like you were really struggling inside as all
that talk was going on.

Deborah went on to describe the depth of her struggle, even to the point of making her physically ill.

Mentor: How do you feel now as you talk about that experience?

Deborah: I am still angry but less raw. I shared a bit of that
experience with my pastoral supervisor, but I did
not have the time to get into details. As I tell you
the story, it's like I am looking at myself angry and
seeing that I really got caught in a corner that evening. As I look back on that event, I could almost
kick myself. How could I have gotten myself into
that situation?

This level of conversation was an opportunity for greater self-awareness, particularly in how Deborah claimed her feelings as her own. This is not enough, however, for transformation. After being fairly satisfied that they had sufficiently explored the internal response at the time of the event, the mentor then invited Deborah to name the feelings that she shared during the mentoring conversation. This opened the way for taking some distance from the event itself. They then turned to the next level of conversation.

Interpretative Level
The goal of this level of questions is to draw out significance from the data for a wider understanding of the event and context. Questions relate to the significance and implications of the event, opening up possibilities for consideration of alternatives and options.

Mentor: Deborah, I wonder what this event is all about for
             you. [Here the mentor relied on what she already
             knew of Deborah.] My experience of you has
             shown me that you are always searching for ways
             to integrate your own life story as you grow into
             your new leadership role. This seems like another
             opportunity for you here.

Deborah: I agree. Like I said, I thought I had dealt with my
             mother and my divorce, but here it is rearing its
             ugly head again. I think I have more work to do in
             that area.

Mentor: That is quite possible. You know that there are
             some "things" that will keep coming back to bite
             us, even when we think we have finished dealing
             with them. There are some events that just trigger
             some of those old wounds. And yet, every time
             you reflect on those events, you have an opportu-
             nity to take another look at how you relate to that
             issue. This could be another call to go deeper in
             your healing.

Deborah: Yeah, I know. What do you think I should do
             about this?

Mentor: I don't know. Let's take a moment to think about
             that.

Deborah: (pause) I think that further personal reflection
             on this will help me get a better perspective on
             that trigger. I could still visit with Dr. Stevens, my
             therapist. He might help me take another look at
             that.

Mentor: (after a period of silence) Deborah, what are your
             biggest concerns around this event at this time?

Deborah: (taking a few moments to think) My leadership.
             I have been very clear about my goals for finding
             and using my voice as a woman in a leadership
             role in ministry. I am committed to that goal;

however, attaining that goal is *not* easy. In fact, it
is really difficult. I have come to see that it is not
just learning new skills. It is much more than that.

Mentor: What do you mean by "It is much more than
that"?

Deborah: I have come to see that it is not just enough to be
determined to do something right. I am coming
to see that "finding and using my voice" are also
about paying attention to what keeps me from
doing the very thing I want to do.

Notice that, although the mentor did not dig into Deborah's
"unfinished business" of dealing with her mother and the shame
of her divorce, she did choose to stay with her in that space for a
while. The mentor paused after addressing the question of further
therapy, attentive to Deborah's body language. Even though she
recognized that this issue was interrelated with Deborah's overall
personal and professional development, she took the cue to continue the conversation in a direction that was consistent with the
goals of mentoring rather than therapy. Her experience of Deborah had shown enough mental stability to move into a different
kind of conversation without jeopardizing the quality of her ministry. This did not mean that Deborah would not want to revisit
that part of her story; however, this was not a therapeutic session.
The mentor then pursued the question of what was keeping Deborah from realizing her goal, giving her an opportunity to notice
patterns in her behaviour whenever she felt threatened or judged.

Mentor: Well, let's go back over what you have said. You
said you have not quite established your place as
a leader, a member of that leadership team. You
have observed yourself letting Guy take over, and
you know that this is not healthy for you, your
ministry, or for the group itself. You have also
observed yourself feeling deep compassion for

> Emily. You have shown that you really care for
> Emily's well-being. (pause) I have a question. As
> you look at that event and other experiences of
> that same group, do you notice a pattern in how
> you act in this group?

Deborah once again brought up her mother's judgment and expectations as partly affecting her behaviour in that incident and reiterated her need to visit her therapist. The mentor then moved into a level of conversation that allowed Deborah to articulate her own moral horizon, her belief in mutuality as a fundamental way of being in leadership and in the world. The meaning that Deborah gave to her quest for finding her voice and establishing her place in leadership opened the way for exploring options for future action.

Mentor:	What are some alternative ways of responding to Guy's behaviour?
Deborah:	I guess that "responding" is the key word here. I have been reacting, not responding. I am often having those "knee-jerk" reactions. I had not realized how much Guy pushes my buttons; it's much more than about divorce.

In an androgogical approach to mentoring, the conditions that make meaning a learning process are both external and internal to the learner. Deborah made meaning of her experience through a reality shaped by her own internalized experience as well as the ecclesial, the external structures in which she was engaged. In her struggle for authenticity, Deborah attempted to free herself from some of the rules that no longer fit her experience yet continued to define her existence. This level of conversation also gave her the space to articulate her own moral horizon, her belief in mutuality as a fundamental way of being in leadership and in the world. This level of awareness will allow her to be more responsive or proactive than reactive in such situations.

Decision Level

The goal of this level of questions is to make the conversation relevant for the future. The questions focused on new directions and implications for the choices that Deborah named. If this level was omitted, the conversation would remain speculative, and there would be little opportunity for Deborah to experiment with her new awareness—her more expanded "form" of knowing—in real life. However, the mentor was attentive to offering the right kind of "consciousness bridge" for Deborah at this time. She checked out Deborah's level of readiness for making some kind of decision. She also used this opportunity to allow Deborah to plan for accessing other forms of one-on-one accompaniment, such as her spiritual director and pastoral supervisor, and then offered her own support for the next step.

> Mentor: You are certainly covering your bases. Is there any-
>   thing I can do to support you? Would it be helpful
>   for you to talk about your plan before actually car-
>   rying it out?
>
> Deborah: It might be. Give me a couple of days to think
>   about it. If I do, I will call you. As you said, this is
>   for the long haul, and for that what I need is this
>   kind of conversation. It's not easy, but I know I
>   need it to help me see things differently.

If Deborah chose simply to continue to reflect on the incident and mentoring conversation, then that would have been the right action for her at that time. No matter what decision she made, it would be helpful to return to that decision at the next mentoring meeting. Her subsequent reflection itself or the anticipated encounter with the team members would then become the issue for the subsequent focused conversation. The mentor's offer of support assured Deborah that she was not walking this path alone. In closing the conversation, the mentor affirmed the challenge and threat inherent in mental growth. She ended by pointing to the mutuality of the learning experience as well as the potential for her environment to develop.

Conclusion

In this chapter, I have explored mentoring using particular theological, philosophical, and androgogical approaches that affirm the fundamental call to the fullness of life. While each approach offers a particular lens for understanding the practice of mentoring, together they underline the complexity of human development and show how mentoring can accompany persons in their mental growth. Effective mentoring offers hospitable spaces for enabling learners to articulate and reflect on their reality. Effective mentoring accompanies persons in their quest toward greater freedom for responsibly meeting their needs for both autonomy and belonging. The focused conversation method for guiding mentoring conversations aims at engaging the whole person in the reflective and decision-making process. As a helping relationship that is educative, mentoring provides opportunities for mentees to surface, critique, and, where needed, expand their meaning systems through which they interpret experience and choose to act. As we gain greater consciousness of our ultimate meaning and purpose, we gain greater clarity about our identities, values, and visions, along with deeper confidence in the continuous process of change into which we are all called. In our search for authenticity, we "need relationships to fulfill but not define ourselves" (Taylor, 1991, p. 34). My understanding and experience of mentoring have shown this to be possible.

References

Basseches, M. A. (1984). *Dialectical thinking and adult development.* Norwood, NJ: Ablex.

Daloz, L. (1999). *Mentor: Guiding the journey of adult learners.* San Francisco: Jossey-Bass.

Englander, H. (2005). Difficult conversations: The heart on mentoring. *Compass: A Magazine for Peer Assistance, Mentoring, and Coaching, 17*(1), 15–18.

Eurich-Rascoe, B. (2000). Hendrika Van de Kemp as mentor: Using, finding, giving voice. *Journal of Psychology and Christianity, 19*(4), 345–349.

Kegan, R. (1994). *In over our heads: The mental demands of modern life.* Cambridge, MA: Harvard University Press.

Kegan, R. (2000). What "form" transforms? In J. Mezirow et al. (Eds.), *Learning as transformation: Critical perspectives on a theory of progress* (pp. 35–69). San Francisco: Jossey-Bass.

Laske, O. (2006). *Measuring hidden dimensions: The art and science of fully engaging adults.* Medford, MA: Interdevelopmental Institute Press.

Mezirow, J. (2000). Learning to think like an adult. In J. Mezirow et al. (Eds.), *Learning as transformation: Critical perspectives on a theory of progress.* San Francisco: Jossey-Bass.

Nouwen, H. (1996). *Ministry and Spirituality.* New York: Continuum.

Palmer, P. (1993). *To know as we are known: A spirituality of education.* San Francisco: Harper San Francisco.

Saint Paul University, Centre for Ministry Formation. (2006). *Members' Handbook.* Unpublished handbook, Saint Paul University, Ottawa.

Stanfield, R. B. (Gen. Ed.). (2000). *The art of focused conversation: 100 ways to access group wisdom in the workplace.* Gabriola Island, BC: New Society Publishers and Canadian Institute of Cultural Affairs (ICA Canada).

Taylor, C. (1985). *Human agency and language: Philosophical papers I.* Cambridge, UK: Cambridge University Press.

Taylor, C. (1989). *Sources of self: The making of the modern identity.* Cambridge, MA: Harvard University Press.

Taylor, C. (1991). *The malaise of modernity.* Concord, ON: Anansi Press.

Vanier, J. (1979). *Community and growth.* London: Dartman, Longman, and Todd.

Vanier, J. (1998). *Becoming human.* Toronto: Anansi Press.

IX

The Helping Relationship in CPE Supervision

Marsha Cutting

The word *ezer* ("helper") in its various forms is widely used in the Hebrew Bible—120 times, to be exact. If we examine the passages where *ezer* is used, we find that a helper keeps one from being alone and can be a partner (Genesis 2:18), the powerless have particular need of a helper (Job 29:12), God is appealed to as a helper (Psalm 30:10), and God delivers those who have no helper (Psalm 72:12). Also, if God opposes you, you won't prevail, even with help (Jeremiah 47:1–7), people are foolish to put faith in helpers who oppose God (Isaiah 31:1), and the help of people may be in vain (Psalm 108:12).

So what does this have to say about the helping relationship as it relates to clinical pastoral education (CPE) supervision? One thing that it suggests is the importance of attending to power in helping relationships, power that can be used for good or ill. Supervisory helping relationships are intended to provide guidance and support for supervisees learning to do therapy, chaplaincy, and ministry; they are also relationships of unequal power and thus contain the potential for abuse. This unequal power also suggests the likelihood of anxiety in the supervisee, who is almost certainly aware, on some level, of the inequality of power.

Some of the theological assumptions about helping relationships that undergird this chapter are the following:

- We are most human when we are in relationships.
- Relationships can take us beyond ourselves, let us do more and better than we could alone—or bind us and make it impossible for us to do our best work. They can create a holy space between two or more people or, when they go awry, create if not a demonic space at least one in which the unredeemed parts of our humanity are most prominent.
- Yet the power of relationships is such that, even in the distorted relationships, growth for the supervisee often still takes place, though sometimes apparently in spite of the relationship rather than because of it.

Literature Review

Numerous authors have offered personal and theoretical reflections on CPE, and at least two have published anecdotal reports about negative CPE supervisory experiences (Cutting, 2007). However, with a couple of notable exceptions (e.g., Fitchett & Johnson, 2001; VandeCreek & Glockner, 1993), the empirical study of CPE supervision, and of the factors that differentiate effective from ineffective CPE supervision, has been neglected. The empirical work that has been done tends to focus on CPE as a whole or on CPE outcomes rather than on the process of supervision per se, and the articles on supervision tend not to be empirical research.

Psychologists, however, have begun to study the supervision that is a component of nearly all mental health training, and one important focus of that work has been the supervisory relationship. It has been argued that "a strong supervisory relationship serves as the foundation for positive experiences, because a relationship characterized by empathy, a sense of affirmation, and a nonjudgmental attitude allows a supervisee to tolerate the anxiety engendered by the challenge to his or her skills" (Cutting, 2007, p. 122). Authors such as Worthen and McNeill (1996) have found that supervisees who said that their supervision was positive reported that their supervisors were empathic, non-defensive, validating, non-judgmental, and willing to examine their assumptions. These supervisors help their trainees to feel accepted, and they normalize the challenges that trainees experience, thus helping trainees to remain open to supervisory input and lessening the need for defensiveness.

The supervisory relationship in negative experiences has also been examined, as reflected in a literature review by Ellis, Swagler, and Beck (2000), who reported that between a third and a half of supervisees "are likely to encounter truly harmful supervision" (p. 2). Their review found that 7% to 10% of supervisees give up working in mental health because of such experiences. They defined *bad supervision* as those instances "when the supervisor is unable or unwilling to meet [the supervisee's] training needs as an emerging professional counselor or psychologist" (p. 2), in contrast to *harmful supervision,* those instances that result in "psychological, physical or emotional trauma, or harm to the supervisee or to the supervisee's clients" (Cutting, 2007, p. 124). Nelson and Friedlander (2001) studied conflictual supervision and found that negative supervision experiences "exacted a toll on [supervisees'] health and well-being and their sense of trust in others, particularly authority figures" (p. 394). Ramos-Sanchez et al. (2002) reported that the supervisory alliance in supervision events that trainees characterize as negative most often was characterized by goals and tasks that were incongruent and by a lack of trust, confidence, and mutuality.

Although much of supervision research has focused on the views of trainees, research focused on both supervisees and supervisors has found that they "tend to evaluate the supervisory alliance similarly, and a strong supervisory alliance enables students to make the best use of supervision" (Cutting, 2007, p. 123).

This chapter is based in part on my dissertation, for which I studied, from the viewpoint of supervisees, both positive and negative supervisory experiences. Not surprisingly, the supervisory relationship played a significant role in both, either for good or for ill.

Method

Participants

I recruited a nationwide US group of participants (N = 16; 11 women, 5 men) by posting notices on web-based bulletin boards and distribution lists, placing notices in chaplaincy association newsletters, and emailing seminary directors of field education. The solicitation notices sought participants who had had a particularly positive or negative CPE supervision experience at least 6 months but not more than 3 years ago. This time frame was specified so that participants would have had time to consider their experiences while still being able to remember the details. The wisdom of this time specification, adopted from Nelson and Friedlander (2001), was confirmed when participants in the pilot interviews, who had done CPE more than 3 years previously, had difficulty recounting their experiences in detail. Since this study was a replication and an extension of Nelson and Friedlander, I used their definition of a negative experience as one that the trainee experienced "as harmful or having had a decisively negative impact on the training experience" (p. 385). I adapted this definition for the positive experiences, so that they were defined as ones "that the trainee experienced as especially helpful, that had a decisively positive impact on his or her training experience or that challenged him or her to grow personally and professionally" (Cutting & Friedlander, 2008).

I interviewed the first eight respondents in each group (positive and negative experiences) who met the inclusion criteria and returned the study materials. This yielded a group of participants who were European American and whose ages ranged from 25 to 69 years (M = 48.07, SD = 15.60). There were 13 Christians who belonged to 11 theologically diverse denominations; 3 participants were of other faiths (unspecified to protect confidentiality). General hospitals were the setting for 12 of the CPE programs, 1 was in a psychiatric hospital, and the other 3 were in a variety of health care and community settings. The experience being discussed was the first one for all but 2 people (1 in each group), and 4 people (2 in each group) had been involved in subsequent CPE units. Volunteers who were currently CPE supervisors or supervisors in training were excluded because their memories of being supervised might have been confounded by the experience of being a supervisor.

For reasons of confidentiality, I asked participants not to name their site or supervisor; thus, I cannot say with certainty that all were from different CPE sites, though I am confident based on their descriptions that no more than two participants were from the same site. It is possible that these two (both in the positive group) had the same supervisor. CPE students have some choice over their supervisor. Typically, they apply to a site and often are interviewed by the supervisor. They may have a choice of supervisor if they are accepted by more than one site, and, obviously, they have the option of withdrawing their applications from sites where they do not wish to work with the supervisor. However, their options may be constrained if they are required to do CPE, if they wish or need to remain within a given geographic area, or if they wish to do CPE at a particular type of site. I did not ask about choice of supervisor in my study, and this would be an interesting question for further study. All of the participants discussed the supervision that was part of one 400-hour unit of CPE. There were 7 same-sex supervisory dyads (4 women, 3 men); of these, all were in the positive group except 1 female dyad. Of the 9 mixed dyads (1 with a female supervisor and 8 with male supervisors), only 3 of the female supervisee/male supervisor dyads were in the positive group.

Nearly half of the participants (N = 7) were in seminary at the time of the CPE experiences that they discussed, and the same number had already completed CPE (one of these participants had finished seminary more than two decades earlier). The remaining two people had medical backgrounds instead of seminary educations and were working in pastoral care when they were interviewed.

Procedure

When possible participants contacted me, in response to the notices that I had circulated, I sent them the informed consent letter approved by the Research Review Board, a demographic questionnaire, and three quantitative instruments, the Supervisory Working Alliance Inventory (SWAI; Bahrick, 1990); the Supervisory Styles Inventory (SSI; Friedlander & Ward, 1984), and the Role Conflict Role Ambiguity Inventory (RCRAI; Olk & Friedlander, 1992). After they returned these materials, I arranged, conducted, and audiotaped a telephone interview. After having the audiotapes transcribed, I reviewed the transcripts to make sure that they were accurate, sent them to participants to make sure that they reflected what they had wanted to convey, and incorporated their comments into the transcripts.

Interview Guide

In developing the guide for the semi-structured interview (Appendix A), I began with the interview used by Nelson and Friedlander (2001) and added questions about positive supervision and questions raised by Veach (2001) about process and supervision groups. My intent was to invite participants to offer detailed descriptions of their experiences and to discuss how they felt these experiences impacted their professional development, behaviour, and self-concept. I began the interviews by asking for information on the CPE site and requesting that interviewees not refer to either the site or the supervisor by name. Using the same interview guide for both groups, I then asked the interviewees to tell me about their supervisor and about their relationship with him or her. The interview guide also included questions about things that might have resulted in participants feeling particularly positive or negative about their experiences as well as encouragement for them to share information that they thought would help us to gain a complete understanding of their experiences.

Instruments

Supervisory Styles Inventory

The Supervisory Styles Inventory (Friedlander & Ward, 1984) was chosen for comparison with Nelson and Friedlander's (2001) results. The SSI was developed inductively from interviews with experienced supervisors. The measure has 33 unipolar items (25 items plus 8 fillers) that make up 3 scales that estimate trainees' perceptions of supervisors' attractiveness, interpersonal sensitivity, and task orientation. The attractive scale (7 items) includes the items *warm, supportive, friendly,* and *open;* the interpersonally sensitive scale (8 items) includes the items *invested, committed, therapeutic,* and *perceptive;* and the task-oriented scale (10 items) includes the items *goal oriented, thorough, focused,* and *structured.* Respondents are asked to rate their supervisor on each item from 1 (*not very important*) to 7 (*very important*). Because there are different numbers of items per scale, ratings on each scale are averaged to provide a score that ranges from 1 to 7. The SSI has been used in at least six published supervision studies (Efstation, Patton, & Kardash, 1990; Herbert, Ward, & Hemlick, 1995; Ladany & Lehrman-Waterman, 1999; Nelson & Friedlander, 2001; Prieto, 1998; Reeves, Culbreth, & Greene, 1997; Usher & Borders, 1993). Results have consistently shown the scales to be highly reliable and to relate in expected ways to supervisors' theoretical orientations, supervisees' developmental levels, and supervisees' satisfaction with supervision.

In previous research (Friedlander & Ward, 1984), Cronbach's alphas for each of the three scales ranged from .76 to .93, and item-scale correlations ranged from .70 to .88 (attractive), from .51 to .82 (interpersonally sensitive), and from .38 to .76 (task oriented). Test-retest reliabilities over a period of 2 weeks were .92 for the combined scale, .94 for the attractiveness scale, .91 for the interpersonally sensitive scale, and .78 for the task-oriented scale. High scores on the interpersonally sensitive scale, indicative of a focus on the supervisory relationship, were found to predict trainees' responses to a question about how supervision affected their professional development. A methodical, content-focused approach to supervision is indicated by high scores on the task-oriented scale, and warm collegiality is indicated by high scores on the attractive scale. Psychodynamic and humanistic supervisors viewed themselves (and were perceived by trainees) as more interpersonally sensitive than task oriented. In addition, Friedlander and Ward found that supervisors working with practicum trainees rated themselves as more task oriented than did supervisors who worked with interns, who tended to see themselves as attractive and interpersonally sensitive. Trainees' responses were consistent with these views. In the present study, only interpersonal sensitivity and attractiveness were examined, although the entire measure was administered because there was no empirical or theoretical basis on which to expect group differences on the task-oriented scale, nor had it been used by Nelson and Friedlander (2001).

Role Conflict and Role Ambiguity Inventory

The Role Conflict and Role Ambiguity Inventory (Olk & Friedlander, 1992) was chosen for comparison with the results of Nelson and Friedlander (2001). A self-report instrument that estimates supervisees' role conflict and role ambiguity in supervision, this 29-item questionnaire has two scales, role conflict (13 items), and role ambiguity (16 items). Role conflict refers to situations in which trainees are confronted with conflicting expectations for their actions, and role ambiguity refers to instances in which trainees are unclear about what supervisors expect of them or how they will be evaluated. Items on the role ambiguity scale include "My supervisor's criteria for evaluating my work were not specific" and "Everything was new and I wasn't sure what would be expected of me" (p. 394). Items on the role conflict scale include "I have wanted to intervene with one of my clients in a particular way and my supervisor has wanted me to approach the client in a very different way. I am expected both to judge what is appropriate for myself and also to do what I am told" and "Part of me wanted to rely on my own instincts with clients, but I always knew that my supervisor would have the last word" (p. 394). Respondents use 5-point Likert scales, from 1 = *not at all* to 5 = *very much;* raw scores are summed and divided by the total number of items in the scale, so that scores on each scale can range from 1 (low) to 5 (high).

In a factor analysis, no items loaded greater than .40 on both factors, and all items loaded at least .40 on one factor (Olk & Friedlander, 1992). Item-scale correlations ranged from .37 to .77 (r = .91) on the role conflict scale and from .50 to .72 on the role ambiguity scale. In prior research, role conflict was uniquely associated with work-related anxiety and dissatisfaction with clinical work and supervision, and role ambiguity was uniquely associated with less counselling experience, when the contribution of role conflict was taken into account (Olk & Friedlander). Used in two subsequent studies (Ladany & Friedlander, 1995; Nelson & Friedlander, 2001), both scales of the RCRAI predicted dissatisfaction with supervision as well as work-related anxiety and general work dissatisfaction.

Because a few of the RCRAI items (e.g., "My supervisor wanted me to use an assessment technique that I considered inappropriate for a particular client" [Olk & Friedlander, 1992]) are not applicable to CPE supervision, the RCRAI was developed for psychology trainees, and the respondents were instructed to mark items not applicable to their CPE experience as 1 (*not at all*).

Supervisory Working Alliance-Trainee Version

The Supervisory Working Alliance-Trainee version (Bahrick, 1990) was chosen because it is a 36-item self-report instrument adapted from the Working Alliance Inventory (Horvath & Greenberg, 1986). Its three subscales were originally intended to estimate how trainees perceive Bordin's (1983) three factors of the supervisory working alliance (agreement on the goals of supervision, agreement on the tasks of supervision, and an emotional bond). When Bahrick revised the WAI, originally designed to examine the strength of the working alliance within the therapeutic relationship, she made minor changes in the wording. Words such as *therapist* and *client* became *supervisor* and *trainee,* respectively, and references to *client problems* became *trainee issues* or *trainee concerns*. Each of the three subscales (goals, tasks, and bond) contains 12 items, which are rated on seven-point Likert-type scales ranging from 1 (*never*) to 7 (*always*). The agreement on tasks subscale includes items such as "We agreed on what was important for me to work on," and the agreement on goals subscale has items such as "I worried about the outcome of our supervision sessions" (Bahrick, 1990). Included on the emotional bond subscale are items such as "I believed that (_____) was genuinely concerned with my welfare." Items for each subscale are summed to produce a subscale score that ranges from 12 to 84; higher scores reflect a stronger emotional bond between trainee and supervisor and greater perceived agreement with the supervisor on the goals and tasks of supervision. Because the three dimensions have recently been found not to be distinct in supervision (as opposed to therapy), and the authors of a recent meta-analysis (Ellis, Russin, & Deihl, 2003) recommend using the total score, I did so in this study. The only exception is in the triangulation section, where I used the subscale scores to allow me to more closely compare the SWAI scores and the narrative data.

Ladany and Friedlander (1995) found that high scores on the SWAI were negatively related to supervisee role conflict and role ambiguity, and Ladany, Brittan-Powell, and Pannu (1997) found a positive relationship between high scores on the SWAI and positive interactions around racial identity during supervision. VandeCreek and Glockner (1993) made unspecified adaptations of Horvath and

Greenberg's (1986) WAI for CPE supervision and found that students viewed their supervisory relationships more positively than did their supervisors. These authors also reported that female students had higher scores on the bond subscale than did male students and that students' WAI scores were related to their levels of self-esteem, death anxiety, depression, and parental attachment style.

Qualitative Analysis

Consensual Qualitative Research (CQR; Hill, Thompson, & Williams, 1997), a qualitative methodology that uses a team of judges who follow an inductive analytic process and make consensual decisions and an auditor who reviews the work of the judges, was employed to analyze the transcribed interviews. None of the three women, two European American and one Taiwanese, who served as judges had had any experience with CPE; in fact, they were unaware of the program's existence prior to their work on the study. Their ages ranged from 23 to 52; two were master's students in counselling psychology, and one was a marital and family therapist. I served as the primary auditor, and my dissertation advisor, a PhD-level psychologist, served as the second auditor.

I asked the judges to read Hill, Thompson, and Williams' (1997) article on CQR, after which we met to discuss it. At this meeting, I asked them to write down any expectations that they were aware of and asked them to record any ideas or biases that they noticed while working on the analysis. We then coded two transcripts from pilot interviews and discussed how the group dynamics impacted the coding. I also invited a CPE supervisor who directed the pastoral care department of a local hospital (which included a CPE program) to do an orientation to CPE for the judges.

They then read the transcripts independently, recording any impressions, themes, or patterns they noticed. In developing the code list, they started with the eight categories from Nelson and Friedlander (2001) (initiation of relationship, impasse characteristics, contributing factors, supervisee perceptions of supervisor reactions, supervisee reactions, supervisee coping strategies, positive outcomes, and negative outcomes) and added domains to reflect the positive experiences (Friedlander and Nelson had interviewed only trainees who had had negative experiences). The judges added new codes as needed throughout the analysis, and each time a new domain or code was added they reread the previously analyzed transcripts to see if there were sections of text to which the new domain or code applied, in the constant comparison method recommended by Corbin and Strauss (1990).

Working independently, they decided on codes for each block of data (sentences or paragraphs), subsequently meeting to discuss their coding and reach consensus on the best codes for each block of data. I reviewed their decision to make sure that they did not overlook any data and were consistent in their decisions, and I offered them feedback. After they had developed the final list of codes (N = 199), I compared the transcripts, identifying the prevalence of the codes, and developed the central concepts or themes. I met with the second auditor to identify separate themes for the positive and negative narratives and then met with the judges to discuss the themes and get their feedback.

Following the procedure recommended by Stiles (1993) to obtain testimonial validity, I sent the description of the themes to all of the participants, asking for their feedback on the extent to which they reflected their experiences. Only 2 of the 12 who responded chose to expand on some of the themes; the rest said that they had nothing to add. I incorporated the expansions into some of the themes as seemed appropriate.

Bracketing of Biases and Expectations
I am a counselling psychologist and a former board-certified chaplain who had two negative experiences in CPE supervision many years ago. However, I have had the opportunity to speak with CPE supervisors whose opinions I respect about changes in CPE in recent years and with several individuals who had both positive and negative experiences. I expected the results specifically related to the supervision relationship to show that (a) confron-

tation plays a role in negative supervision experiences, and that (b) participants experience lasting effects from both positive and negative supervisory relationships.

I asked a member of my dissertation committee, a CPE supervisor who has published extensively on the subject of CPE, to review the transcripts of the first two negative and first two positive interviews, to be sure that my biases and expectations were not influencing participants' responses as I interviewed them. He decided that my biases did not seem to be influencing the direction of the interviews.

Results

Quantitative Group Comparisons

A quantitative analysis was conducted to determine whether the two groups differed significantly from each other on three instruments: the Supervisory Styles Inventory (SSI; Friedlander & Ward, 1984), the Role Conflict Role Ambiguity Inventory (RCRAI; Olk & Friedlander, 1992), and the Supervisory Working Alliance Inventory-Trainee version (SWAI; Bahrick, 1990).

Preliminary Tests

Boxes M test for normality and homogeneity of variance (done via multivariate analysis of variance) demonstrated that none of the major variables significantly deviated from normality or homogeneity of variance, $F(6,1420) = 1.95$, $p = .07$.

Correlations among the dependent variables were conducted to assess whether to use a univariate or multivariate analysis. To control for Type I error, a modified Bonferroni procedure (Holland & Copenhaver, 1988) was used to determine the per comparison alpha. The results are presented in Table 9.1. As is evident, all the dependent variables were substantive and significantly intercorrelated, all $p < .01$. Therefore, multivariate procedures were indicated (cf. Haase & Ellis, 1987).

Table 9.1
Intercorrelations among the self-report variables

	SWAI-T	IS	AT	RC	RA
SWAI-T	---	.92**	.91**	-.74**	-.86**
IS		---	.98**	-.75**	-.89**
AT			---	-.76**	-.85**
RC				---	.77**
RA					---

Note: SWAI-T = Supervisory Working Alliance-Trainee version (Bahrick, 1990); IS = interpersonally sensitive scale on the Supervisory Styles Inventory (Friedlander & Ward, 1984); AT = attractive scale on the Supervisory Styles Inventory (Friedlander & Ward, 1984); RC = role conflict scale on the Role Conflict Role Ambiguity Inventory (Olk & Friedlander, 1992); RA = role ambiguity scale on the Role Conflict Role Ambiguity Inventory (Olk & Friedlander, 1992). ** p < .01.

Major Analyses

Scores on the three instruments were subjected to a multivariate *t* test. To control for intercorrelations among dependent variables, standardized discriminant function coefficients (*sdfc*s) were used to follow up significant multivariate *t* tests (Haase & Ellis, 1987). Shrunken effect sizes (`$r^2$`) are reported, as recommended by Haase, Ellis, and Ladany (1989).

Table 9.2 presents the means and standard deviations by group on the three instruments. As shown in the table, on the SSI, as expected, the positive group scores were significantly higher than the negative group scores for the interpersonally sensitive scale, $F(1,14) = 33.92$, $p < .0001$, `$r^2$` = .69, *sdfc* = -.75, and for the attractive scale, $F(1,14) = 32.28$, $p < .0001$, `$r^2$` = .68, *sdfc* = -.03. On the RCRAI, the negative group scores were significantly higher on both the role conflict scale, $F(1,14) = 23.62$, $p < .0001$, `$r^2$` = .60, *sdfc* = -.49, and the role ambiguity scale, $F(1,14) = 43.12$, $p < .0001$, `$r^2$` = .74, *sdfc* = -.37. Finally, SWAI total scores for the positive group were also significantly higher

Table 9.2

Means and standard deviations on the self-report instruments

Variable	Positive group		Negative group		$F(1,14)$	$p <$	p^2	$sdfc$
	M	SD	M	SD				
SWAI-T	222.25	12.28	100.75	34.28	89.09	.0001	.86	1.23
SSI								
Attractive	6.00	.53	2.93	1.43	32.28	.0001	.68	-.03
Interpersonally sensitive	6.36	.29	3.03	1.59	33.92	.0001	.69	-.75
RCRAI								
Role conflict	1.25	.21	2.81	.88	23.62	.0001	.60	-.49
Role ambiguity	1.63	.42	3.74	.81	43.12	.0001	.74	-.37

Note. N = 16. SWAI-T = Supervisory Working Alliance-Trainee version (Bahrick, 1989); SSI = Supervisory Styles Inventory (Friedlander & Ward, 1984); RCRAI = Role Conflict Role Ambiguity Inventory (Olk & Friedlander, 1992). *sdfc* = standardized discriminant function coefficient.

than for the negative group, $F(1,14) = 89.09$, $p < .0001$, `$r^2 =$ .85, $sdfc = 1.23$. The mean for the positive group was 222.25 ($SD = 12.28$), whereas the mean for the negative group was 100.75 ($SD = 34.28$). In sum, the quantitative data clearly demonstrated substantial differences between the positive and the negative supervisory groups.

Because all of the self-report variables were highly correlated, $rs > .74$, $ps < .01$, effect sizes were inflated. For this reason, standardized discriminant function coefficients were used to determine which variables accounted for the greatest amount of variance. Results showed that most of the variance was attributable to the SWAI ($sdfc = 1.21$) and to the interpersonally sensitive scale of the SSI ($sdfc = -.75$), with the role ambiguity and role conflict scales of the RCRAI contributing the next greatest amounts, $sdfc = -.37$ and -.49, respectively (Haase, Ellis, and Ladany, 1989).

Qualitative Results

Themes that applied to all of either the positive or the negative cases were termed *general*, themes that applied to at least half of the cases (four to seven) in each group were termed *typical*, and themes that were relevant to two to three cases in each group were termed *variant* (Hill, Thompson, and Williams, 1997). There were notable differences in the ways that participants in the two groups described their relationships with their supervisors. The themes that relate to this chapter are found in Table 9.3.

Positive Group Results

As might be expected, supervisees in the positive supervision group offered a variety of positive attributes when speaking of their supervisors. Discussing their supervisors' interpersonal characteristics, supervisees typically used words such as *empathic, compassionate, supportive, affirming,* and *validating.* One general theme was found, in which supervisees described their supervisors' cognitive characteristics with words such as *sharp, astute, competent, experienced,* and *knowledgeable.* Supervisees tended to

Table 9.3

Themes of Supervisee Experiences of Positive and Negative Supervision

Category	General	Typical	Variant
Initiation of Relationship			
Positive Group			
Supervisee had prior knowledge of or relationship with supervisor			X
First response different from final response			X
Negative Group			
Supervisee had prior knowledge of supervisor			X
Relationship with Supervisor			
Positive Group			
Perceptions of the Supervisor's Characteristics			
Competent, experienced, knowledgeable, sharp, astute	X		
Empathic, compassionate, supportive		X	
Present, invested		X	
Respectful		X	
Validating, affirming		X	
Interactions with Supervisor			
Warm, trusting, comfortable relationship		X	
Supervisor skilled at dealing with personal issues that influenced clinical work		X	
Supervisor was skilled at teaching			X
A place to unwind and process things			X
Respected supervisor			X

Table 9.3 (continued)
Themes of Supervisee Experiences of Positive and Negative Supervision

Category	General	Typical	Variant
Relationship with Supervisor			
Negative Group			
Perceptions of the Supervisor's Characteristics			
Not "present," not invested, did not listen well		X	
Arrogant, patronizing, disrespectful, demeaning		X	
Critical, judgmental		X	
Hostile, abusive, enraged		X	
Rigid			X
Threatened			X
Had issues with women			X
Unfair, manipulative, played favorites			X
Burned out			X
Interactions with Supervisor			
Supervisor attempted to function as counselor		X	
Inappropriate sexual talk or behavior		X	
Supervisor threatened retaliation			X
Supervisor scapegoated a group member			X
Supervision a waste of time			X
Supervisor self-disclosed			X
Supervisee noticed power struggles			X

Table 9.3 (continued)
Themes of Supervisee Experiences of Positive and Negative Supervision

Category	General	Typical	Variant
Critical Incident or Turning Point			
Positive Group			
Supervisor offered helpful insight or shared understanding			X
Epiphany			X
No conflict			X
Received positive response to work			X
Brought personal information to supervision			X
Negative Group			
Demeaned by supervisor's attitude		X	
Confronted or expressed frustration to supervisor		X	
Supervisor responded negatively to confrontation		X	
Supervisee wanted more/different learning opportunities			X
Supervisor accused supervisee of inappropriate behavior			X
Supervisee reactions			
Threatened		X	
Sought outside support		X	
Third party responsive			X
Third party unresponsive			X
Traumatized			X
Misunderstood			X
Alone, overwhelmed, and stressed			X
Harassed			X
Helpless, "don't rock the boat"			X

Table 9.3 (continued)
Themes of Supervisee Experiences of Positive and Negative Supervision

Category	General	Typical	Variant
Critical Incident or Turning Point (continued)			
Negative Group, continued			
Supervisee reactions, continued			
Angry			X
Guarded, self-protected			X
Disillusioned			X
Outcomes			
Positive Group			
Personal growth		X	
Supervisee gained insight		X	
Increased confidence		X	
Learned when to risk			X
General learning: gained knowledge and skills		X	
Call to ministry affirmed		X	
Career change		X	
Continued mentor relationship with supervisor			X
Questioned call to ministry (subsequently resolved)			X
Negative Group			
Personal growth		X	
Supervisee gained insight			X
Self-affirmation			X
Empowered by confrontation			X
Learned when to risk			X
General learning, gained knowledge and skills		X	

Table 9.3 (continued)
Themes of Supervisee Experiences of Positive and Negative Supervision

Category	General	Typical	Variant
Outcomes (continued)			
Negative Group (continued)			
Questioned call to ministry or chaplaincy			X
Concerned about certification or ordination (not realized)			X
Negative impact on grades			X
Conflict unresolved		X	
Personal resolution			X
Contributing Factors			
Positive Group			
Personal differences from supervisor or group			
Religion/denomination		X	
Education/employment history		X	
Age			X
Gender/cultural background			X
Retirement			X
History of personal loss, trauma		X	
Negative Group			
Personal differences from supervisor or group			
Religion/denomination		X	
Age		X	
Gender/cultural background		X	
Traumatic personal history		X	
Supervisor in training (SIT)		X	
SIT's sessions being taped			X

emphasize experiencing the supervisor as present and invested; as one said of her supervisor, "She just drew it out of me in her warm, compassionate way and just listened. It wasn't like she was just there with me, she listened. At some level, she was emotionally involved" (Participant #8).

Supervisees in the positive group generally reported that their supervisors respected their boundaries while using their skills to help them deal with personal issues that influenced their clinical work. One participant said, "He was excellent at very gently pointing out areas of resistance and asking seemingly innocuous questions to get at a ... deeper level of understanding of both me personally and my interactions with the group as a whole and my interactions with the patient" (Participant #7). Another participant (#4) described his supervisor by saying, "He's not going to let you get away with anything. He'll push you, and if you're not ready to be pushed too far he recognizes that."

Participants typically used words such as *warm, trusting, comfortable,* and *collegial* to describe their interactions with their supervisors. One participant (#7) noted, "For me it was the intimacy of that relationship that helped me survive it. If that had not been, if I hadn't felt that my supervisor had my best interests at heart, I would have quit."

For several participants in the positive group, being affirmed stood out as a turning point in the supervisory relationship (variant theme). One participant reported, "And at the conclusion he said, 'This was an exquisite.' I mean this was his word, 'This was an exquisite visit.' And now he had plenty of things to say to improve it, but he said, 'You did very well with this.' He was basically giving me affirmation" (Participant #6).

A few participants in the positive experience group also talked about having epiphanic moments or moments of sudden insight. One participant described confronting a situation in which she felt overwhelmed: "So it was really an eye-opener for me, certainly in terms of looking at my desire to continue to do this as well as looking at my capabilities and where I needed to grow, not coming into this thinking I've worked in the church for [number] years, I can handle most things. Well, this was a real eye-opener" (Participant #1).

Two participants spoke about bringing personal information to supervision:

> I hadn't really grieved my younger brother's death. He died in [year], and I thought I had, and [in] one of our conversations … she drew it out of me. Since the day that I found out that he was going to die, I completely, I was devastated and completely fell apart. I hadn't cried that hard again until my session with her. It was like cleansing. (Participant #8)

In both the positive and the negative groups, participants saw differences in age, in denomination or religion, in educational or employment background, or in gender, sexual orientation, or culture as contributing to their positive or negative experiences. When some participants in the positive group spoke about these differences, they appeared to value the diversity and saw it as enriching their experiences. For example, one participant reported,

> I was worried about [not being Christian] when I started, but it ended up being a learning experience for the group as a whole, because we, rather than doing a lot of kind of biblical study, we did a lot more theological discussion, looking in more depth at kind of the meaning behind things, because we weren't focused just on the Christian milieu, we were talking in more, in kind of more general spiritual things. (Participant #7)

Other participants seemed impressed at how little diversity issues were problematic; one participant (#8) in the positive group said of her supervisor, "She has a very different sexual orientation and background than I do, so we couldn't be more opposite than any two people in the world. And I don't know, she was just wonderful."

Participants in both groups also cited a variety of personal factors, particularly those involving family of origin issues, as contributing to their experiences of supervision. One supervisee who had a positive experience reported that the supervisor was supportive of him while he was dealing with his father's terminal illness, and another participant in the positive group (#2) stated, "I was very nervous going into it, because the reason I left the church initially [number] years prior was because of clergy abuse, actually."

Participants in the positive supervisory experience group related a number of positive outcomes under the theme of personal growth, including personal insight and increased confidence and, less frequently, learning when to take risks. One participant (#2) stated, "I think conflict's always been hard for me. It's hard for a lot of women, I think, and I had to learn to, that I can do that." Another participant reported,

> There were a number of personal issues that came out as a result of CPE in regards to my familial relationships and with how ... I made choices and that in some ways I'm still exploring, in particular the interpersonal relationships and some of the behaviour patterns that I wasn't aware of. But going through the CPE experience where you do that self-reflective model helped me reflect not just on how I interacted with patients but how I interacted with my family as well. (Participant #7)

Participants in the positive group also reported growth in knowledge and skills, including one supervisee (#4), who said that the program "helped me to understand what my relationship to a patient was all about." Participants also reported gaining mentors and seeing the need for ongoing supervision as well as affirming a call to ministry or making a career change. A variant theme was the questioning of a call to ministry when confronted with the difficulty of the work.

Negative Group Results

In describing their experiences, supervisees in the negative group used words such as *critical, judgmental, not supportive, disrespectful, hostile, abusive,* and *enraged* (typical themes). One (#13) related, "The primary thing that comes up for me is disrespect, maybe even misogyny—a total lack of civility. It was an ongoing onslaught of criticism." Several participants mentioned working with a supervisor-in-training, and one participant stated, "It basically, in part at least, had to do with his lack of experience. I felt the person had potential of being a supervisor at some point, but I didn't feel that he really had the experience or the know-how or even the maturity. He really needed to grow a bit in the role of supervisor" (Participant #14).

Many supervisees in the negative group experienced their supervisors as not present, invested, able, or willing to listen. For example, one supervisee reported, "He was not interested in really doing supervision. I had a terrible time scheduling a meeting time with him because of his absences. I mean, not only was he gone for the vacation, but then he was out on Friday, he was out on Tuesday ... " (Participant #13).

In describing their interactions with their supervisors, a few participants in the negative group experienced their supervisors as threatening retaliation, as scapegoating, or as attempting to function as a counsellor in a way that did not respect their boundaries. One participant reported,

> I also felt a number of times as though rather than try to super-
> vise ministry, she was trying to be a counsellor to me. I've been
> through therapy a number of different times just for myself with
> my issues, and in fact I'm married to a counsellor. So it was the
> kind of thing, I saw what she was doing, I knew what she was
> doing, and she wasn't doing it all that well. (Participant #12)

A variant theme was feeling traumatized by the experience. One participant (#14) stated, "When I woke up the next morn-

ing, I literally felt like I had been raped." In addition, many participants in the negative group experienced their supervisors as being
involved in inappropriate sexual talk or behaviour. One reported,
"One of the inappropriate things my supervisor shared with our
group was 'You haven't heard anything until you have heard a nun
sexually please herself in the middle of the night.' He then went
on to describe more about this" (Participant #15). Another participant (#5) observed that the director of the program and the
associate supervisor "flirted with" students in the program, and a
third (#16) stated that her supervisor told her he had "a theology
of swearing." An additional variant theme was observing power
struggles: "I noticed some power struggles going on. If I were to
say something that he felt that he should have said, or I was getting into territory that he hadn't gone into yet in our discussion,
he would cut me off and say, 'I'm the supervisor here. You're not
the supervisor'" (Participant #15).

In the negative supervisory group, participants typically confronted their supervisors about behaviour that they considered
inappropriate or unfair. One participant, who reported the supervisor to the human relations department for a situation involving
sexual harassment, stated,

> I was stunned, and I told him when he, he was reaming me out
> and cussing me out, and I, I sat, and I looked him in the eye,
> and I said, "You are way off base, and you are totally inappro-
> priate, and you're out of line, and you're being abusive," and, of
> course, I knew, I was already in the system, so to speak, and I
> knew I had backup. (Participant #9)

Another participant, who was denied permission by her supervisor
to make a presentation to the family members of patients that had
been requested of her, said,

> I said to [name], I said, "I've given you two weeks' notice." She
> said, "I don't care." I said, "So what I hear you saying is that you

don't take pride in your interns being asked to do things. Is that what I'm hearing you say?" And she said, "You know you cannot miss your classes," and I said, "You mean to tell me, all the work that I've done, I cannot miss one class?" (Participant #10)

Typically, participants had a turning point when they experienced a negative response to confrontation. One participant who confronted a supervisor about a group experience said,

I don't remember exactly what happened, but there was something that was entirely inappropriate that happened in the group, and I went to him to complain, to say, "Look, this is not acceptable, you should've stepped in and told the person, you know, cool it off, and you didn't, and I really don't accept that," and he basically said to me, "Our program is built on criticism, and if you don't like it, tough." (Participant #13)

Two participants in the negative group reported being accused of inappropriate behaviour, which they denied. One participant (#15) reported being accused of a breach of confidentiality after discussing her CPE experience with her counsellor (without using patient or peer names), and the other participant (#10) was accused of lying in a verbatim (a report of a pastoral care interaction). She stated that her supervisor "took the paper, threw it across the table at me, and she said, 'This is ludicrous. I don't believe a word in it.'"

Participants in the negative group described experiencing a variety of emotional responses to these conflicts, most often feeling threatened but also feeling helpless, stressed out, or frustrated. One participant (#10) reported, "I mean, I was devastated, and that particular moment I realized that she was trying to get rid of me." Some responded by becoming more guarded, and some sought outside support from colleagues, clergy, a counsellor, or family members. For many participants, the conflicts remained unresolved, although one individual found a personal resolution, and one found "healing" in a subsequent CPE program.

As mentioned above, participants saw differences in age, in denomination or religion, in educational or employment background, or in gender, sexual orientation, or culture as a source of problems, as one supervisee stated: "I tend to be a little, somewhat more conservative. I see scripture as the inspired word of God and operate accordingly. She [supervisor] didn't share that particular view and had some different ideas and opinions, which did affect some of how ministry would be done and especially in this kind of setting" (Participant #12). Four participants' negative experiences involved relationships with supervisors-in-training (typical theme), at least three of whom were videotaping their supervision sessions for their own training purposes. One of these participants (#10) reported, "she supervised us by herself, which I have since then found out, at least in this CPE program, is never done when you're a first-year supervisor-in-training."

Some participants in the negative group mentioned backgrounds that included abuse or family alcoholism and saw them as connected to their negative experiences:

> I would ask her [supervisor] questions like "Where does it say in the Bible that Jesus treated people the way I feel I'm being treated in this group?" And she could never answer me. I said, "I don't understand how, where does this kind of treatment come from?" She also was very much aware of the abusive background from which I came, not only from my parents, but also from my former husband. I was a battered wife.
> (Participant #10)

Participants in the negative experiences group did report positive outcomes, although less frequently than those in the positive experiences group. The themes in this group were general learning and, for a few participants, increased personal insight and learning when to take risks. One participant said, in reference to her experience with her supervisor, "It was something I would never go through again or want to, but it gave me the opportunity to deal with a crisis and ... abuse and harassment in a healthier way than I'd ever done before" (Participant #9).

Triangulation with Quantitative Data

The positive and negative groups had mean scores on the three self-report instruments that were significantly different in the expected directions (see Table 9.4). Participants in the positive group rated their supervisors significantly higher than the scale norms on the attractive and interpersonally sensitive scales of the SSI, and on the bond subscale of the SWAI, and significantly lower than the scale norms on both the role conflict and the role ambiguity scales on the RCRAI, all $ps < .001$ (see Table 9.4). Participants in the negative group rated their supervisors significantly lower than the scale norms for the SSI and SWAI and significantly higher on both parts of the RCRAI, all $ps < .001$.

I compared each participant's scores on the three instruments (see Table 9.5) with their individual narrative data as an additional means of assessing triangulation and found striking consistencies between the qualitative and the quantitative results. In one instance, a participant (#3) in the positive group described his supervisor's style as collegial, adding, "He really worked to get his point across without appearing to be 'I'm the boss, I'm the supervisor.'" This participant rated his supervisor very highly on both the interpersonally sensitive and the attractiveness scales of the SSI (more than one SD above the normative means). Another supervisee (#4) in the positive group scored her supervisor well above the normative means on attractiveness and interpersonal sensitivity and reported, "it was a very easy relationship in that I felt very comfortable. I learned very quickly what sacred space was all about. He was someone that was, and I'm not sure what the chemistry was that kind of allowed that relationship to develop quickly, but I had ... I just felt that I could pretty well open up with him." In contrast, a participant (#10) in the negative group who rated her supervisor extremely poorly on both attractiveness and interpersonal sensitivity, three to four standard deviations

Table 9.4

Comparison of Means and Standard Deviations between the Current Sample and the Normative Means

	SSI		RCRAI		SWAI-T
	AT	IS	RC	RA	
Negative group					
M	2.93	3.03	2.81	3.74	100.75
SD	1.43	1.59	.88	.81	34.28
Z -17.83	-19.83	21.00	23.00	-32.27	
p	.00	.00	.00	.00	.00
ρ^2	.98	.98	.98	.99	.99
Positive Group					
M	6.00	6.36	1.25	1.63	222.25
SD	.53	.29	.21	.42	12.28
Z 5.97	7.92	-5.00	-7.14	9.06	
p	.00	.00	.00	.00	.00
ρ^2	.81	.89	.75	.86	.91
Normative Data					
M	5.23	5.41	1.55	2.13	195.62
SD	1.09	.98	.54	.66	30.41

SSI = Supervisory Styles Inventory (Friedlander & Ward, 1984); AT = attractive scale; IS = interpersonally sensitive scale. RCRAI = Role Conflict Role Ambiguity Inventory (Olk & Friedlander, 1992); RC = role conflict scale; RA = role ambiguity scale; SWAI-T = Supervisory Working Alliance-Trainee version (Bahrick, 1989).

below the normative means, described the supervisor by saying, "She was not what I would call an inviting kind of person" and "She treated me like dirt."

On the RCRAI, all but one participant in the positive group had scores that were below the norm (2.13) on role ambiguity (Olk & Friedlander, 1992). One participant in this group,

Table 9.5
Participants' Scores on the Self-Report Measures

Participant	SWAI				SSI RCRAI			
	Goal	Task	Bond	Total	AT	IS	RC	RA
Positive Experience Group								
1	65	58	78	201	5.71	6.25	1.6	2.45
2	81	76	82	239	7.00	6.50	1.3	1.68
3	74	72	80	226	6.57	6.88	1.4	1.26
4	76	69	74	219	6.00	6.13	1.1	1.32
5	68	69	80	217	5.57	6.63	1.4	1.95
6	77	73	68	218	5.43	6.38	1.0	1.26
7	71	68	81	220	6.00	6.00	1.2	1.74
8	81	76	81	238	5.71	6.13	1.0	1.37
Negative Experience Group								
9	37	35	34	106	2.14	2.63	3.4	3.58
10	21	21	27	69	1.14	1.00	1.8	4.58
11	31	28	29	88	4.43	4.38	1.8	3.47
12	36	33	39	108	3.85	4.63	2.3	1.95
13	14	20	13	47	1.43	1.00	4.0	4.26
14	56	41	65	162	4.71	5.00	3.3	3.89
15	40	32	37	109	1.86	2.13	3.7	4.16
16	43	28	46	117	3.86	3.50	2.2	4.00

Note: SWAI-T = Supervisory Working Alliance-Trainee version (Bahrick, 1989), range = 36 – 252, subscales range from 1 - 7; SSI = Supervisory Styles Inventory (Friedlander & Ward, 1984); each scale ranges from 1 - 7, AT = attractive scale, IS = interpersonally sensitive scale; RCRAI = Role Conflict and Role Ambiguity Inventory (Olk & Friedlander, 1992), RC = role conflict scale, RA = role ambiguity scale; each scale ranges from 1 - 5.

whose role ambiguity score (1.32) was one standard deviation below the normative mean (i.e., indicating low ambiguity), spoke about learning what to expect as time went on: "And the more I was within the CPE studying, the more comfortable I was that realizing that this was a safe place to let down a lot of things, talk about a lot of things that I had pretty well filed away" (Participant #4).

In contrast, participants in the negative experience group had scores above the norm for role ambiguity, and all but one had scores that were at least two standard deviations above the normative mean. One participant (#16) reported, "It was just really unclear what his expectations were for us, in what we should be doing. He'd just say, 'Well, go do ministry.'" This participant's role ambiguity score, 4.00, was more than two standard deviations above the normative mean.

One aspect of role conflict involves the supervisee expecting to perform in an expert role but simultaneously not being allowed the freedom by the supervisor to decide how to do the work. All members of the positive experience group had role conflict scores below the normative mean of 1.55 (Olk & Friedlander, 1992). Two members (#4 and #8) in this group reported being unable to recall any conflicts with their supervisors; their role conflict scores (1.1 and 1.0, respectively) were more than one standard deviation below the normative mean of 1.55 (Olk & Friedlander), indicating very low role conflict. (Scores on the role conflict scale range from 1 to 7, with 1 as the lowest possible score.) Another participant (whose score of 1.0 also was more than one standard deviation below the normative mean) described conceding to his supervisor about theoretical orientation. He reported, "And so I simply said to the supervisor, 'Is this your Torah, or is this the Torah of CPE?' and he said, 'It's the Torah of CPE.' I said, 'All right.' That was it" (Participant #6).

On the other hand, all members of the negative group had role conflict scores above the normative mean; six members of this group had scores at least one standard deviation above the normative mean, reflecting high role conflict. One member of this group reported,

It was really weird, because at the very beginning he gave a pep talk to the entire group, because he was the head of the entire department, about how we should take risks and try things. And that he could, if something went wrong, he would just say, "Oh, they're in training blah, blah, blah." So I really took that to heart and really tried things and did things that I wasn't comfortable in doing just because I wanted to see, you know, how it'd go. But then when I did that he became very angry. (Participant #13)

This participant's score (4.00) was more than three standard deviations above the normative mean.

Supervisory Working Alliance

The bond subscale of the SWAI refers to the perceived emotional closeness between supervisor and supervisee. In comparison with the normative means (Ladany, Ellis, & Friedlander, 1999), the negative group was significantly lower, $Z = -32.27$, $p < .0001$, `$r^2$ = .99, and the positive group was significantly higher, $Z = 9.06$, $p < .0001$, `r^2 = .91.

One participant (#13) in the negative group described her relationship with her supervisor by saying, "The primary thing that comes up for me is disrespect, maybe even misogyny—total lack of civility." This participant's score was 13, more than three standard deviations below the normative mean for the bond subscale, 65.91 (Ladany, Ellis, & Friedlander, 1999).

On the other hand, a participant (#2) in the positive group, whose score was more than one standard deviation above the normative mean, stated, "I really trusted him implicitly, ... and I trusted that he trusted us."

The agreement on tasks subscale focuses on a common understanding of how supervision should be used. A participant in the positive group, whose score was nearly one standard deviation above the previously published normative mean, 65.96 (Ladany, Ellis, & Friedlander, 1999), reported that, although there was no explicit agreement on how to approach supervision, the supervisee appreciated the latitude: "I just took the steps that I needed to take in that process, and I never felt pushed by him in any way, which really helped me a lot because I was able to open up to the experience, as I felt ready to do that" (Participant #2).

The agreement on goals subscale has to do with whether both parties have the same goal for the supervision and see supervision as a means of reaching that goal. One member (#10) of the negative group stated, "My supervision time was a total waste of time." This participant's score was more than three standard deviations below the normative mean for this scale, 64.52 (Ladany, Ellis, & Friedlander, 1999).

Discussion

The results of this study reinforce the centrality of the helping relationship that supervision can be highlighted by the contrast between participants' positive and negative experiences in CPE supervision. Those who reported positive supervisory relationships testified to the healing power of the relationship—one participant who had experienced clergy abuse many years previously resumed her journey toward ordained ministry. However, participants who had negative supervisory experiences reported experiencing significant pain and traumatization.

This finding is consistent with results reported in the supervision literature in psychology (Bernard & Goodyear, 2003; Bordin, 1983; Efstation, Patton, & Kardash, 1990; Ekstein & Wallerstein, 1972; Ladany, Friedlander, & Nelson, 2005; Mueller & Kell, 1972). It also has a high degree of internal consistency, as demonstrated by the triangulation reported previously as well as by the opposing terms used by participants in the two groups to detail their relationships with their supervisors and to describe their supervisors as professionals and as people.

The descriptions by participants in the positive group were far more consistent with each other than were the descriptions by participants in the negative group. For example, all participants in the positive group saw the supervisor as competent, experienced, knowledgeable, sharp, or astute, but supervisees in the negative group reported widely varying perceptions of their supervisors. This result echoes the report of McCarthy, Kulakowski, and Kenfield (1994), who described the responses of participants regarding the least helpful aspects of supervision as "more idiosyncratic" (p. 179) than their reports of helpful supervision. I was reminded of Tolstoy's (1968) comment "All happy families resemble each other; every unhappy family is unhappy in its own way" (p. 3).

Participants in both groups mentioned probing of personal issues by supervisors, often during group sessions. Within the context of a positive supervisory relationship, this probing was experienced as helpful, but in the context of a negative supervisor relationship participants experienced it as painful and intrusive. It may be that, because the focus in CPE is on formation for ministry, rather than on training students to do therapy, as in the mental health disciplines, CPE supervisors may feel free to pursue a range of personal issues in a way that psychotherapy supervisors do not unless these issues are seen as having a direct impact on the therapy that the trainee is doing (Bernard & Goodyear, 2003).

CPE supervision also occurs within the context of a program in which the supervisor typically has multiple roles, such as group supervision, experiential groups, and individual supervision. Participants in the negative group had difficulty separating their experiences of their supervisors in these multiple roles, with the interesting exception of one participant who had a different supervisor for individual and group supervision. This participant reported fewer negative consequences of supervision and in fact seemed to have derived more benefits from the overall CPE experience than most other participants in the negative group. This role confusion makes it difficult to determine the source of an individual's problems in CPE supervision, because a negative experience in individual supervision may lead the supervisee to act in ways that alienate him or her from the peer group and result in difficulties in the experiential group. A second possibility is that the supervisor may be influenced in his or her perceptions of the supervisee by a group that has scapegoated the supervisee. A third possibility is that a negative experience in individual supervision may lead the supervisor to treat the supervisee in ways that contribute to difficulties within the group. And a fourth possibility is that a supervisee's negative experience in either group supervision or the experiential group may influence his or her reaction to the individual supervisor.

Finally, more than half the participants in the negative group saw their supervisors as involved in inappropriate sexual talk or behaviour and as failing to limit inappropriate sexual talk within the group. At least two participants noted that if the behaviour or talk that they observed happened in a business setting it would clearly be third-party sexual harassment. Although future research will need to focus on this point, it may be that, just as some religious leaders in the past have seen themselves as being exempt from concerns about sexual abuse, some CPE supervisors may not be aware that their behaviour is viewed as sexual harassment.

Limitations and Strengths
Participants in this study were not randomly selected since this was a qualitative investigation, and due to the reliance on self-selection there may have been sampling bias. Perhaps people who had extreme difficulty coping with a negative CPE experience did not respond to the call for volunteers. Alternatively, those who had negative experiences may have been more eager than those who had positive experiences to discuss them with the investigator. Diversity, in particular ethnic diversity, was limited in this small sample. Although the results do not speak to the prevalence of positive and negative supervisory experiences in CPE, they do provide guidance for subsequent research along these lines.

This was a retrospective study that relied on self-reporting, which raises the possibility that participants' memories may have been faulty. Other limitations included the small sample, which lacked racial diversity, included more women than men, and thus may not have been representative. The judges were all women, so it is possible that they made decisions differently than a mixed group might have. The biases of the investigator might have influenced the study, either because of her exclusively negative memories or because of overcompensation in the other direction. Due to the limitations imposed by confidentiality, it was not possible to determine how long ago the supervisors were trained, which is unfortunate because of the gradual modification of supervision over the years (Gleason, 1993; VandeCreek, personal communication, April 29, 2002). The study also did not include behavioural data. Because of time limitations, the study did not address the question of whether supervisees who had negative experiences eventually came to regard them as positive and vice versa. Further, it is impossible to know how the interviews may have been affected by social desirability or by having the participants fill out the questionnaires prior to being interviewed.

Finally, the study did not speak to the perspectives of supervisors who were involved in the experiences described by participants. The veracity of the supervisees' experiences thus cannot be determined. The study was phenomenological, and the narrative data only represented a single party in the supervisory dyad.

On the other hand, the triangulation provided strong support for the consistency of the results, as did the internal consistency of the positive and negative groups and the clear differentiation between the two groups. Participant feedback also supported the results of the study. The use of two auditors provided internal checking for the judges and the investigator, and the initial interviews were examined for bias, with none noted.

Implications for Practice
In light of the fact that more than half of the participants in the negative group reported a traumatic personal history, the following comment from Nelson and Friedlander is particularly poignant:

If the supervisor responds to the supervisee in a way that reen-
acts the supervisee's painful relationship with prior authority
figures, the supervisee may become resistant and refuse to
cooperate. Thus, it behooves supervisors to anticipate what
impasses could occur, to avoid what is possible to avoid, and to
plan for creatively addressing the inevitable conflicts, large or
small, that will come up. (2001, p. 393)

I agree with Nelson and Friedlander that the responsibility for
anticipating difficulties, avoiding them to the extent possible, and
taking the lead in addressing those that cannot be avoided lies
with the supervisor as the person with more power in the situation. At the beginning of this chapter, I noted that in the Bible the
notion of a helper is connected with questions of power and that,
when helping relationships are considered, including the supervisory relationship, the question of power must be attended to.
I would argue that the person with the most power also has the
most responsibility for resolving difficulties.

It seemed that negative experiences tended to become problematic early in supervision, which suggests the importance of CPE
supervisors seeking consultation as soon as they become aware of
problems in their relationships with students. The isolated nature
of many CPE sites and the fact that many have only one supervisor may make this difficult, but the extra effort might prevent distress for supervisees as well as supervisors. Given that supervisees
in the present study identified the contribution to their difficulties
of personal differences in the areas of religious outlook, age, culture, gender, and sexual orientation from either the supervisor or
the rest of the group, supervisors may wish to exercise particular
care when such differences are part of a supervisory relationship.

The fact that many of the negative experiences involved
supervisors-in-training (SITs) suggests that it could be important to provide SITs with an independent avenue for consultation outside the evaluation process so that they might be quicker
in seeking assistance. SITs may be in a particularly vulnerable

position, with a significant amount of responsibility but less power than the full supervisors who have much to say about their careers. It also could be helpful to provide SITs with training on how to establish an effective supervisory working alliance and on how to respond to ruptures in the alliance, as suggested by Nelson and Friedlander (2001).

Conclusion

I said at the beginning of this chapter that one of my theological assumptions is that relationships can take us beyond ourselves, let us do more and better than we could alone—or bind us and make it impossible for us to do our best work. The supervisory helping relationships that I was privileged to learn about have reinforced that assumption. Participants for whom the supervisory relationship was indeed a helping one grew in ways that they could not have anticipated and clearly valued what they had learned. Unfortunately, participants who experienced negative supervisory relationships testified to the difficulties that such relationships create. Yet even in the distorted relationships, growth for the supervisee often took place, sometimes apparently in spite of the relationship rather than because of it.

References

Bahrick, A. S. (1990). Role induction for counselor trainees: Effects on the supervisory working alliance. *Dissertation Abstracts International, 51,* 1484B. (University Microfilms No. 90-14, 392).

Bernard, J. M., & Goodyear, R. K. (2003). *Fundamentals of clinical supervision.* Needham Heights, MA: Allyn & Bacon.

Bordin, E. S. (1983). A working alliance based model of supervision. *The Counseling Psychologist, 11,* 35–41.

Corbin, J., & Strauss, A. L. (1990). *Basics of qualitative research: Grounded theory procedures and techniques.* Thousand Oaks, CA: Sage.

Cutting, M. L. (2007). Psychology clinical supervision research: Possible contributions to CPE supervision. *Reflective Practice, 27,* 120–135.

Cutting, M. L., & Friedlander, M. L. (2008). Supervisees' positive and negative experiences in clinical pastoral education. In T. S. J. O'Connor, C. Lashmar, & E. Meakes (Eds.), *The spiritual care giver's guide* (pp. 169-192). Waterloo, ON: CAPPESWONT/Waterloo Lutheran Seminary.

Eckstein, R., & Wallerstein, R. (1972). *The teaching and learning of psychotherapy* (2nd Ed.). New York: International Universities Press.

Efstation, J. F., Patton, M. J., & Kardash, C. M. (1990). Measuring the working alliance in counselor supervision. *Journal of Counseling Psychology, 37,* 322–329.

Ellis, M. V., Russin, A., & Deihl, L. M. (2003, August). *Dimensionality of the supervisory working alliance: Supervisees' perceptions.* Poster paper presented at the meeting of the American Psychological Association, Toronto.

Ellis, M. V., Swagler, M. A., & Beck, M. (2000, August). Harmful clinical supervision from the supervisee's perspective: Survival, recourses, and prevention. In N. Ladany & M. V. Ellis (Co-Chairs), *Hot topics in supervision and training, 2000.* Roundtable presented at the meeting of the American Psychological Association, Washington, DC.

Fitchett, G., & Johnson, M. (2001). Sexual contact in the CPE supervisor-student relationship. *Journal of Supervision and Training in Ministry, 21,* 90–112.

Friedlander, M. L., & Ward, L. G. (1984). Development and validation of the Supervisory Styles Inventory. *Journal of Counseling Psychology, 31,* 541–557.

Gleason, J. J. (1993). Guest editorial: The impact of feminism on clinical pastoral education. *Journal of Pastoral Care, 52,* 3-6.

Haase, R. F., & Ellis, M. V. (1987). Multivariate analysis of variance. *Quantitative Foundations of Counseling Psychology Research* [Special issue]. *Journal of Counseling Psychology, 34,* 404–413.

Haase, R. F., Ellis, M. V., & Ladany, N. (1989). Multiple criteria for evaluating the magnitude of experimental effects. *Journal of Counseling Psychology, 36,* 511–516.

Herbert, J. T., Ward, T. J., & Hemlick, L. M. (1995). Confirmatory factor analysis of the Supervisory Styles Inventory and the Revised Supervision Questionnaire. *Rehabilitation Counseling Bulletin, 38,* 334–349.

Hill, C. E., Thompson, B. J., & Williams, E. N. (1997). A guide to conducting consensual qualitative research. *The Counseling Psychologist, 25,* 517–572.

Holland, B. S., & Copenhaver, M. D. (1988). Improved Bonferroni-type multiple testing procedures. *Psychological Bulletin, 104,* 145–149.

Horvath, A. O., & Greenberg, L. S. (1986). The development of the Working Alliance Inventory. In L. S. Greenberg & W. M. Pinsof (Eds.), *The psycho-therapeutic process: A research handbook* (pp. 529–556). New York: Guilford.

Ladany, N., Brittan-Powell, C. S., & Pannu, R. K. (1997). The influence of supervisory racial identity interaction and racial matching on the supervisory working alliance and supervisee multicultural competence. *Counselor Education and Supervision, 36,* 284–304.

Ladany, N., Ellis, M. V., & Friedlander, M. L. (1999). The supervisory working alliance, trainee self-efficacy, and satisfaction. *Journal of Counseling & Development, 77,* 447–455.

Ladany, N., & Friedlander, M. (1995). The relationship between the supervisory working alliance and trainees' experiences of role conflict and role ambiguity. *Counselor Education and Supervision, 34,* 220–231.

Ladany, N., Friedlander, M. L., & Nelson, M. L. (2005). *Critical events in psychotherapy supervision: An interpersonal approach.* Washington, DC: American Psychological Association.

Ladany, N., & Lehrman-Waterman, D. E. (1999). The content and frequency of supervisor self-disclosures and their relationship to supervisory style and the supervisory working alliance. *Counselor Education and Supervision, 38,* 143–160.

McCarthy, P., Kulakowski, D., & Kenfield, J. A. (1994). Clinical supervision practices of licensed psychologists. *Professional Psychology: Research and Practice, 25,* 177–181.

Mueller, W. J., & Kell, B. L. (1972). *Coping with conflict: Supervising counselors and psychotherapists.* Englewood, NY: Prentice-Hall.

Nelson, M. L., & Friedlander, M. L. (2001). A close look at conflictual supervisory relationships: The trainee's perspective. *Journal of Counseling Psychology, 48,* 384–395.

Olk, M. E., & Friedlander, M. L. (1992). Trainees' experience of role conflict and role ambiguity in supervisory relationships. *Journal of Counseling Psychology, 39,* 389–397.

Prieto, L. R. (1998). Practicum class supervision in CACREP-accredited counselor training programs. *Counselor Education and Supervision, 38,* 113–123.

Ramos-Sanchez, L., Esnil, E., Goodwin, A., Riggs, S., Touster, L. O., Wright, L. K., et al. (2002). Negative supervisory events: Effects on supervision satisfaction and supervisory alliance. *Professional Psychology: Research and Practice, 33,* 197–202.

Reeves, D., Culbreth, J. R., & Greene, A. (1997). Effect of sex, age, and education level on the supervisory styles of substance abuse counselor supervisors. *Journal of Alcohol and Drug Education, 43,* 76–86.

Stiles, W. B. (1993). Quality control in qualitative research. *Clinical Psychology Review, 13,* 593–618.

Tolstoy, L. N. (1968). *Anna Karenin* (L. Wiener, Trans. and Ed.). New York: AMS Press.

Usher, C. H., & Borders, L. D. (1993). Practicing counselors' preferences for supervisory style and supervisory emphasis. *Counselor Education and Supervision, 33,* 66–79.

VandeCreek, L., & Glockner, M. (1993). Do gender issues affect clinical pastoral education supervision? *Journal of Pastoral Care, 47,* 253–262.

Veach, P. M. (2001). Conflict and counterproductivity in supervision:When relationships are less than ideal: Comment on Nelson and Friedlander (2001) and Gray et al. (2001). *Journal of Counseling Psychology, 48,* 396–400.

Worthen, V., & McNeill, B. W. (1996). A phenomenological investigation of "good" supervision events. *Journal of Counseling Psychology, 43,* 25–34.

Appendix A

Opening Questions

1. "Where are you now in your ... training [for ministry], or have you completed your degree?"
2. "How long ago was the supervision experience that you will be talking about?"
3. Where were you in your training for ministry at that time?
4. At what kind of site was the CPE program based (general hospital, prison, psychiatric hospital, etc.)?
5. Did the experience involve primarily one supervision session, or was it an ongoing experience?
6. Did the experience involve one-on-one supervision or group supervision?
7. How many units of CPE had you completed prior to this one?
8. How many units of CPE have you completed since this one?

Questions about Supervision

1. "Can you describe in as much detail as possible your relationship with your [CPE] supervisor? How would you describe the supervisor? How would you describe yourself in relation to the supervisor?"
2. "Can you describe a *critical* incident or incidents, or a turning point that occurred with your supervisor that resulted in your feeling [either especially positive or especially] negative about the experience?" Or was there an incident or incidents that represent why you felt especially positive or negative, or was it the experience as a whole?
3. "What factors seemed to contribute to this experience? (personal, interpersonal, client, institutional," other).
4. Did your experience in the CPE group have an impact on the supervisory experience? How did the group members respond to you and to the supervisor? If there was a conflict, did group members side with you or with the supervisor?

5. "Did the experience in any way impede or assist your progress through CPE? If so, how?" How has that supervisory experience affected you professionally?

6. How has that supervisory experience affected you personally?

7. Were there any conflicts with your supervisor? If so, "Did you resolve the conflict directly with the supervisor at any point? How did that take place? [If relevant: What factors seemed to influence the resolution?] Did the supervisor do anything or could the supervisor have done anything to help the situation? If so, what? Have you resolved the conflict for yourself without the participation of the supervisor? If so, what factors have contributed to that resolution?"

8. "Have any positive benefits emerged from the situation?"

9. "Is there anything else you would like to tell me that you haven't mentioned?"

Note: The interview questions in quotation marks were taken from Nelson and Friedlander (2001, p. 395).

X

The Pastorate as Helping Relationship[1]

Bradley T. Morrison

Spiritual care is rapidly replacing pastoral care in institutional settings. While the assumptions of spiritual counselling may be a better fit for hospitals, nursing homes, and counselling centres, the pastoral paradigm remains the better fit for congregational care. This chapter argues that the pastoral paradigm provides a productive framework for addressing developments in the field of pastoral care and congregational ministry. The chapter correlates the psychotherapy outcome research of the common factors model with features of the pastoral paradigm to identify the ways in which the pastoral paradigm leverages the relational and communal dimensions of congregational life. The pastorate is a helping relationship.

Challenging the Pastoral Paradigm

The newly expanded *Dictionary of Pastoral Care and Counseling* (Hunter, 2005) includes a set of essays analyzing developments in the field since the dictionary's publication 20 years ago. A major trend in clinical and institutional contexts has been to rename pastoral counselling, spiritual counselling (Association for Clinical

Pastoral Education, 2001). This trend recognizes that the word *pastoral* may not adequately describe the faith-based care offered in institutional contexts. Pastoral categories do not necessarily apply in institutional helping relationships. The helper or helpee may not belong to a pastorate. Even if one is pastor or parishioner, this fact may not inform the helping process.

VanKatwyk (2002) argues that the turn to a spiritual paradigm creates an identity crisis in pastoral care and counselling. With the secularization of society, most people seek their care outside the church. The concept of a pastorate becomes irrelevant to the giving and receiving of faith-based care in institutional settings. Increasingly, pastoral counsellors are trained in non-congregational contexts with no operative pastoral relationship. Ironically, the ideal pastoral client is located apart from the congregational context—often in counselling centres or institutional settings. Consequently, the ideal pastoral helping relationship is framed in clinical or institutional terms.

In addition to the fault lines developing between spiritual and pastoral care, the adequacy of individual-based interventions is being questioned. In her article in the expanded edition of the *Dictionary of Pastoral Care and Counseling*, Miller-McLemore warns that pastoral care and counselling "consume significant resources to reach a relatively small population in need" (2005, p. 1378). She is not alone in challenging our field to make pastoral theology "public theology" with societal interventions. Within this emerging model, training programs need to equip pastoral caregivers and counsellors for social and public policy ministry beyond the congregation's walls.

In the expanded dictionary, Townsend notes that formation and integration of pastoral identity are no longer limited to pastors or lay specialists. Rather, the move is away from "teaching basic clinical skills to ministers ... and instead [teaching] basic ministry and theological reflection skills to clinicians" (2005, p. 1411). Training and formation of pastoral caregivers and counsellors are described as an "integrative bridge discipline" (p. 1410)

that holds together ministry and clinical practice. The art of theological reflection becomes a resource for anyone involved in care
or social action.

These challenges recognize the potential of congregations for
ministry beyond the church's walls. Even though pastoral care and
counselling are increasingly located in clinical and institutional
contexts, focusing on societal and public interventions, and equip-
ping community leaders outside ecclesial structures, the health
of congregations themselves must remain a priority or at least a
consideration. The importance of congregations as an engine for
pastoral theology cannot be underestimated or reduced to an aux-
iliary function or role. Pastoral theology must not overlook the
congregation's fundamental need for communal self-care to sus-
tain it for broader ministry. The shift in pastoral care from private
to public focus, individual to societal interventions, and clergy to
laity-based training in a pluralistic society need not undermine
congregational-based care and counselling. On the contrary, the
pastoral paradigm offers theological and ethical resources necessary to satisfy these public, social, and lay shifts in our discipline—
perhaps in ways inaccessible to the spirituality paradigm.

The Pastoral Paradigm

The pastoral paradigm arises from a well-established biblical narrative: the care of God's children is assigned to a shepherd named
David (1 Samuel 16). The image of shepherd and sheep describes
the Hebrew people, and this image continues into the gospel narratives, where Jesus is described as shepherd to God's children.
The pastoral paradigm is the framework for biblical community,
and through the ages the Christian Church has described itself as
pastorate.

The pastoral paradigm has its fullest expression as pastoral community. The pastorate is a community. Contemporary usage of the
word *pastoral* has lost sight of this communal dimension. Pastoral

is often reduced to a description of what a pastor does. Too often pastoral is merely a virtue, synonymous with the caring qualities befitting a pastor. The biblical narration of the pastoral paradigm, however, encompasses more than the character of the shepherd or the needs of the sheep. Pastoral is not reduced to the relationship of the shepherd to the sheep.[2] Pastoral refers to an entire community or society and the matrix of pastoral relationships therein: pastor, parishioner, stranger, and God—and the landscape that they inhabit. These relationships are pastoral, not because of some quality or virtue, but because they are expressions of a particular community: namely, the human pastorate.

The pastorate or congregation is a form of community. The word *community* derives from the word *common,* which in turn derives from the Latin *com-* "together" and *munis* "bound," "under service," which derives from *munus* "gift," "service," "duty" and is related to *munire* "to wall around," from *murus* "wall" (*The Compact Oxford English Dictionary,* 1991). Put simply, community is the gathering together of gifts and services toward a common purpose or common good.[3] In the pastoral community, the gathering together of gifts and services toward a common good is informed by the pastoral paradigm. People and their gifts are shepherded on God's behalf, with an explicit claim that these people and gifts belong first to God.

The pastoral paradigm claims God to be a communal participant. God participates in the gathering of gifts and services; moreover, God's communal participation interprets communal goods through a theological aim. The pastoral community claims that goods originate from God, making them gifts. As gifts, they are expressions of God's grace. In general, creation and its life-giving and -sustaining power are interpreted as God's gifts. These divine gifts and services to humanity are, in turn, gathered by the community and symbolically offered back to God as gifts and services.

An economy arises in any community. The word *economy,* from *eco* "household" and *nomos* "to manage or control," is the management of gifts and services toward a common purpose or good. In the pastoral economy, the human other is understood to be a gift from God; moreover, the self is understood as a gift from God. Communal ethics arise from the economy or stewardship of this gift.[4] The ethos of self and other as gift is recognized and sustained in the pastorate through the equitable management of communal gifts and services. The pastorate understands the aetiology of human suffering to arise from the mismanagement of this human ethos. The mismanagement is a forgetting of humanity's ethos as gift.

This brings us to pastoral care and counselling. Care and counsel in the pastoral economy are a response to this human suffering. Or, to borrow from Foucault (1988), pastoral care is a *technē* of the self and other. The helping relationship in the pastoral economy is a service aimed at countering the forgetting of human ethos. Pastoral care responds to human suffering and contributes to the common good by remembering and reminding others of God's gift economy. Meech (2006) argues that community, in tending to human suffering, uncovers the ways in which the ethical aim and common good remain unfulfilled. Pastoral care and counselling, responding to human suffering, have a similar uncovering or revelatory effect that can inform public policy and debate on what constitutes the just society.

Pastoral Anthropology

The pastoral paradigm differs from the spiritual paradigm in terms of anthropology. The spiritual paradigm sees human beings as ontologically marked (ethos)—people are categorically, by nature, receptive to an encounter with God. Compare the Association for Clinical Pastoral Education's 2001 white paper, which describes spirit as the "natural dimension of every person" (p. 82) and describes spiritual care as the treatment of a "specific dimension of a person" (cf. Townsend, 2005, p. 1407). Some questions arise. Can one be free not to be spiritual if spirit is a natural dimension of every person? Can one choose not to be spiritual if spiritual identity is an ontological imperative? Or, drawing on Taylor's (2007) analysis of Western culture's process of secularization, is this definition of spirituality as an ontological imperative counterintuitive given secular society's core values of personal freedom, choice, and self-determination?

The pastoral paradigm, however, frames its anthropology within a human community that makes a claim to God's participation. One is free to choose participation in that community's economy. The pastoral community's participants may choose to relate to communal participants and non-participants. The pastoral paradigm is built upon the concept of relationship rather than the individual's ontological or naturalist status, leaving space for ontological and moral differences to be honoured. As Taylor's (2007) analysis of secularization points out, however, modern society has come to reject the authoritarian claims—and even abuses—that have marked the pastoral paradigm's relationships.

Congregation as Worshipping Community

The word *congregation* itself reflects this unsavoury authoritarianism of the pastoral paradigm. Congregation, deriving from the Latin *gregare* "herd (of livestock)," calls to mind the sheepherder or animal husbandry image. Acknowledging the historical and problematic character of this paradigm's language, I recognize the terms "pastorate," "pastoral community," and "congregation" to refer interchangeably to the context out of which the pastoral helping relationship arises.

Of all the unique characteristics that mark the pastorate or congregation, the practice of corporate worship is fundamental. In the pastoral paradigm, the gathering of communal gifts and services includes the specific practice of worshipping God. In worship, the community's gathered gifts and services are symbolically offered to God and for God's purposes. This worship is a public, corporate act that distinguishes it from other communities. Yes, other institutions such as hospitals and nursing homes include public, corporate worship in their activities. Even institutions involved in counselling—seminaries and pastoral counselling centres—may participate in corporate worship. But unlike congregations, a health care community or academic community can remain as such apart from expressing faith in God through corporate worship.

I argue that public, corporate worship is the defining characteristic of a congregation. Worship liturgy and ritual enact the remembering of God's presence and participation in communal life. Keeping with the pastoral paradigm, worship claims God as a participant. Worship is understood to be an encounter with God. Herein is the unique difference that contextualizes the helping relationship in the pastorate. The congregation is built around the public, corporate claim that God is encountered—unlike clinical and institutional contexts, where any alleged encounter with God may remain a private, individual claim exempt from public, corporate discourse, argumentation, and conflict of convictions.

In the congregational context, the individual's alleged encounter with God must take into account those of others in the faith community—not necessarily the case in other helping institutions. As well, the public dimension of worship allows the individual's integration of one's life experience with the alleged encounter with God. In the clinical context, the encounter with God may be discussed in the helping relationship; however, that encounter with God is not intentionally shared corporately, beyond the helper and helpee. The clinic's or institution's public, corporate ethos is not established in or sustained by a public, corporate encounter with God in worship.

Perhaps the spirituality paradigm seems better suited to clinical and institutional settings because the spirituality paradigm is what remains when the pastoral paradigm is divested of corporate worship and public discourse on encounters with God.

The Helping Relationship

Having distinguished between pastoral and non-pastoral community, as well as between the pastoral paradigm and the spirituality paradigm, it remains possible to correlate social science models of the helping relationship with that of the pastoral paradigm. I have chosen the common factors model to represent the social science literature because of its emphasis on the helping relationship in successful therapeutic outcomes.

The common factors model developed out of the debate on evidenced-based practice in counselling psychology (Levant, 2004; Sprenkle & Blow, 2004). The common factors literature identifies four primary factors impacting therapeutic outcome: extra-therapeutic factors, relationship factors, hope and expectancy, and models and techniques (Lambert & Barley, 2002; Norcross, 2002).

Extra-therapeutic factors refer to the client's functioning: client strengths, talents, unique coping skills, resiliency, support system, concept of and readiness for change, presenting problem, and pre-treatment changes. Relationship factors refer to the therapist's functioning: therapist ability to join and develop alliance, caring, empathic ability, validation and support, structuring skills, and use of identity. Hope and expectancy factors refer to the client's capacity for hope: the client's pre-existing hope regarding the presenting problem, expectation that change is possible, and openness to the therapist's hope. Models and techniques refer to the therapist's ability to make interventions related to a specific helping model, skill set, and treatment selection.

Lambert and Barkley (2002) found that extra-therapeutic factors and relationship factors account for the majority of positive therapeutic outcomes. Model and technique factors account for a relatively minor portion of positive therapeutic outcomes. Figure 10.1 organizes these common factors along a double axis: (1) a horizontal axis moving from therapist regard for other to therapist use of self, and (2) a vertical axis moving from therapeutic content to process. The result is a quadrant model of therapeutic factors. In this model, Quadrant I underscores that the helping relationship can reach beyond itself, having recourse to extra-therapeutic factors such as social and public policy.

Praxis and Bridging Method

Townsend (2005, p. 1410) describes pastoral theology as an integrative bridge discipline, where theological method correlates or holds together counselling practice and religious care. The distance to be bridged is short, but that distance has an unknown depth. The double axis in Figure 10.1 provides the structure for a bridge that connects pastoral praxis with the social science literature on the helping relationship. Figure 10.2 organizes pastoral praxis into quadrants that correspond to the common factors literature. A triangle at the centre symbolizes God's presence (cf. Peterson, 1987) in the helping relationship—a factor not accounted for in the social science paradigm but fundamental to the pastoral paradigm's claim to God's communal participation.

The overlap between the common factors model and pastoral practice centres on the economy of relationship and action—both therapeutic and pastoral. A translation of common factors language into pastoral language allows for some differences in emphasis. For example, extra-therapeutic client factors applied to the pastoral relationship can refer to parishioner functioning beyond congregational life; however, this quadrant of factors also

Figure 10.1

Factors contributing to client success in treatment

		Therapist's regard for other	Therapist's use of self
Therapeutic	**process**	I EXTRA-THERAPEUTIC FACTORS *(Client's functioning)*	II RELATIONSHIP FACTORS *(Therapist's functioning)*
Therapeutic	**content**	III HOPE AND EXPECTANCY FACTORS *(Client's capacity for hope)*	IV MODEL/TECHNIQUE FACTORS *(Therapist's ability to intervene)*

Note: Adapted from Lambert and Barley (2002).

Figure 10.2
Stewardship model of pastoral care and counselling

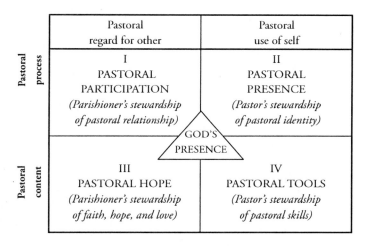

accounts for parishioner functioning within congregational life but situated outside a structured pastoral care or counselling intervention. Hope and expectancy factors applied to the pastoral context can refer to a three-fold response to God's teleological grace: namely, faith, hope, and love. Most importantly, a translation of common factors language into the pastoral context must account for the unique ethos of the pastorate as a worshipping community.

The proposed stewardship model of pastoral care and counselling organizes four primary functions in pastoral care: pastoral participation, pastoral presence, pastoral hope, and pastoral tools.

Pastoral participation refers to the parishioner's stewardship of his or her pastoral relationships. Pastoral relationships are formed between parishioners, as well as between parishioner and pastor, and they are shaped by a variety of contextual issues: gender, cultural, class, and theological differences. These pastoral relationships are more than friendship, civic, or therapeutic bonds—they are covenantal relationships arising within a worshipping community. Pastoral participation is openness to receiving pastoral care from any who are in the pastoral relationship, including other parishioners and identified pastor. When parishioners join a congregation, they make a public promise to participate in the life and work of the congregation. Their stewardship of that pastoral relationship makes pastoral care possible.

Pastoral presence refers to the pastoral caregiver's stewardship of pastoral identity and authority. Pastoral caregivers—clergy and lay—do ministry within the pastoral relationship. Everyone in a worshipping community, because he or she is part of the network of pastoral relationships, is able to provide pastoral care (Gerkin, 1997). Some individuals are specifically identified or set apart for pastoral care ministry (e.g., clergy, elders, parish nurses, pastoral counsellors, lay visitors). These pastoral caregivers are commissioned or "sent" by the congregation to do pastoral care ministry. They are given pastoral authority and identity, which help to establish pastoral trust and competence.

Stewardship of pastoral authority carries with it a responsibility for recognizing and respecting contextual differences, tending to power and control issues, including boundary violations and abuse of pastoral power. In general, codes for the helping professions are built on five common principles: autonomy, beneficence, non-maleficence, justice, and fidelity (Zygmond & Boorhem, 1989). No doubt there are theological correlates to these five principles. However, principles to apply to ethical decision making in pastoral practice must derive from the economy of God's gift: where the other is a gift from God to oneself and the other.

Pastoral hope refers to the parishioner's stewardship of faith, hope, and love. Participation in a worshipping community means participation in God's gracious presence. In that relationship, God gifts us with faith, hope, and love, and believers are called to be good stewards of these primary gifts from God.

Pastoral tools refer to the pastoral caregiver's stewardship of pastoral skills. The pastoral caregiver's ministry is focused corporately on the parishioner's relationship with God, self, and others. In response to parishioners' problems of living and crises, the pastoral caregiver has a number of pastoral resources or tools available. Experienced and trained pastoral caregivers and counsellors bring more specialized helping models, assessment and diagnostic tools, techniques, referrals, supervision, and oversight to the pastoral relationship. More specialized interventions allow a best fit of helping tool to the pastoral need. Evidence-based practice (O'Connor, 1998) finds its expression in this quadrant of pastoral practice.

Bridging Mutual Influence

Correlation of the common factors model and the above pastoral care model allows for mutual influence. Pastoral community, with its broad aim of transforming the world, is reminded of its obligation toward the individual. We are reminded that our tradition includes giving the individual stranger and friend an individual cup of water—and that doing so is not poor stewardship. Miller-McLemore observes that "Pastoral theology has spawned congregational programs focused almost entirely on individual care, such as Stephen Ministries or Parish Nursing. Such programs consume significant resources to reach a relatively small population in need" (2005, p. 1378). We can appreciate her critique without collapsing into an either/or thinking that would cause us to abandon allocation of pastoral resources for individual care programs.

The correlation underscores the importance of the helping relationship and the value of developing relational competence in the person providing help. In the pastoral paradigm, whether the helper is clergy or laity, specialist or generalist, the relationship ability of the helper is crucial. This capacity for healthy and helpful pastoral relationship has recourse to more than mere skill training. There is value in developing pastoral identity and a sense of calling or commissioning related to the pastoral community, which correlates with the dynamics of ascribed power in helping relationships. The management of differences in ascribed power is just as important in the pastoral helping relationship. Pastoral care cannot lose sight of power differentials. Good intentions cannot lose sight of the ethos of the other as God's gift, perverting it to a commodification of the other to serve one's own ends.

The pastoral paradigm impacts the social science understanding of helping relationships. The common factors literature needs to explore the extra-therapeutic factors that reach beyond the client's intrapersonal makeup or immediate interpersonal environment. The pastoral paradigm with its broader aim of transforming the world challenges the therapeutic model of clinical and institutional care to explore communal and societal transformation through public policy interventions. The common factors model is challenged to move from the narrow debate on ideal helper and ideal helpee to a debate on the ideal community of helpers and the ideal helpee's community.

This correlation reminds us that Quadrant 4 considerations need not be limited to traditional helping tools and techniques. In the common factors model, the helper can reach beyond psychological helping techniques. In the pastoral model, the caregiver can reach beyond traditional helping tools such as prayer and scripture and engage critical, political, sociological helping, and advocacy models. These non-traditional tools and techniques may, in many cases, provide the best content for the clinical or pastoral helping relationship.

Further Study

The above correlation of the common factors model and pastoral paradigm raises a number of questions for further study and discussion. What method arises from this correlation and its mutual influencing? Is this method context specific? Is this question itself critiqued by the common factors model, which puts minimal emphasis on the model used? Does this response, therefore, promote eclecticism or an integration model, promoting whatever works best in the situation? Does the "method" question, too quickly asked, negate the role of theological reflection? Or does it underscore the importance of working out pastoral identity and relationship issues prior to the helping encounter, so that the best model can be effectively employed? How do these pastoral models inform clinical and institutional contexts that are not overtly corporate worshipping communities? How are more complex interventions for specific conditions and problems of living derived from the fundamental aetiology of human suffering as amnesia or mismanagement of fundamental human ethos?

Notes

[1] Reprint of sections of Morrison (2005).
[2] Even within literary criticism, the word *pastoral* is often mischaracterized as reference to idyllic landscapes. In *What Is Pastoral?* Paul Alpers (1996) argues that the pastoral mode in literature refers to shared communal experience represented by shepherds or humble living.
[3] Compare the etymology of the word *fellowship* from Old Norse *félage* "laying together of money in common," from *fé* "property" and *lag* "to lay" (*The Compact Oxford English Dictionary,* 1991).
[4] Compare the notion of economy of the gift in Ricoeur (1992) and Wall (2001).

References

Alpers, P. (1996). *What is pastoral?* Chicago: University of Chicago Press.
Association for Clinical Pastoral Education. (2001). A white paper: Professional chaplaincy: Its role and importance in healthcare. *Journal of Pastoral Care, 55,* 81–98.
Foucault, M. (1988). Technologies of the self. In L. H. Martin, H. Gutman, & P. H. Hutton (Eds.), *Technologies of the self: A seminar with Michel Foucault* (pp. 16–49). Amherst: University of Massachusetts Press.
Gerkin, C. (1997). *An introduction to pastoral care.* Nashville: Abingdon Press.
Hunter, R. (Ed.) (2005). *Dictionary of pastoral care and counseling* (Expanded ed.). Nashville: Abingdon Press.
Lambert, M. J., & Barley, D. (2002). Research summary on the therapeutic relationship and psychotherapy outcome. In J. Norcross (Ed.), *Psychotherapy relationships that work: Therapist contributions and responsiveness to patients* (pp. 17–32). New York: Oxford University Press.
Levant, R. (2004). The empirically validated treatments movement: A practitioner/educator perspective. *Clinical Psychology: Science and Practice, 7,* 219–224.

Meech, J. (2006). *Paul in Israel's story: Self and community at the cross.* American Academy of Religion Series. New York: Oxford University Press.

Miller-McLemore, B. J. (2005). Pastoral theology as public theology: Revolutions in the "fourth area." In R. Hunter and N. J. Ramsay (Eds.), *Dictionary of pastoral care and counseling* (Expanded ed.) (pp. 1370–1380). Nashville: Abingdon Press.

Morrison, B. (2005). Stewardship models of pastoral care, counselling, and supervision: The Commonians meet Ricoeur at worship. *Pastoral Psychology, 53,* 435–446.

Norcross, J. (Ed.). (2002). *Psychotherapy relationships that work: Therapist contributions and responsiveness to patients.* New York: Oxford University Press.

O'Connor, T. (1998). *Clinical pastoral supervision and the theology of Charles Gerkin.* Editions SR, 22. Waterloo, ON: Wilfrid Laurier University Press/Canadian Corporation for Studies in Religion.

Peterson, E. (1987). *Working the angles: The shape of pastoral integrity.* Grand Rapids, MI: W.B. Eerdmans Publishers.

Ricoeur, P. (1992). *Oneself as another* (K. Blamey, Trans.). Chicago: University of Chicago Press.

Sprenkle, D., & Blow, A. (2004). Common factors and our sacred models. *Journal of Marital and Family Therapy, 30,* 113–129.

Taylor, C. (2007). *A secular age.* Cambridge, MA: Belknap Press of Harvard University Press.

The Compact Oxford English Dictionary (2nd ed.). (1991). New York: Oxford University Press.

Townsend, L. L. (2005). Ferment and imagination in training in clinical ministry. In R. Hunter and N. J. Ramsay (Eds.), *Dictionary of pastoral care and counselling* (Expanded ed.) (pp. 1404–1415). Nashville: Abingdon Press.

Vankatwyk, P. (2002). Reconciliation and forgiveness: A practice of spiritual care. In A. Meier & P. Vankatwyk (Eds.), *The challenge of forgiveness* (pp. 125–139). Toronto: Novalis.

Wall, J. (2001). The economy of the gift: Paul Ricoeur's significance for theological ethics. *Journal of Religious Ethics, 29,* 235–260.

Zygmond, M., & Boorhem, H. (1989). Ethical decision making in family therapy. *Family Process, 28,* 269–280.

Contributors

Editors

Augustine Meier, PhD, is a certified clinical psychologist in private practice and a professor emeritus in the Faculty of Human Sciences, Saint Paul University, Ottawa. He provides advanced training in object relations therapy and self psychology. For more than 20 years, he taught graduate courses in psychotherapy and psychopathology and trained graduate students in individual counselling. He has co-authored over 40 articles on psychotherapy and psychopathology in refereed journals. He is the editor of *In Search of Healing* and a co-editor of *The Challenge of Forgiveness, Spirituality and Health: Multidisciplinary Explorations,* and *Through Conflict to Reconciliation.* Dr. Meier and Micheline Boivin published *Counselling and Therapy Techniques: Theory and Practice* (Sage). Professor Meier is the founder and president of the Ottawa Institute for Object Relations Therapy.

Martin Rovers, PhD, is a professor and an AAMFT-approved supervisor in the Faculty of Human Sciences, Saint Paul University, Ottawa. He is the coordinator of the Certificate in Couple Counselling and Spirituality and provides training and supervision within the master's program. Dr. Martin has published several books, including *Healing the Wounds in Couple Relationships* (Novalis, 2005) and *Through Conflict to Reconciliation* (co-editor, Novalis, 2007), and numerous refereed articles. He has written extensively on the synthesis of attachment theory and family of origin theory, in a new approach that he termed Attachment in Family Therapy (AFT). Dr. Martin is a psychologist and marriage and family therapist and has his own private practice.

Contributing Authors

Micheline Boivin, **MA,** is a certified clinical psychologist working with traumatized children and their parents at the Programme enfance jeunesse famille du centre local des services communautaires de Gatineau, Québec. She is the author of "L'exploitation sexuelle des enfants: Ouvrir les yeux and tendre la main," published in *In the Search of Healing,* and the co-author of "The Treatment of Depression: A Case Study Using Theme-Analysis," published in the journal *Counselling and Psychotherapy Research.* She has co-authored articles on psychotherapy published in refereed journals, presented workshops on child sexual abuse and the use of puppets in child therapy, and co-presented advanced workshops on the use of mental imagery in psychotherapy. Micheline Boivin and Dr. Meier published *Counselling and Therapy Techniques: Theory and Practice* (Sage).

Shelley Briscoe-Dimock, PhD (Cand.), is an individual and couple therapist in private practice in Ottawa. She is a Canadian certified counsellor and certified object relations therapist. She obtained her BA (Honours) in psychology from Carleton University and is currently completing her PhD in counselling and spirituality at Saint Paul University, Ottawa. She has given workshops and presented at various conferences in the area of object relations couple therapy. She has co-published in the *Journal of Relationship and Couple Therapy* (2006). Her research interests include the dynamics of the therapeutic relationship in individual and couple therapy as well as the needs underlying maladaptive patterns in distressed couple relationships.

The Rev. Marsha Cutting, PhD, is an associate professor of pastoral care and counselling at Waterloo Lutheran Seminary, Waterloo, ON. She is a board certified chaplain. She is ordained in the Presbyterian Church (USA). Dr. Cutting's research areas are supervision research and religiosity scales. She currently is conducting research through a web-based survey, The Religiosity Scales Project. She also studies clergy careers and impediments to religious participation by mental health services recipients. In her free time, she sails, plays folk music, reads mysteries, and listens to jazz.

John Dimock, MB Ch B., Dip. Psych., FRCPC, is in private practice of psychiatry in Ottawa and Stittsville, ON, and is the consultant psychiatrist to the Canadian Armed Forces, Petawawa Base. He was previously a clinical assistant professor at the University of Ottawa and the director of Ottawa Family Court Clinic, Royal Ottawa Health Care Group, where he worked for 10 years after completing undergraduate training at Birmingham Medical School, UK, and a postgraduate residency in the University of Ottawa program. He completed a clinical fellow-ship in forensic psychiatry and worked in the Ottawa Forensic Psychiatry Program, both at the Family Court Clinic and at the Adult Forensic Sexual Behaviours Clinic. He then entered private practice and worked as the consultant psychiatrist to the Armed Forces at Health Care Clinic Ottawa 1996–99. After 9/11, he worked in Pennsylvania and returned to full-time private practice in 2003. He now works in Ottawa, Stittsville, and Petawawa. He has three book chapters and a number of refereed papers pub-lished. Highlights of his career include acting as invited expert on a distinguished panel of American child forensic psychiatrists in San Diego at the American Academy of Psychiatry and the Law Meeting. He gave expert evidence in the first successful battered woman defence to manslaughter in Canada, dramatized in the CBC documentary *Life with Billy* and in two books. His chapter is dedicated to his wife, Shelley, who works alongside him and their children, Emma, Amy, Stephen, and Alexander, and their grandchildren Callum, Ceci, and Ryan.

Kristine Lund, PhD, has been an assistant professor in contextual theology and pastoral counselling at Waterloo Lutheran Seminary since 2005. She is a specialist in pastoral counselling and a pastoral counselling teaching supervisor with the Canadian Association of Pastoral Practice and Education (CAPPE). Kristine is interested in the teaching and learning experiences for both supervisor and supervisee. In her spare time, she plays violin with the Kitchener-Waterloo Chamber Orchestra.

Molisa Meier, PhD (Cand.), is a first-year clinical psychology student at the School of Psychology at the University of Ottawa. Her research interests include the use of attachment theory to explain externalizing behaviours in adolescence, with a focus on young offenders, as well as to investigate the influence of childhood attachment disorganization and role reversal in the psycho-social adjustment of adolescents. She has co-authored articles in refereed journals and has presented and co-presented scientific papers at annual conferences.

Brad Morrison, D.Min., is an ordained minister in the United Church of Canada. He is also a clinical member of the American Association for Marriage and Family Therapy. In addition to his church work, Brad maintains a private counselling practice. His academic interests include the philosophy of Paul Ricoeur and theories of community. His related publications include "Stewardship Models of Pastoral Care, Counselling, and Supervision: The Commonians Meet Ricoeur at Worship" in *Pastoral Psychology.*

Tricia Schöttler, Ph.D., received her doctoral degree in clinical psychology from the University of Windsor in 2004. She has worked as a clinical supervisor and trainer in the counselling program at Saint Paul University. She is currently working as a psychologist in private practice in Ottawa. She has previously published in the area of clinical competence.

Lorraine Ste-Marie, D.Min., holds an MA (Theology) in ethics from Saint Paul University and a Doctor of Ministry from

McMaster Divinity College at McMaster University. An assistant professor in the Faculty of Human Sciences at Saint Paul University, she teaches in the area of reflective practice and practical theology in the Master of Pastoral Theology and the Doctor of Ministry Programs. Her research focuses on the connection between adult development and pastoral leadership education. Lorraine's professional training includes transformative facilitation, conflict resolution, and process developmental coaching. She is currently the vice-chair of the Association for Theological Field Education. She is the author of *Beyond Words: A New Language for a Changing Church* (Novalis, 2008), in which she examines the relationship between language and processes of change.

Index

psychiatrist's journey learning
about, 86–94
psychoanalytic treatment, 53
as reaction of client, 70
resistance and, 12
separation/individuation, xiv
theoretical understanding, 69–74
therapeutic relationship, 50–51
as unconscious creation of
analyst, 56
working with, 84–86
transformational learning, xvi,
148, 163
transformative learning, 146–48, 163
treatment manuals,
psychotherapy, 38–40, 42

U

unconditional positive regard, 4–5
unconscious, 71, 74
conflicts, 80–81
fantasies, activation of, 16
processes, 61
sensitivity of psychoanalyst, 61
state of mind, 61
strivings, 16

understanding, 5, 19, 24, 43–44
universal health schemes, 131
universal love, 156
unresolved separation/
individuation pattern, 101–2,
104–5, 125, 127

V

validation, 90
value judgment, 11
Vanier, Jean, 156–57, 176

W

Wampold, B. E., 32–34, 37–38,
40, 42–46
Weinsheimer, J., 139, 152
Wolf Man, 11
Wolitzky, D. L., 49, 60, 62, 64,
78
working alliance, therapeutic,
33–34, 43, 48–49
written consent, 113

Y

Yalom, I., 32, 46
Yates, A. Y., 1, 31